First Nations, Inuit, and Métis Peoples

EXPLORING THEIR PAST, PRESENT, AND FUTURE

Gy
JOHN ROBERTS
Mohawk College

with activities by

RANDY MONTGOMERY
Edmonton Public School Board

FRED SPROULE
Edmonton Public School Board

2006
Emond Montgomery Publications Limited
Toronto, Canada

Printed in Canada.

We acknowledge the financial support of the Government of Canada through the Book Publishing Industry Development Program (BPIDP) for our publishing activities.

Library and Archives Canada Cataloguing in Publication

Roberts, John A., 1944-
First Nations, Inuit, and Métis peoples : exploring their past, present, and future / John Roberts; with activities by Randy Montgomery and Fred Sproule.

Includes index.
ISBN 1-55239-167-1

1. Native peoples—Canada—Textbooks.
I. Montgomery, Randy II. Sproule, Fredrick C. III. Title.

E78.C2R558 2006 971.004′97 C2005-906547-8

Publisher
Tim Johnston

Developmental editors
Loralee Case
Elaine Aboud

Editorial assistant
Joyce Tannassee

Production editor, copy editor, & image researcher
Francine Geraci

Image researcher & permissions editor
Lisa Brant

Cover designer, interior designer, & compositor
Shani Sohn, WordsWorth Communications

Assistant compositor
Tara Wells, WordsWorth Communications

Proofreader
David Handelsman, WordsWorth Communications

Indexer
Paula Pike, WordsWorth Communications

Production coordinator
Jim Lyons, WordsWorth Communications

Reviewers
Doug Gordon
Thames Valley District School Board (formerly)

Ross Hoffman, PhD
Smithers, British Columbia

Blain Knott
Edmonton, Alberta

Table of Contents

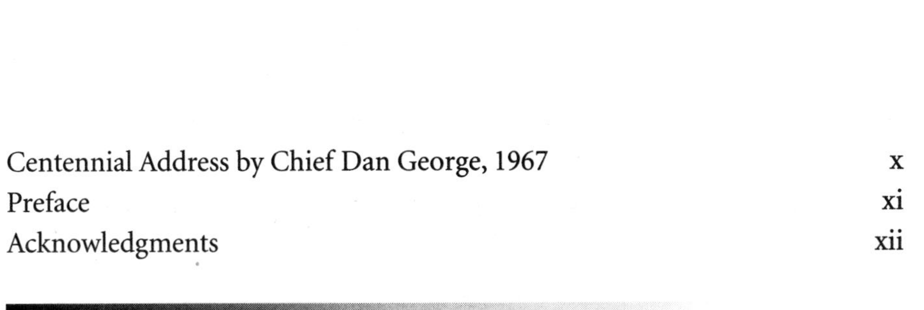

Centennial Address by Chief Dan George, 1967 x
Preface xi
Acknowledgments xii

PART I

FIRST NATIONS AND INUIT CULTURES PRIOR TO EUROPEAN CONTACT

CHAPTER 1: Origins of the First Peoples **3**
Introduction 3
Oral Tradition 4
- Understanding Our Past 4
- Storytelling 4
- Interpreting the Stories 7
- Close-Up: Stories of the Siksika and the Haida 7
- Close-Up: Written Records of First Nations History 8
- The Value of Oral Stories 9

Theories of Origins of the First Peoples 10
- The Beringia Theory 10
- Other Theories of Origins 12
- First Nations and Inuit Theories of Origins 12
- Close-Up: Some Myths about Origins 13

The First Peoples and the Land 15
- Medicine Wheel Teachings 15
- Close-Up: The Importance of the Number Four 17

Culminating Activity: Getting Your Life in Balance **19**

CHAPTER 2: Characteristics of First Nations and Inuit Cultures 23

Introduction 23
Cultural Periods 24
- The Role of Archaeology 24
- The Wisconsin Glaciation Period (70,000–12,000 Years Ago) 24
- The Palaeo-Indian Culture (12,000–7,000 Years Ago) 24
- The Archaic Period (7,000–3,000 Years Ago) 26
- The Woodland Period (3,000 Years Ago to Contact) 26

Connections to the Land 27
- Spirituality 27
- Respect for All Things 28
- Interdependence 28
- Gender Roles 30
- Close-Up: The Role of Children 30
- Trade 31

Language Families 33
Distinctions among Cultural Groups 35
- The Peoples of the Woodland 36
- The Peoples of the Plains 38
- Close-Up: The Travois 38
- Close-Up: Making Pemmican 41
- The Peoples of the Interior Plateau 41
- The Peoples of the Pacific Coast 43
- The Peoples of the Subarctic 44
- The Peoples of the Arctic 46

Culminating Activity: First Nations and Inuit Cultures and the Influence of Geography 48

PART II

EFFECTS OF EUROPEAN ARRIVAL ON ABORIGINAL PEOPLES AND CULTURES

CHAPTER 3: The Impact of Colonization on Aboriginal Peoples 51

Introduction 51
The First Europeans 52
- Contact with the Beothuk 52
- Jacques Cartier 53
- Opportunities in the New World 54

The Growth of European Settlements 54
Living Together 55
Close-Up: Coureurs de Bois 56
Impact of the French and British Governments on Aboriginal Peoples 57
Britain and France at War 57
The Fur Trade on the Plains 58
Life in the Northwest 58
Close-Up: The Siksika and the Fur Trade 59
The Plains and Western Subarctic Peoples 62
Profiles of the Plains and Western Subarctic Cultures 63
Biography: Isapo-muxika (Crowfoot) 64
Biography: Red Crow 65
Biography: Pitikwahanapiwiyin (Poundmaker) 67
Biography: Mistahimaskwa (Big Bear) 68
Settlement in the West 71
The Métis 71
The Red River Settlement 72
Annexing the West 73
The Red River Rebellion 74
Dominion Lands Act 75
Growth of European Settlements 75
Biography: Louis Riel 76
The Impact of European Settlement on Aboriginal Cultures 77
Changes in the Barter System 77
The Notion of Wealth 77
Disappearance of the Clan System 78
Selection of Leaders 79
Dependence on Europeans 79
Close-Up: Aboriginal Peoples and the Trading Posts 80
Collapse of the Fur Trade 80
Dependence on Government 81
Missionaries 81
Culminating Activity: The Plains Peoples: European Contact and Change 84

CHAPTER 4: Treaty Making and the Loss of First Nations' Lands and Autonomy 87

Introduction 87
Early Treaty Making between First Nations and Europeans 88
Close-Up: The Great Peace Treaty of 1701 88

The Fur Trade 89
Land and Resources 89
Why Treaties Were Established 90
Treaties before and after Confederation 91
Pre-Confederation Treaties and the *Royal Proclamation of 1763* 91
The Numbered Treaties (1871–1921) 94
Close-Up: Who Was Included in the Treaties? 95
Land Claims 103
Usufructuary Right 103
Land Claims prior to 1973 103
Comprehensive Land Claims 104
Specific Land Claims 105
Resolving Land Claims 105
Bill C-6 106
Culminating Activity: Treaties with First Nations: Fair or Flawed? 110

CHAPTER 5: The Challenges to Aboriginal Sovereignty 113
Introduction 113
Assimilation 114
The *Indian Act* of 1876 115
Indian Agents 115
The Impact of the *Indian Act* 116
Close-Up: Government in First Nations Communities 117
Residential Schools 118
The Structure of Residential Schools 119
The Impact of Residential Schools 120
Abuse at Residential Schools 121
Close-Up: The Legacy of Residential Schools 121
The "Lost" Métis Nation 123
Scattered to the Wind 124
The Emergence of Aboriginal Political Activism 125
Close-Up: The Allied Tribes of British Columbia 126
Restricting Aboriginal Rights 126
The Union nationale Métisse Saint-Joseph du Manitoba 127
Biography: Malcolm Norris 127
The Renewal of Aboriginal Activism 127
The National Indian Council 128
The National Indian Brotherhood/The Assembly of First Nations 128
Close-Up: The White Paper of 1969 129

The Native Council of Canada/The Congress of Aboriginal Peoples 130
National Métis Organizations 130
The Inuit Tapiriit Kanatami 131
The Issue of Self-Government 132
The Complexity of Self-Government 133
Culminating Activity: Analyzing Stereotypes in the Media 135

PART III
CONTEMPORARY ABORIGINAL ISSUES

CHAPTER 6: Aboriginal Peoples and Socioeconomic Issues 139

Introduction 139
The Aboriginal Population 140
Aboriginal Ancestry and Identity 140
Growth Rates 141
Decrease in Birth Rate 142
Increase in Life Expectancy 142
Aboriginal Seniors 142
Provincial and Territorial Distribution of Aboriginal Populations 143
Migration to Cities 144
Education 146
Elementary and Secondary Schools 146
Close-Up: Band Schools 147
Postsecondary Education 148
The Education Gap 148
Health 151
Physical Health 151
Close-Up: Aboriginal Diabetes Initiative 153
Mental Health 155
Close-Up: Factors in Aboriginal Suicide 157
Administration of Health Services 158
Close-Up: National Native Alcohol and Drug Abuse Program 159
Living Conditions 160
The Environment 161
Employment 163
Unemployment Rate 163
Employment Rate 163
Level of Education 164

Close-Up: Employment Rates and Educational Attainment 165
Place of Residence 165
Aboriginal Representation in Employment Sectors 165
Income 168
Average Employment Income 169
Social Assistance 169
A Cycle of Dependence 170
Funding of Services and Programs 170
The Future 170
Close-Up: The History of Social Assistance for Aboriginal People 171
Close-Up: Working toward Self-Determination 172
Culminating Activity: Aboriginal Peoples and Affirmative Action Programs 174

CHAPTER 7: Aboriginal Peoples and the Canadian Justice System 177

Introduction 177
Traditional Social Control 178
Resolving Disputes in Selected Cultures 179
Early Judicial Conflicts between Aboriginal and Non-Aboriginal Laws 179
Imposing Foreign Laws 179
Banning the Potlatch 180
Legal Rights 182
Hunting and Fishing Rights 182
Treaty Rights versus the Law 183
Land Claims and Self-Government 183
Biography: John Amagoalik 184
Domestic Violence 185
The Roots of Domestic Violence 185
A Culture of Violence 186
Addictions and Violence 187
Eliminating Domestic Violence 187
Close-Up: Facts about Domestic Violence 187
Aboriginal Peoples and the Justice System Today 189
Crime among Aboriginal Youth 191
Aboriginal Peoples within the Justice System 191
Close-Up: Facts about Aboriginal Peoples and the Justice System 192
Biography: Fauna Kingdon 193
Alternative Methods of Justice 194
Community Policing 194

Court Workers 195
Legal Clinics 195
Biography: Roberta Jamieson 195
Justices of the Peace 196
Restorative Justice 196
Close-Up: A Sentencing Circle in Action 197
Young Offenders and the Justice System 197
Creating a Fairer System of Justice 198
Culminating Activity: Conflict over Hunting and Fishing Rights 199

CHAPTER 8: The Resurgence of Aboriginal Cultures 201
Introduction 201
Rebuilding Languages 202
Relearning and Renewing 203
Reclaiming Ancient Artifacts 205
Close-Up: Haida Repatriation (*Yaghudangang*—To Pay Respect) 205
A Resurgence in the Arts 207
Blending the Old with the New 207
Biography: Jane Ash Poitras 208
Métis Cultural Revival 209
Blending Past and Present in Inuit Society 210
Biography: Maria Campbell 211
Aboriginal Tourism 211
Close-Up: Head-Smashed-In Buffalo Jump 212
Conclusion 213
Culminating Activity: The Resurgence of Aboriginal Cultures 214

GLOSSARY 217
INDEX 221
CREDITS 228

Centennial Address by Chief Dan George, 1967

How long have I known you—Oh Canada? A hundred years? Yes—a hundred years—and many, many years more. Today, when you celebrate your hundred years, Oh Canada—I am sad for all the Indian people throughout the land. For I have known you when your forests were mine. When they gave me food and my clothing. I have known you—in your brooks and rivers—where your fish splashed and danced in the sun, and whose waters said, "Come and eat of my abundance." I have known you in the freedom of your winds and my spirit like your winds—once roamed this good land. But in the long hundred years since—the white man came—I have seen my spirit disappear—just like the salmon as they mysteriously go out to sea. The white man's strange ways and customs—I could not understand—thrust down upon me until I could no longer breathe. When I fought to protect my home and my land—I was called a savage. When I neither understood nor welcomed this new way of life—I was called lazy. When I tried to rule my people—I was stripped of my authority. My nation was ignored in your history textbooks. We were less important in the history of Canada than the buffalo that roamed the plains. I was ridiculed in your plays and motion pictures—and when I drank your firewater—I got drunk—very, very drunk—and I forgot. Oh Canada—how can I celebrate with you this Centennial Year—this hundred years? Shall I thank you for the reserves that are left me of my beautiful forests? Shall I thank you for the canned fish of my river? Shall I thank you for the loss of my pride and authority—even amongst my own people? For the lack of my will to fight back? Shall I thank you for my defeat? NO—I must forget what is past and gone. Oh God in Heaven—give me the courage of the olden chief. Let me wrestle with my surroundings. Let me once again as in the days of old—dominate my environment. Let me humbly accept this new culture and through it rise up and go on. Oh God—like the Thunderbird of old—we shall rise again out of the sea—we shall grasp the instruments of the white man's success—his education—his skill—and with these new tools, I shall spirit my race into the proudest segment of your society: and before I follow the great chiefs that have gone before us—I shall see these things come to pass. I shall see our young braves and our chiefs sitting in the house of Law and Government—ruling and being ruled by the knowledge and freedom of our great land. So shall we shatter the barriers of our isolation. So shall the next hundred years be the greatest in the proud history of our tribes and nations.

Preface

The authors and publisher would like to acknowledge the support of the Aboriginal Education Department at Sault College in the preparation of the first edition of this book.

In the past, the history that was taught in elementary and secondary schools in Canada began with Christopher Columbus "discovering" North America in 1492. Students learned little about the history of the many First Nations and Inuit cultures that once thrived in the Americas *before* the arrival of Columbus. For the most part, history books presented these cultures as one homogeneous group. The information and images about the First Peoples were stereotypical. Often, they were subtly—and at times overtly—demeaning. Such histories were neither accurate nor objective. While it is human nature to view other people and events from one's own cultural perspective, to do so ignores the points of view of many who played a part in the past. When we fail to include these perspectives, our history becomes biased. Perhaps the Shawnee Chief Chiksika summarized this most simply: "When a white army battles Indians and wins, it is called a great victory, but if [the white army] loses, it is called a massacre."

In recent years, however, those who write about the past have made greater efforts to present a more inclusive history of Canada. Today, history books present not only the perspectives of Aboriginal cultures, but also the perspectives of other groups who have been marginalized by traditional interpretations of the past. By acknowledging these multiple perspectives, we have the opportunity to learn about all those who have contributed to the building of the Canadian nation.

The goal of this book is to create a greater awareness of Aboriginal cultures and the issues that have affected them, both in the past and the present. To achieve this goal, first we need to understand the foundation of all Aboriginal cultures—the traditional belief in the importance of spirituality. It is impossible to discuss the history of Aboriginal peoples in any other context. Although Aboriginal spirituality has its roots thousands of years in the past, it still lies at the heart of Aboriginal communities today. By providing insights into Aboriginal peoples, cultures, and issues in the past, we can better understand the issues and challenges that Aboriginal peoples face today.

Acknowledgments

I would like to acknowledge the invaluable assistance provided by many people in the creation of this book.

Tim Johnston of Emond Montgomery Publications deserves credit for conceiving this project and guiding it through its development, and for his invaluable advice along the way. Randy Montgomery and Fred Sproule developed excellent activities for the book and also offered expert advice regarding its contents.

A special debt of gratitude is owed to Francine Geraci and Lisa Brant for their editorial skills and attention to detail.

The book would never have been completed without the outstanding work of Loralee Case and Elaine Aboud, who edited, wrote, and advised on all aspects of the text. I can't say enough about the quality of their work and the obvious enthusiasm they put into the project.

Jim Lyons is the complete wordsmith; I have never worked with anyone as competent in the English language.

It would not have been possible to produce a book of this quality without the assistance of WordsWorth Communications—Shani Sohn in cover and text design, Tara Wells in composition, David Handelsman in proofreading, and Paula Pike in indexing. Thank you.

Paul Emond—thanks for believing in the project.

John Roberts
Hamilton, Ontario
September 2005

PART I

First Nations and Inuit Cultures Prior to European Contact

CHAPTER 1

Origins of the First Peoples

LEARNING OBJECTIVES

In this chapter, you will

- recognize the differences in oral creation stories among specific First Nations and Inuit cultures
- discover the significance of oral traditions in these cultures
- compare scientific theories about the origins of the First Peoples in the Americas
- recognize the significance of the land in First Nations and Inuit cultures

INTRODUCTION

First Nations and **Inuit** cultures have lived across North America for thousands of years. While some groups have disappeared, most continue to thrive today.

There are six distinct cultural groups in Canada: the Woodland, Plains, Pacific Coast, Interior Plateau, Subarctic, and Arctic. These **cultures** share many common characteristics. Yet within each culture, there are many diverse **subcultures**. The goal of this book is to help you gain a greater knowledge about **Aboriginal** cultures in the past and develop a greater understanding of Aboriginal issues and peoples in Canada today.

Since there are many cultures and subcultures living across Canada, it is not possible to study them all in a single book. This book provides an overview of all Aboriginal cultures, with particular emphasis on the First Nations cultures of the West.

First Nations
an Indian band or community, excluding Inuit and Métis

Inuit
an Aboriginal people living in the Arctic regions of Canada

culture
the abstract values, beliefs, and perceptions of the world that are shared by a society and reflected in the behaviour of its people

subculture
a group that has the general characteristics of a culture, but also has distinctive features in its values, norms, and lifestyle

Aboriginal
in Canada, includes First Nations, Inuit, and Métis peoples

First Peoples
First Nations and Inuit peoples

VOICES

Only by being willing to see the world from another point of view can we gain the knowledge, and thereby the understanding, of the history and culture of the **First Peoples**:

"If we choose to try to understand and sensibly appreciate Aboriginal culture, way of life, and spirituality, we must be willing, first, to accept that there is ... a very special way of 'seeing the world.' Secondly, ... we must make an attempt to 'participate' in this way of seeing. The implications are very serious. Quite simply, if we are not willing to consider another way of 'seeing the world' and take it seriously, we limit ourselves critically, or eliminate entirely our chances of ever really appreciating North American Aboriginal mythology and legend."

James Dumont, "Journey Through Daylight-land: Through Ojibwa Eyes," Laurentian University Review, *8, 31–43, February 1976.*

ORAL TRADITION

To understand the cultures of the First Peoples, we need to study their origins. As you read this chapter, you will discover why any discussion about origins is, and will continue to be, the subject of lively debate.

Understanding Our Past

Throughout time, all peoples have attempted to answer questions about the mystery of our existence and about those things that are beyond our control. For example:

- Where did we come from?
- Who am I?
- Where will I go when I die?

These questions are part of our quest to understand ourselves, not only as people in a specific culture, but also as individuals. Understanding our past is an attempt to make greater sense of our future. Each culture responds to these questions with its own explanations—stories that are unique to that culture.

Storytelling

oral tradition
information that is passed from one person to another by word of mouth

Storytelling is an **oral tradition**. Many cultures pass down their knowledge of themselves from generation to generation through the stories they tell. Each culture answers the question "Where did we come from?" in its own way. The storytellers themselves are unique. They are judged according to their eloquence and their ability to spark their listeners' imagination. Because

Cultural Name	European Name	What the Cultural Name Means
Abenaki; Alnombak	Abenaki	People from the east; The people
Ah-ah-nee-nin	Gros Ventre	White clay people
Anishnaabe	Plains Ojibwe; Saulteaux; Chipewyan	First man lowered; Original people
Attiwandaron	Neutral	Those who speak differently
Chinook	Chinook	Snow-eater
Dakota	Sioux	The allies
Dene	Chipewyan; Dogrib	Pointed skins
Dene-thah	Slavey	Captives
Dunne-za	Beaver	Our people
Haida	Haida	Children of Eagle and Raven; People of the ocean
Haudenosaunee	Iroquois	People of the Long House
Inuna-ina	Arapaho	Our people
Kainai	Blood	Many chiefs
Kanien'Kehaka	Mohawk	Keepers of the eastern door
Ktunaxa	Kootenay	Deer robes; Water people
Lakota	Sioux	The allies
Mi'kmaq	Micmac	My friends
Nakoda	Assiniboine	Those who use cooking stones
Nehiyaw	Cree	The people; True men; The four-directions people
Nisga'a	Nisga'a	People of the Nass River
Odawa	Ottawa	To trade
Piikunii; Apatohsi Piikunii; Amoskapi Piikunii	Peigan; North Peigan; South Peigan	Badly tanned robes
Potawatomi	Potawatomi	Those who make a fire
Seneca	Seneca	Keepers of the western door
Siksika	Blackfoot	Black foot; Black moccasins
So-sonreh	Shoshoni	Our people
Tionantati	Tobacco	On the other side of the mountain
Tsuu T'ina	Sarsi	Many people
Wendat	Huron	Island dwellers
Wuastukwiuk	Maliseet	Broken talkers

Figure 1.1 Cultural Names in This Book When Europeans came to North America, they gave names to the different peoples they met. In the past, these names were commonly used in Canada. However, First Nations and Inuit peoples had their own names for themselves. Today, most nations prefer to be known by their original names. This table identifies the First Nations and Inuit names found in this book.

in the past, few First Nations and Inuit cultures kept written records of their history, customs, and traditions, oral tradition is a vital link between past, present, and future.

Common Characteristics of Stories

First Nations and Inuit stories share some common characteristics:

- Stories reflect the culture and the natural environment in which the people live. Cultures that live near the ocean, such as the Haida, include elements of the sea, such as water and conch shells, in their stories. Groups that live on the plains, such as the Siksika (Blackfoot), describe such things as prairie grasses and buffalo herds in their stories.
- Stories provide answers to the meaning and order of the world in which the people live. The Inuit, for example, tell a story about the meaning of the Aurora Borealis, or Northern Lights. They believe that the Aurora Borealis are giants who are great hunters and fishers. Although these giants are not visible, they are perceived to be friendly. The Inuit believe that when these giants hunt animals and spear fish, they use torches. These torches appear as the Northern Lights.
- Stories often include places that a culture deems sacred. They describe how these places came to have **spiritual** significance. For example, Dreamer's Rock on Birch Island, near Manitoulin Island in Ontario, is a sacred place where the Anishnaabe go to **fast** and receive a vision. Traditionally, the vision provides direction and a purpose for living for the vision seeker.
- Stories are rich in symbolism that helps explain the origins of the First Peoples as well as their **worldview**.
- Stories are about living and real spirits—beings that are as alive as people. First Nations and Inuit peoples believe that their stories have lived longer than humans have. As these stories are passed down from generation to generation, they provide a **legacy** for each culture.
- Stories are linked to the season in which they are told. This is an important aspect of storytelling. The Nehiyaw (Cree), for example, tell certain stories at specific times of the year. To do otherwise would invite revenge and punishment from the spirits.

spirituality
in Aboriginal cultures, a belief that all things in the world are alive, have a role in the land, and are therefore worthy of respect

fast
to abstain from food and, in some cultures, water to purify one's self and to connect with the spiritual world

worldview
a group's view of the world and its relationship to it

legacy
something that is handed down from a predecessor

Creation Stories

One of the most important themes in First Nations and Inuit stories is their origins—that is, where did the people come from? In all stories, the people were either born from the land in which they traditionally lived or they moved there from some other place.

The Reliability of Oral Stories

Through their stories, First Nations and Inuit cultures establish continuity and stability among their people.

Some historians argue that the problem with oral tradition is that it is oral. They believe that without a written record the messages in oral stories may be misunderstood, misinterpreted, or embellished.

Interpreting the Stories

Even in cases where oral stories are in writing, there are questions about their reliability. Stories translated from their original language lose some of their meaning. First Nations and Inuit symbolism is unfamiliar to people of other cultures. Their connections to nature and the spirits are unique to their societies. Therefore, the images and symbols associated with the natural and spiritual worlds are meaningless to outsiders.

STORIES OF THE SIKSIKA AND THE HAIDA

While creation stories share many similarities, there are differences, too. In what ways are these two stories different? In what ways are they the same?

A Siksika (Blackfoot) Creation Story

Long ago there was a time when water covered the entire world. Napi the creator wanted to know what happened below all this water. He sent a duck, an otter, and then a badger, but all came up with nothing. Finally, a muskrat dove beneath the water and was down a very long time. He returned with a ball of mud in his paws. Napi took the lump and blew on it until it dried and was transformed into the Earth. He molded the hills, valleys, and mountains with his hands. He created grooves in the Earth for rivers and lakes. The first people were molded from this Earth, and Napi taught men and women how to hunt and to live. Once Napi felt his work was complete, he climbed up to a mountain peak and disappeared.

Source: R.D. Francis, R. Jones, and D.B. Smith, Origins: Canadian History to Confederation, 5th ed. *(Toronto: Thomson/Nelson, 2004), p. 3; found at http://www.ucalgary.ca/applied_history/tutor/firstnations/earth.html.*

A Haida Creation Story

Raven was wandering on the beach, when he heard noise coming from a clamshell. He looked more closely and saw that it was full of little human creatures. They clearly looked terrified by Raven and the great big world outside the shell. So Raven leaned his great head close to the shell, and with the smooth trickster's tongue, that had got him out of so many misadventures in his troubled and troublesome existence, he coaxed and cajoled and coerced the little creatures to come and play in his wonderful, shiny, new world.

Source: Bill Reid of the Haida Nation, at http://www.virtualmuseum.ca/Exhibitions/Inuit_Haida/haida/english/raven/index.html.

WRITTEN RECORDS OF FIRST NATIONS HISTORY

Prior to European contact, few First Nations and Inuit cultures had written records of their histories. In South America, some groups created *hieroglyphics.* These pictures and symbols represented specific words. The Haudenosaunee (Iroquois) recorded laws, teachings, and historical events, such as treaty signings, on *wampum.* These shells were placed in certain designs to depict meanings. The Anishnaabe (Ojibwe) and Nehiyaw (Cree) wrote symbols and scripts on birch bark to record their historical events and teachings. Many cultures created *pictographs* (drawings and paintings on rock walls) and *petroglyphs* (carvings and inscriptions on rocks). Both methods represented the spiritual experiences, such as dreams, visions, and prophecies, of the chiefs and shamans.

The Europeans who first met the First Nations created most of the written records we have of these societies. In the 1600s, Jesuit priests wrote descriptive accounts about their contact with these cultures as they tried to convert them to Christianity. The stories told to the Jesuits by First Nations peoples are consistent with the stories told by the Elders and other storytellers today. Therefore, the Jesuits' journals reinforce the idea that these stories are timeless.

Figure 1.2 A Pictograph at Writing-on-Stone, Alberta
The Siksika of southern Alberta named this site along the Milk River *Aisinai'pi,* meaning "it has been written." The site contains the largest single concentration of rock art in North America.

Some people question how these stories should be interpreted. Are they based on facts? Or are they based on **mythology**? Most scientists maintain that these are stories created to find answers to phenomena in the natural world. **Anthropologists** and **archaeologists** base their beliefs and theories on scientific evidence.

Some people believe that Christianity is based on symbolism and **allegory** rather than scientific evidence. In fact, faith is the basis of all religions. Therefore, it may be just as valid to accept faith-based stories that are told through oral tradition as it is to accept the creation stories of other religions.

mythology
traditions or stories involving supernatural characters that embody popular ideas about nature and society

anthropologist
a scientist who studies human beings, their societies, and their customs

archaeologist
a scientist who studies human history and prehistory through the excavation of sites and the analysis of physical remains

allegory
a story in which the meaning or message is represented symbolically

shaman
a person who has access to the spiritual world

The Value of Oral Stories

Indeed, there are many good reasons to accept oral stories at face value. There is evidence that they have been told consistently for hundreds—perhaps thousands—of years. Stories told by various First Nations and Inuit groups are found in the records and journals of European explorers, fur traders, government officials, and others. These stories remain virtually unchanged today.

Oral stories are not told casually or spontaneously. They are carefully passed down from generation to generation and are told with great precision. Storytellers memorize their stories. They repeat them many times over the course of their lifetimes in teaching circles and other ceremonies. Storytellers are highly honoured and respected members of their communities because they are the keepers of the historical record of a people's culture. To forget any part of a story would be like a **shaman's** forgetting a key ingredient in a medicine. Oral records are vital to the continuity of these cultures. Therefore, storytellers take great care and pride to ensure that these records remain accurate.

1. What creation stories do you believe?
2. Consider the two creation stories on page 7.
   a) What values and beliefs are important to each of the cultures in these creation stories? Give reasons for your answers.
   b) What role does the environment play in each story? What role do humans play?
3. In your opinion, what are the strengths and weaknesses of the oral tradition and archaeology as sources of historical evidence? Give reasons for your answers.
4. How reliable is scientific evidence? Provide an example of scientific evidence that was subsequently proven to be inaccurate.

THEORIES OF ORIGINS OF THE FIRST PEOPLES

The Beringia Theory

theory
a system of ideas based on general principles that explains a fact or event

There are many scientific **theories** to explain the presence of the First Peoples in the Americas. The most common theory is that the First Peoples came to the Americas over a land bridge called Beringia that once linked Siberia and Alaska. (See Figure 1.3.) During the last ice age, vast ice sheets froze 5 percent of the world's oceans. For a time, however, these glaciers melted. When they did, they exposed a land bridge across what is now the Bering Strait. It was during this time, many researchers believe, that the First Peoples came to the Americas. They were in pursuit of migrating herds of big game.

The Evidence

What evidence is there to support this theory? The coastal areas of Siberia and Alaska share similar types of plant and animal life. The people who live in these two areas speak similar languages. They have similar dental patterns. They have similar spiritual practices. Their tools for hunting, fishing, and other practices in their daily lives share similarities, too.

A recent archaeological discovery appears to reinforce the Beringia theory:

> A people who may have been ancestors of the first Americans lived in Arctic Siberia, enduring one of the most unforgiving environments on Earth at the height of the ice age, according to researchers who discovered the oldest evidence yet of humans living near the frigid gateway to the New World.
>
> Russian scientists uncovered a 30,000-year-old site where ancient hunters lived on the Yana River in Siberia, some ... 480 kilometres north of the Arctic Circle and not far from the Bering land bridge that then connected Asia with North America... .
>
> Finding evidence of human habitation at the Yana site "makes it plausible that the first peopling of the Americas occurred prior to the last glacial maximum" ... 20,000 to 25,000 years ago.
>
> *Source: Associated Press, January 1, 2004; found at http://www.msnbc.msn.com/Default.aspx?id=3855039&p1=0.*

Once the First Peoples crossed the bridge, experts believe they travelled south down the only passable route—along the present border between Alberta and British Columbia. Not everyone agrees, though. Some researchers suggest that this corridor was impassable during this period. They base their opinion on glacial deposits, ancient pollen, and other organic materials found in the area.

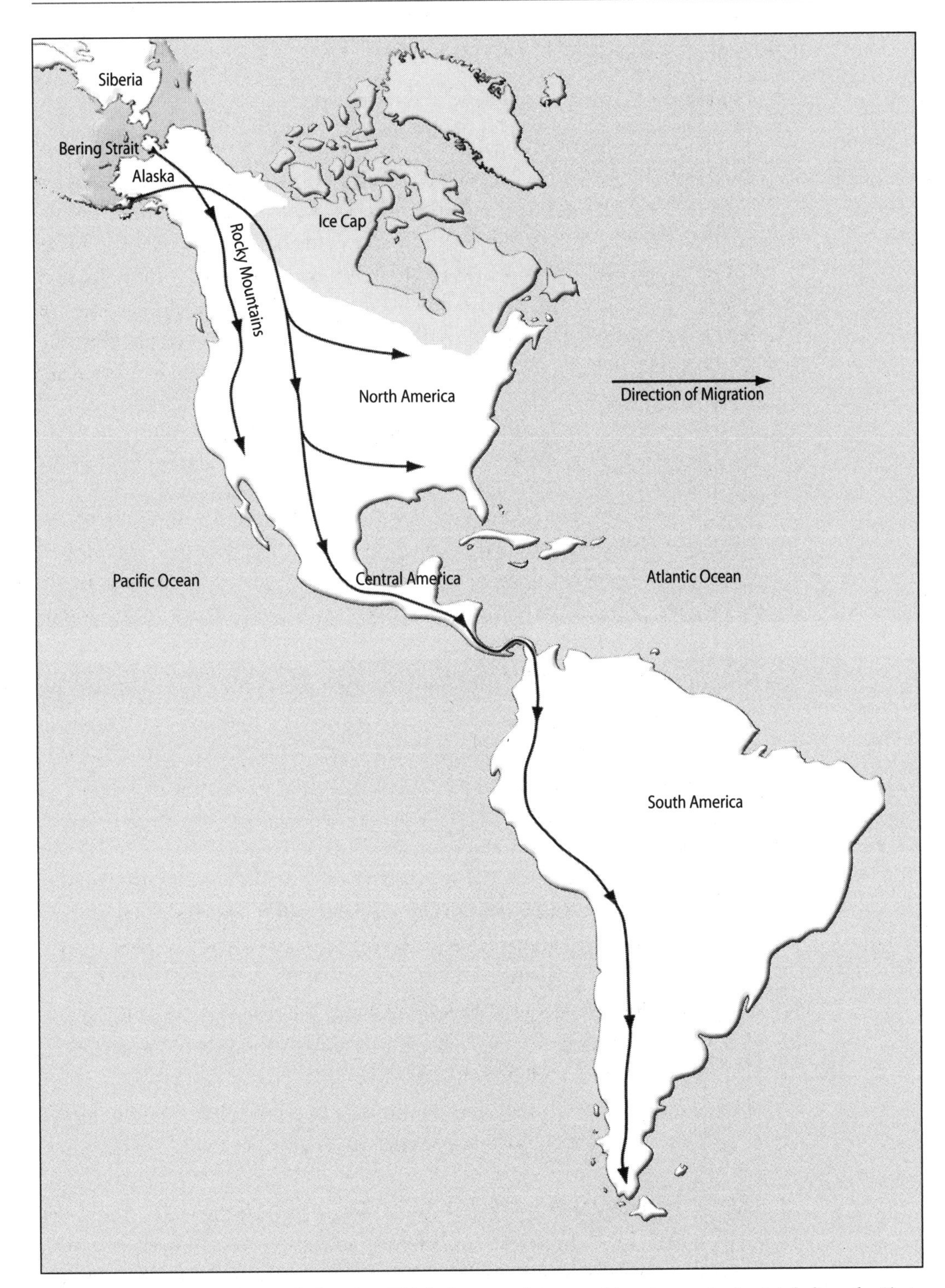

Figure 1.3 The Beringia Theory of Migration This is the route that many historians and scientists believe the First Peoples took to the Americas. (The shaded area represents the Beringia land bridge.) Exactly when this migration took place, however, is widely debated. It could have been anywhere from 10,000 to 40,000 years ago. It is also unclear whether the First Peoples crossed Beringia in a single mass migration or at different intervals over time.

Doubts about Beringia

The Beringia theory has been widely accepted for many years. Yet there are recent discoveries that cast some doubt on its validity. For example, primitive stone tools found in the Bow River Valley in Alberta in 1996 suggest that prehistoric people may have lived here even before the last ice age. The truth is, it is impossible to know for sure. Many researchers believe that the evidence needed to solve this puzzle lies hidden deep beneath the waters of the Bering Strait.

Other Theories of Origins

There are other scientific theories to explain how the First Peoples came to be in the Americas. One theory suggests that these early migrants came by sea. They crossed the Pacific and then travelled down the coast of the Americas. Some of the most persuasive evidence to support this theory was found in South America. Ancient **artifacts** discovered in southern Chile and northeastern Brazil indicate that the First Peoples may have occupied the Americas earlier than the Beringia theory suggests. However, there is some debate over whether these tools were made by humans or by natural forces. Therefore, the evidence is inconclusive.

artifacts products of human skill or activity

Another theory suggests that prehistoric groups may have crossed the Pacific by boat from Southeast Asia. DNA evidence from some **indigenous** groups suggests that each continent has a different pattern of DNA **mutations**. First Nations and Inuit peoples in the Americas have distinct DNA mutations that indigenous peoples from Siberia lack. But this particular mutation pattern is found in indigenous peoples in Southeast Asia and the islands of the South Pacific. Some scientists suggest that this means that the First Peoples came across the Pacific—not across the Bering Strait.

indigenous people born in a region

mutations distinct forms produced by genetic change

First Nations and Inuit Theories of Origins

While the scientific theories of origins are varied, they all suggest that the First Peoples came here from some other place. But as you have seen in their creation stories, the First Peoples have a different theory about their origins. They believe that this is their homeland. They know no other place. They have lived here since time began.

The Theory of American Genesis

An American archaeologist named Jeffrey Goodman has a theory that supports this perspective. In 1981, he put forth the theory of American **genesis**. According to Goodman, a unique **evolutionary** line occurred in the Americas. It was separate from any evolutionary line in Asia or Africa. Over time, this line evolved into the First Nations and Inuit cultures of today. Accord-

genesis the origin of something

evolutionary gradually developed from a simple to a more complex form

ing to Goodman's theory, the First Peoples did not come to the Americas by way of the Bering Strait. In fact, the reverse happened. They evolved here in the Americas. Later, they migrated to Asia. (See Figure 1.4.)

Goodman bases his arguments on archaeological evidence that suggests that humans were hunting in North America as far back as 100,000 years ago. This is much farther back than the 15,000 to 40,000 years ago cited in the classic theories.

VOICES

Although few scientists accept Goodman's theory, many First Nations and Inuit peoples support it.

"Many of Goodman's arguments are intriguing; they suggest new realms of possibility. If some of his interpretations are ever firmly supported by new evidence, certainly any arguments that Indigenous people are relative newcomers can be set aside. Goodman does not reject the importance of the Bering Land Bridge, but he reverses the direction of the current; certainly ... his model is more credible than some of the other proposed Aboriginal theories."

P. Brizinski, Knots in a String: An Introduction to Native Studies in Canada *(Saskatoon: University of Saskatchewan, 1989), p. 35.*

SOME MYTHS ABOUT ORIGINS

Some myths revolve around the theory that the First Peoples came to North America from somewhere other than Asia. One myth holds that they were ancestors of the Twelve Lost Tribes of Israel. After being banished from the Middle East in pre-Christian days, these people made their way to the Americas. There may even have been two such migrations. The second migration, which took place 600 years BCE, split the Israelites into two groups. One founded the ancient civilizations of Mexico and South America. The other created the indigenous civilizations of North America. Another myth suggests that the First Peoples are the survivors of the lost continents of Atlantis, Lemuria, or Mu. How valid are myths in explaining the origins of a people?

Dates	Events	Genesis Theory
2.5 million BCE	Beginning of Pleistocene Era	
1.6 million BCE	*Homo erectus* evolved from earlier forms, possibly in Africa	
1 million BCE	Beginning of ice ages	
200,000–300,000 BCE	Neanderthal Man (*Homo neanderthalensis*) evolved and appeared in Africa, Europe, and Asia	
100,000 BCE	Modern humans (*Homo sapiens*) appear, either in a single location or in Africa, Europe, and Asia	
70,000 BCE	Beginning of last ice age; Bering Strait accessible for human migration	Evolution of modern humans in North America
35,000–40,000 BCE	Spread of modern humans through inhabited world	Migration of humans from North America to Asia
10,000–12,000 BCE	Distinctive fluted points appear in North America, signifying the adaptation of humans to a Palaeo-Indian, big-game hunting way of life; spread of humans throughout the Americas	
	Ancestors of Athapaskan-speaking peoples may have entered North America	Distinctive adaptations arising in North America
	End of ice age; climatic changes	
5,000–7,000 BCE	Domestication of plants for food in Central and South America	
4,500 BCE	Egyptian civilization	
4,000 BCE	Palaeo-Eskimo people spread across the Arctic	
3,500 BCE	Indigenous states (Inca, Maya, etc.) develop in Mexico, Central and South America	
3,000 BCE	Woodland cultures, with agriculture and pottery, found in what is now the eastern United States	
2,500 BCE	Golden Age of Greece	
2,200 BCE	Rise of the Roman Empire	
2,000 BCE	Beginning of Christianity	
1,000 BCE	Thule people, ancestors of modern Inuit, come from Alaska and spread across northern Canada and Greenland	

Figure 1.4 Theory of American Genesis The Evolutionary Scale. Goodman argues that certain cultural features, such as cave art, developed in North America and were later transported to Europe. *Source: Adapted from P. Brizinski,* Knots in a String: An Introduction to Native Studies in Canada *(Saskatoon: University of Saskatchewan, 1989), p. 29.*

BCE = Before the Common Era

In what ways has your family, community, and culture influenced your ideas about our origins? In what ways is this similar to or different from the influences and experiences of First Nations and Inuit peoples prior to European contact?

THE FIRST PEOPLES AND THE LAND

All First Nations and Inuit cultures share a strong bond with nature. Their "ways of being" are closely linked to the land. It is impossible to separate the foundation of all these cultures—their spirituality—from their connections to the land. Coming from the land is part of their cultural heritage. It is a "belief in origin" rather than a "theory of origin."

In the worldview of First Nations and Inuit cultures, all things—organic and living, animate and inanimate—have a spirit. The gifts of the land are to be used and enjoyed. Above all, however, they are to be respected. Understanding this relationship is essential to understanding these cultures. As you will discover later in this book, connections to the land are at the heart of Aboriginal issues past, present, and future.

Medicine Wheel Teachings

Why is the land so important in First Nations cultures? For some First Nations, Medicine Wheel teachings help explain this bond. These teachings provide listeners with a means of understanding and improving themselves and their world from a spiritual perspective.

Medicine Wheel teachings begin with the drawing of a circle. The circle is divided into four directions or teachings. (See Figure 1.5.) Each of these teachings relates to something in the environment, and all four segments are interconnected. The things that happen in one area affect all the other areas of the wheel. For example, if the spring is dry, then the summer crops may be affected. Without the spring rains, the crops do not have a chance to grow healthy roots. This causes them to wither and die in the summer or to be underdeveloped in the fall. Keeping all four aspects in balance enables nature to be healthy and strong. This balance demonstrates the concept of **interdependence**.

Another Medicine Wheel teaching illustrates how balancing the **ecosystem** is critical to the health of the environment. The Earth comprises four main elements: earth, air, fire, and water. When one of these elements is abused, the other three suffer. For instance, when all of a forest's large trees are cut down, **erosion** occurs as rains wash away the nutrient-rich topsoil. Winds blow down the smaller trees that remain because they no longer

interdependence
the state of being influenced by or dependent on one another

ecosystem
a biological community of interacting organisms in a physical environment

erosion
the wearing away of the Earth's surface by wind, water, or glacial action

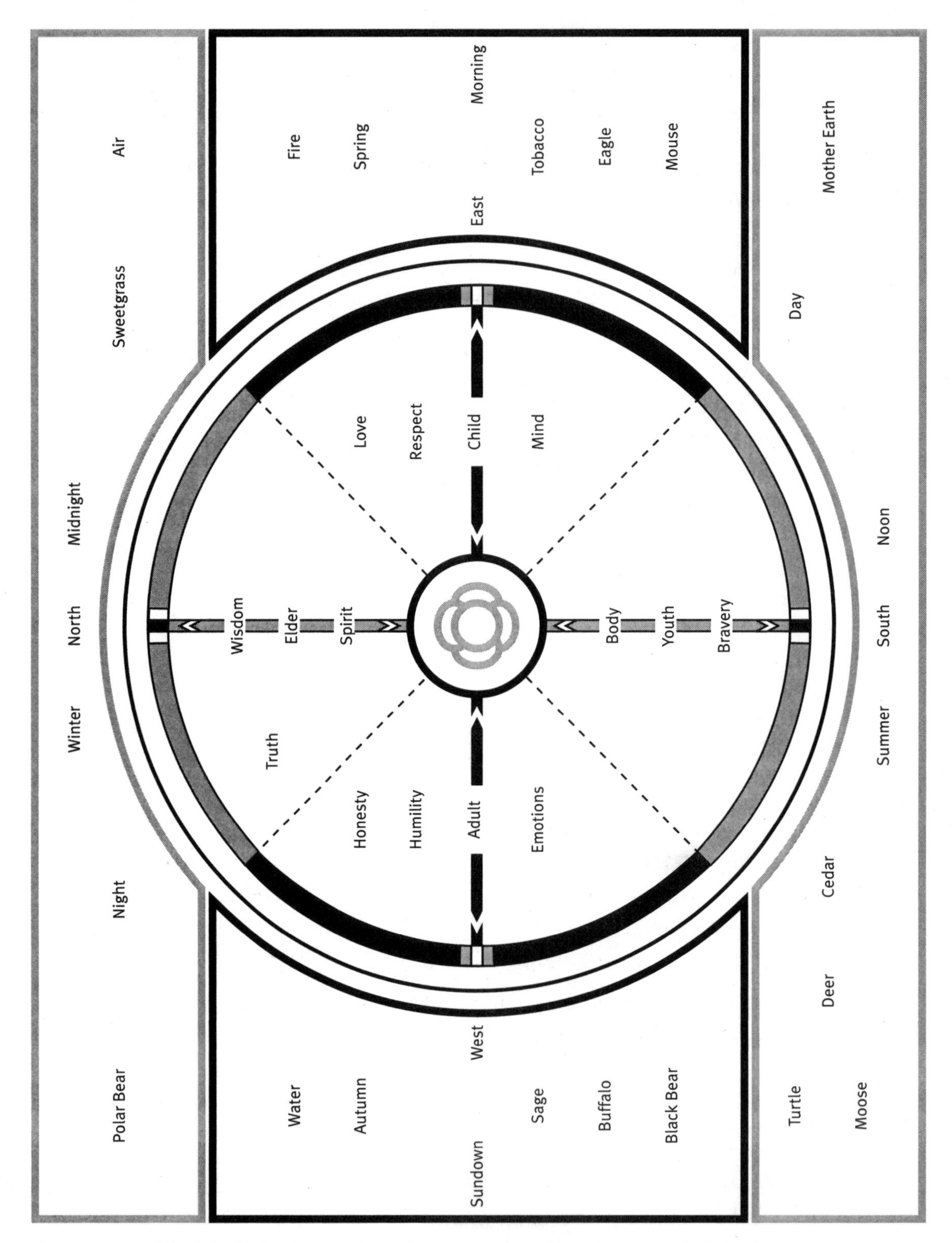

Figure 1.5 A Medicine Wheel This diagram shows the connections and interdependences of a Medicine Wheel based on a drawing by Anishnaabe artist and teacher Henry Angeconeb.

have the protection of a standing mature forest. Fires start easily in the dry bushes of dead foliage and branches that cover the ground. Soil that is overexposed to the sun—because of the absence of trees—dries out. Again, Medicine Wheel teachings show the interdependence of all things in nature. (In Chapter 2, you'll see how the concept of interdependence applies to people and their communities.)

THE IMPORTANCE OF THE NUMBER FOUR

In many First Nations and Inuit cultures, four is an important number. It is also the basis of most Medicine Wheel teachings. Many things take place or exist in fours:

- four seasons (fall, winter, spring, and summer)
- four directions (north, south, east, and west)
- four physical elements (earth, air, fire, and water)
- four aspects of the individual (emotional, physical, spiritual, and mental)
- four stages of life (child, teen, adult, and Elder)
- four sacred medicines (sage, tobacco, sweetgrass, and cedar)
- four colours of humans (red, yellow, black, and white)

Responsibilities to Nature

Another Medicine Wheel teaching demonstrates the First Peoples' connection to the land. In the teaching of the four colours of humans, the Creator has given each group responsibility for different parts of nature:

- White people are responsible for taking care of the air.
- Black people are responsible for taking care of the water.
- Yellow people are responsible for fire.
- Red people are responsible for taking care of the earth.

This teaching is reinforced in many creation stories. As the last to be created, humans were assigned the roles of servants and caretakers for all other creations. This notion contrasts sharply with the Judaeo-Christian belief that humans have "dominion over the fish of the sea, and over the fowl of the air, and over the cattle, and over all the Earth" (Genesis 1:25). You'll have the opportunity to learn more about these contrasting worldviews in Chapter 4.

1. First Nations and Inuit creation stories present a "belief in origin" and a "theory of origin." What is the difference between a belief and a theory?
2. Identify one common belief and one common theory in your culture.
3. What further examples can you think of that demonstrate the concept of interdependence in the environment?

CHAPTER 1 CULMINATING ACTIVITY

Getting Your Life in Balance

Is your life in balance? Regardless of our age, time management is one of the most important skills we need to balance the demands that are placed on our busy lives. For example, if you are so busy with your school work and a part-time job that you do not have enough time for recreation and relaxation, you may be placing your health at risk. Then your life is out of balance. Or if you have plenty of computer games and other technological gadgets, but no friends to enjoy them with, your life is out of balance.

Balancing life's priorities sounds like simple advice, but it can be a difficult task in the real world. Too frequently, burnout, depression, and poor health are the price we pay for not balancing our lives.

In this chapter, you discovered the role of Medicine Wheel teachings in creating balance in the lives of many First Nations peoples. They have recognized the importance of balancing their lives. Instead of living to work, First Nations peoples have worked to live.

This activity simulates the holistic approach to a balanced life as practised in a Medicine Wheel. In no way should it be considered an activity about an actual Medicine Wheel. Medicine Wheel teachings are best left to First Nations Elders and facilitators. Instead, this activity builds upon the concept of living a balanced life as a path toward overall wellness. It asks you to create your own "Balance-of-Life Wheel." Since developing the skills to lead a balanced life requires disciplined habits that are acquired over time, you may want to repeat this activity at the end of the course to measure your growth in the quest to lead a more balanced life.

THE WHEEL OF LIFE

The Wheel of Life provides a graphic representation of the concept of wellness. To attain and maintain harmony and balance in your life, you must focus on each of the eight dimensions of wellness. To neglect or overemphasize any of these dimensions will result in an unbalanced life wheel.

Think of a balanced Wheel of Life as a bicycle tire made up of eight different spokes, with each spoke representing a dimension of wellness. If one or more of these spokes is either too long or too short, the wheel will be unbalanced and the bicycle will provide a very bumpy ride. Therefore, we roll along through life more smoothly when our lives are well-rounded or balanced.

Poor Mental Health

Balanced Mental Health

A balanced Wheel of Life helps you determine whether you are focusing too much on one part of your life while neglecting other parts. The wheel is divided into eight spokes. Rank your level of satisfaction from 0 to 10 for each area of your life. A score of 10 indicates that you are completely satisfied with this aspect of your life. A score of 0 indicates that you are completely dissatisfied. An example is shown below.

My Life (example):

Physical activity: 8

Home and family: 7

Friends: 6

Spirituality: 8

Part-time work: 2

School: 3

Relationships: 1

Fun and recreation: 7

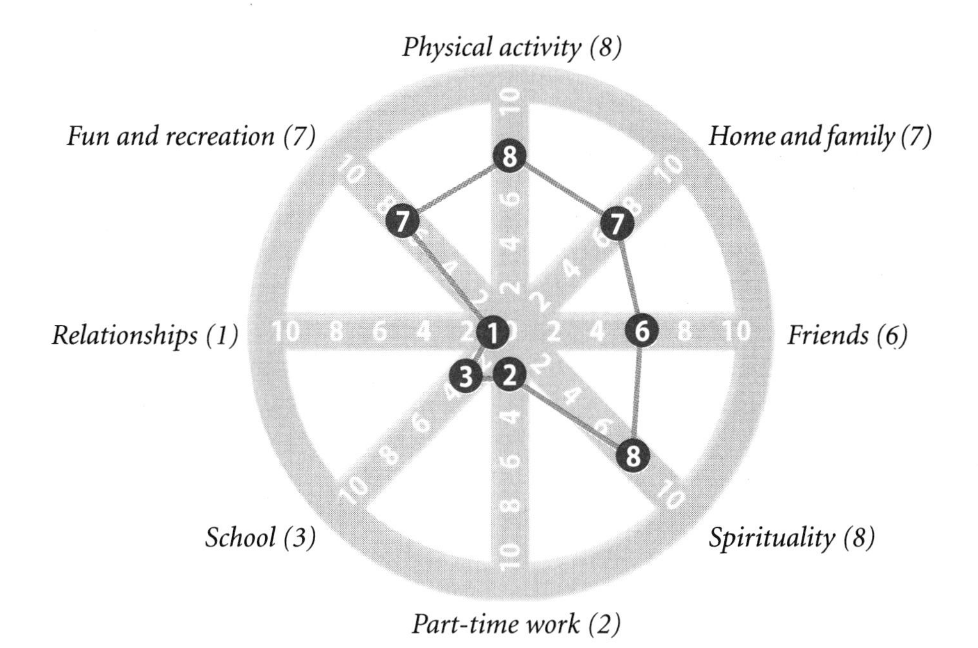

Balancing Life Using a Wheel For this person, the degree of satisfaction for School, Part-time work, and Relationships is low. He or she can now recognize areas of life that need improvement in order to create a more balanced wheel.

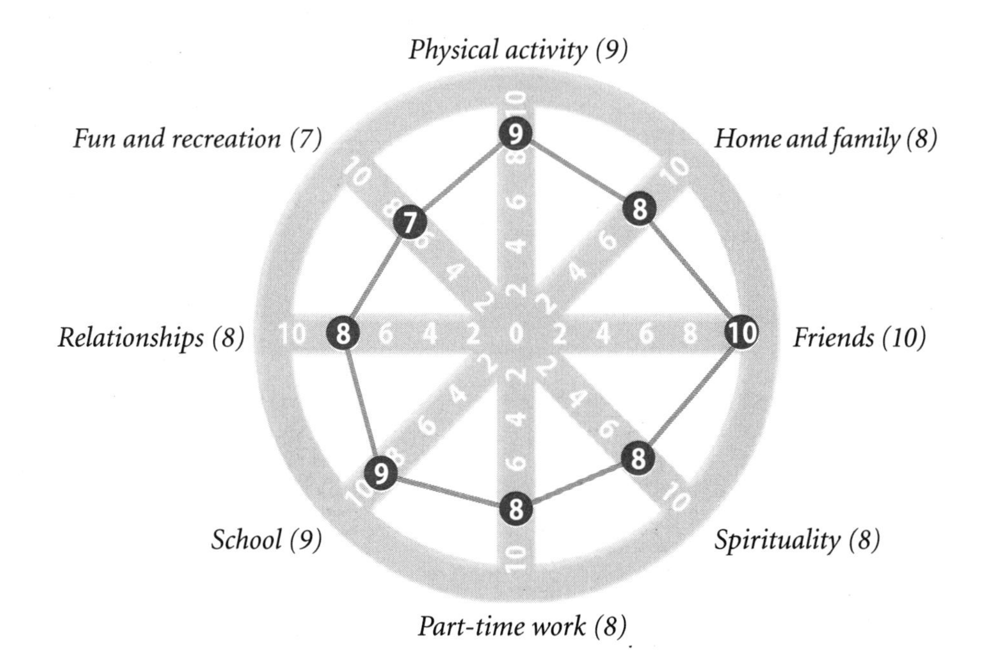

A Balanced Wheel of Life The ideal Wheel of Life is something like this.

Now make a copy of the wheel and try it yourself!

My Life:

Physical activity: _____

Home and family: _____

Friends: _____

Spirituality: _____

Part-time work: _____

School: _____

Relationships: _____

Fun and recreation: _____

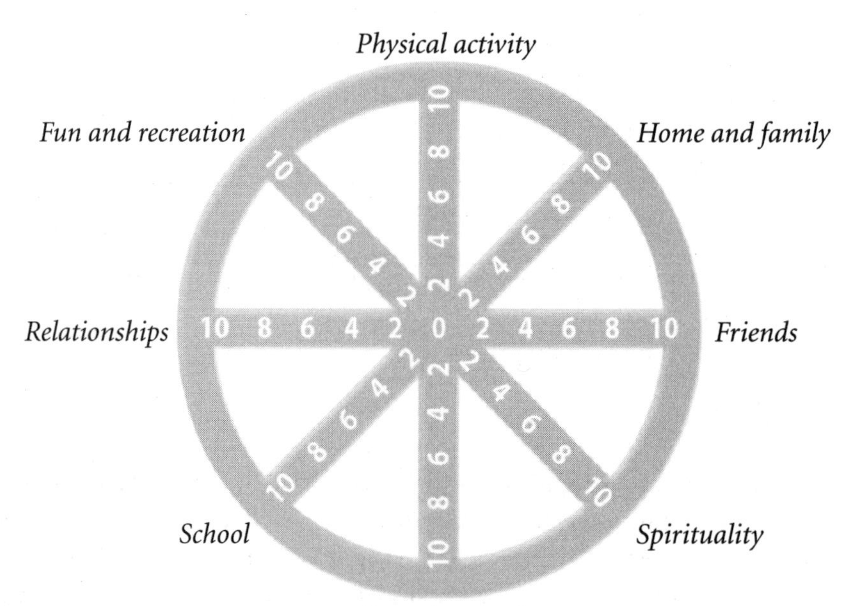

My Balance-of-Life Wheel

CHAPTER 2

Characteristics of First Nations and Inuit Cultures

LEARNING OBJECTIVES

In this chapter, you will

- understand the role of archaeology in interpreting the history of First Nations and Inuit peoples
- identify some of the common cultural characteristics of First Nations and Inuit peoples in Canada
- identify the 11 First Nations and Inuit language families in Canada
- identify the six First Nations and Inuit cultural groups in Canada
- compare and contrast the geographic environment of these six cultural groups
- learn about the buffalo culture of the Plains peoples

INTRODUCTION

In this chapter, you have the opportunity to learn about the six First Nations and Inuit cultural groups that lived in what is now Canada before the arrival of Europeans over 500 years ago. You'll begin by looking at the role archaeology has played in studying their history and identifying cultural time periods. You'll discover that First Nations and Inuit cultures shared a common, yet richly diverse, worldview and spirituality based on their connections to the land. You'll also discover that they had many unique characteristics, too, that resulted from the geographic environments in which they lived. You'll see how these environments led to the evolution of many different languages and cultures across Canada. You'll also have the opportunity to take a closer look at the buffalo culture of the Plains people.

CULTURAL PERIODS

The Role of Archaeology

First Nations and Inuit peoples used legends, songs, and personal stories to pass down their cultures from generation to generation. They did not write history books or keep diaries or official records. Since there were no formal systems of reading and writing, most scientific information about the First Peoples comes from archaeological investigation.

Archaeology is the scientific study of human history and prehistory through the excavation of sites and the analysis of physical artifacts. It provides clues to help us learn about and understand ancient cultures. From this research, archaeologists have created time periods for the First Peoples. They begin with the Palaeo-Indian culture, which emerged around 12,000 years ago as the glaciers began to recede, and end with the Terminal Woodland cultures, which existed at the time of European contact. (See Figure 2.1.)

A Devastating Loss of Population

First Nations and Inuit cultures did not keep census records. Therefore, experts can only estimate the number of First Peoples who once lived in North America. Many estimates suggest that there may have been as many as 3 million First Nations and Inuit people living here prior to the arrival of Europeans.

By 1900, census figures indicated that there were only about 100,000 First Nations and Inuit people in Canada. This low number means that since the arrival of Europeans only 400 years earlier, the population had dwindled by over 95 percent.

The Wisconsin Glaciation Period (70,000–12,000 Years Ago)

The Wisconsin Glaciation period marked the beginning of the last ice age. In the western half of the North American continent, the Cordilleran Ice Sheet covered most of what is now southern Alaska and British Columbia, extending south into the United States. To the east, the Laurentide Ice Sheet extended across Saskatchewan east to the St. Lawrence River and beyond to the region south of the Great Lakes.

It was during this time that *Homo sapiens*, or modern humans, emerged in Asia. Approximately 35,000 to 70,000 years ago, the Beringia land bridge connected Siberia and Alaska. This allowed people to cross from Asia to North America, where they migrated south using an ice-free corridor in what is now Alberta. As the glaciers receded, the people spread across the continent following herds of game animals. As they did, they developed their own societies, cultures, and languages.

The Palaeo-Indian Culture (12,000–7,000 Years Ago)

The Palaeo-Indian culture was the first culture to emerge in North America. However, little is known about the Palaeo-Indians. The only archaeological evidence about them consists of the tools they left behind.

What archaeologists do know, however, is that much of the Palaeo-Indian culture was centred in what is now the United States, in the area south of the glaciers. There is some evidence that the Palaeo-Indians also lived in what is now southeastern Alberta, southern Saskatchewan, and the extreme southwestern part of Manitoba.

The Palaeo-Indians were big-game hunters. Artifacts of a stone spear-point technology found only in North America suggest that they developed their own hunting methods. As the climate warmed and the glaciers receded, the Palaeo-Indians spread into eastern Canada. As they did, a new culture, the Archaic peoples, emerged.

Years Ago	Period	The Environment	The People
70,000	Wisconsin Glaciation	• Cold • Glacial ice covers most of present-day Canada and the northern United States	• People migrate from Siberia to Alaska across the Beringia land bridge • Populate most of the Americas
12,000	Palaeo–Indian	• Cool • Glaciers begin to melt • Tundra and spruce parkland	• As the glaciers melt, people migrate to present-day Ontario • Big-game hunters and gatherers
7,000	Archaic	• Warmer • White pine and oak forests • Many big-game animals, such as the woolly mammoth, become extinct	• People become less nomadic; begin to build seasonal camps • Small-game hunters, fishers, and gatherers • Begin to invent many new tools
3,000	Initial Woodland	• Conditions similar to the Archaic period 2,000 years ago	• Pottery, bows, and arrows introduced from the south • Extensive trade networks established • Burial mounds introduced in east-central United States and southern Ontario • A Point Peninsula band begins to occupy Serpent Mounds c. 200 BCE • Serpent Mounds abandoned as regular camps c. 400 CE
1,000	Terminal Woodland	• Conditions similar to the Archaic period	• Haudenosaunee (Iroquois) cultures established in the upper St. Lawrence and Lake Ontario regions • Development of agriculture based on corn, beans, and squash • Population explosion takes place • Warfare leads to large palisaded villages; longhouses introduced • Mass pit graves introduced • Only intermittent occupation of Serpent Mounds • Europeans arrive in North America

Figure 2.1 Cultural Time Periods The earliest period identified by archaeologists is the Wisconsin Glaciation period, at least 70,000 years ago. *Sources: Adapted from C.W. Ceram,* The First American: A Story of American Archeology *(New York: Mentor, 1971); Ontario Ministry of Education, Independent Learning Centre, "The Meaning of Culture," in* Peoples of Native Ancestry, *Lesson 2 (Toronto: Queen's Printer, n.d.), p. 17.*

The Archaic Period (7,000–3,000 Years Ago)

nomadic moving from place to place in search of food and fresh pasture

The Archaic culture was divided into two groups: the Laurentian and the Shield. The Laurentian culture lived in southern Ontario. Archaeologists believe they were originally a **nomadic** culture that migrated north from the United States. Although the people were big-game hunters, they supplemented their diet with smaller game, fish, berries, and wild plants.

The religious beliefs of the Laurentians included sprinkling the corpses of the dead with red ochre and placing stone, bone, and copper tools and ornaments and shells from the Gulf of Mexico and the Atlantic region in their graves. The shells indicate that the Laurentians had trade relationships with the cultures in these areas. The Laurentian culture lasted almost 3,000 years, until agriculture was introduced to the region.

All the technologies developed by the First Peoples reflected their deep knowledge and understanding of their environments:

"Development of stone and bone tools represented one of humanity's great strides forward into technological sophistication.... It was viable only because of acute and careful observation of nature—still a basic requirement today."

Olive Dickason, Canada's First Nations *(3rd ed.) (Toronto: Oxford University Press, 2002), p. 12.*

The Shield cultures lived in central and northern Ontario. The people shared some of the cultural traits of the Laurentian peoples. They hunted big game and supplemented their diet with smaller game, waterfowl, and fruits and berries. They had their own unique characteristics, too. They developed technologies such as birch-bark canoes and snowshoes to use in a land of many rivers and lakes and cold, snowy winters.

The Woodland Period (3,000 Years Ago to Contact)

The Woodland period was the closest period to European contact. Therefore, more artifacts have been preserved from this period than from any other. This has enabled scientists to learn more about the Woodland peoples than about any of the cultures that preceded them.

The Woodland culture was similar to the Archaic culture. However, the Woodland peoples added pottery to their technologies. The discovery of five different pottery types has led archaeologists to identify five cultures that flourished during the Initial Woodland period between 3,000 and 1,000 years ago:

- the *Laurel* culture in northern Ontario
- the *Point Peninsula* culture in eastern Ontario
- the *Saugeen* culture in southern Ontario
- the *Princess Point* culture in southwestern Ontario
- the *Hopewell* and *Meadowood* cultures in southwestern Ontario and the midwestern United States.

The Initial Woodland period was replaced by the Terminal Woodland period from 1,000 years ago to the time of European contact. This period marked the emergence of the Algonquian-speaking peoples of northern Ontario and the Iroquoian-speaking peoples of southern Ontario.

1. What tools and technologies of First Nations peoples do archaeologists use to investigate the past?
2. How do you think people, ideas, technologies, and cultural traits moved from place to place in the prehistoric era?

CONNECTIONS TO THE LAND

Spirituality

In Chapter 1, you learned that First Nations and Inuit peoples have a strong connection to the land. Land is more than a geographic territory. It is a sacred, living entity, with its own rhythms and cycles. The people are sensitive to these rhythms and they heed the signs in nature. The land reflects the people's way of life and their spirituality. It provides the people with sacred places where power, wisdom, and the meaning of life are granted by the spiritual world. In this way, the land is closely linked to the people's destiny. It keeps them strong as nations.

First Nations and Inuit cultures depended on nature for their survival and had a deep spiritual relationship with their environment:

"Without [the land and animals] our spirits will die. Non-natives sometimes think we are being romantic when we talk about these things. This is not about romance. This is about reality and survival."

Norma Kassi, Gwich'in Nation, in a speech to the First American Congress of Indigenous Peoples, 1989.

Figure 2.2 The Sun Dance The Plains nations held summer celebrations of the buffalo spirits during the annual Sun Dance. Although the Plains cultures had ceremonies to worship other spirits, including the sun, the Thunderbird, and the Old Man of the Dawn, this sacred ceremony was the most important.

Seven Grandfathers traditional teachings of the Anishnaabe that describe the qualities of wisdom, love, respect, bravery, honesty, humility, and truth that should guide a person's life

Respect for All Things

First Nations and Inuit peoples have great respect for the land, and all things of the land have a spiritual significance for them. To show their respect, they developed many spiritual practices. When a deer was killed for food, for example, the hunter laid down tobacco at the site of the killing as an expression of thanks to the spirit of the deer for giving up its life to nurture the hunter and his family. If the hunter offended the deer's spirit, he would face great challenges obtaining food in the future. Therefore, the people had to be alert to their spiritual encounters with nature and to heed their messages. These practices were reflected in the Anishnaabe teachings of the **Seven Grandfathers**. (You can find out more about the spiritual practices of the Plains cultures on page 40.)

Animism

First Nations and Inuit peoples share a common worldview of people and their place in the world called *animism*. They believe all of creation is alive and that all things in the physical world have a spirit. Therefore, all things are to be respected.

Interdependence

As you learned in Chapter 1, all things in life are interdependent in First Nations and Inuit cultures. Each person has four components—physical, emotional, mental, and spiritual. These qualities are interrelated and interconnected. If one element is neglected, then the others are adversely affected and an imbalance is created. To be **holistic**, people must ensure that each area of their lives is cared for equally.

This belief extended to relationships among the people in their communities. Most societies were **egalitarian**. The people relied on one another to contribute the skills the group needed to survive. Each person contributed to the physical, emotional, mental, and spiritual balance that was needed to maintain strong communities. Each person was valued and respected, regardless of age, gender, or status.

Failure to live up to one's responsibilities had grave consequences. When efforts at rehabilitation failed, a person was banished from the community. This inevitably meant death for the banished person because it was not possible to survive without the community's help and support. All members of the group were aware of the consequences of unacceptable behaviour.

holistic
balanced in all aspects of life—physical, emotional, mental, and spiritual

egalitarian
promoting human equality, especially with respect to social, political, and economic rights and privileges

A Code of Ethics

Most First Nations cultures shared a common code of ethics that was closely connected to their spirituality. The code, which offered guidance for all members of a community, was based on the following principles:

1. Give thanks to the Creator when rising each morning and before retiring each evening for the life within you and for all life and for the good things you experience. Consider your actions and words thoughtfully and seek the courage and strength to be a better person in all things.
2. Respect yourself, others, and the world around you and show respect as a basic law of life.
3. Respect and listen to the wisdom of those who make decisions about your world, and share your ideas equally with others.
4. Be truthful at all times and in all situations.
5. Treat your guests with honour and consideration and give the best you have in food, accommodations, and other comforts.
6. Accept the hurt of one as the hurt of all and the honour of one as the honour of all.
7. Welcome strangers and outsiders with kindness and a loving heart because we are all members of the human family.
8. Respect all races as though they are different-coloured flowers in a meadow, and acknowledge that each is beautiful and has an important role to play. Understand that the Creator made each race for a special reason and that we must respect one another's gifts.
9. Serve others because this is the primary reason humans were created. Understand that the secret to true happiness comes to those who dedicate their lives to the service of others.
10. Observe moderation and balance at all times and in all things.
11. Be wise and know the things and actions that will lead to your health and well-being and those things that will lead to your destruction. Know your heart.
12. Listen and follow the guidance in your heart and expect guidance to come in many forms: in prayer, dreams, quiet reflection, and the actions and deeds of Elders and other wise people.

Therefore, there were relatively few contraventions of community norms and taboos.

The egalitarian values of First Nations and Inuit societies were evident in their decision making. In many cultures, decisions were reached by **consensus**. The people discussed an issue until everyone agreed to accept a resolution. Communities were egalitarian with the food supply, too. When a hunter returned with the carcass of an animal he had killed, the meat was distributed among the community.

consensus general agreement of the group

Gender Roles

Women were responsible for gathering and preparing food, making clothing out of furs and skins, raising the children, and managing the homes. Men were responsible for fishing, hunting, and waging war. Elders, both male and female, were highly respected. They were the mediators and advisers in the community. They passed down the people's stories and teachings.

CLOSE-UP

THE ROLE OF CHILDREN

Children in First Nations and Inuit societies had a great deal of personal freedom and independence. Gender determined a child's roles and responsibilities. Girls gathered food and helped around the home. Boys hunted for small game. Both boys and girls ran errands for the Elders. They were respected for the roles they played. Children did not "belong" to their parents. Instead, they were part of a larger extended family. It was not uncommon for children to live temporarily with grandparents or aunts and uncles if their parents were unable to meet their needs or if family members needed help.

Figure 2.3 Children in First Nations and Inuit Societies Children were the future of their communities. Therefore, each member of the community assumed responsibility for the children's care and learning. Children's roles and responsibilities were as valued and respected as those of adults.

Trade

Contact among First Nations and Inuit cultures influenced their customs and traditions. The main benefit of contact was trade. Different cultures traded those things they had in abundance for those things they could not obtain in their own environment. They also traded to maintain friendly relations and forge alliances with neighbouring groups.

Some trade goods were natural resources, such as food and minerals. Other trade goods were products that the people made, such as arrowheads and tools. As the climate became more moderate, agricultural societies developed. Increasingly, these groups began to settle in one place for longer periods of time. This led to more permanent communities that served as trading centres. The people in these communities produced a surplus of food, which they traded for other foods and resources.

As the map in Figure 2.4 shows, First Nations and Inuit peoples had well-established trading networks. Artifacts found in the St. Lawrence Valley

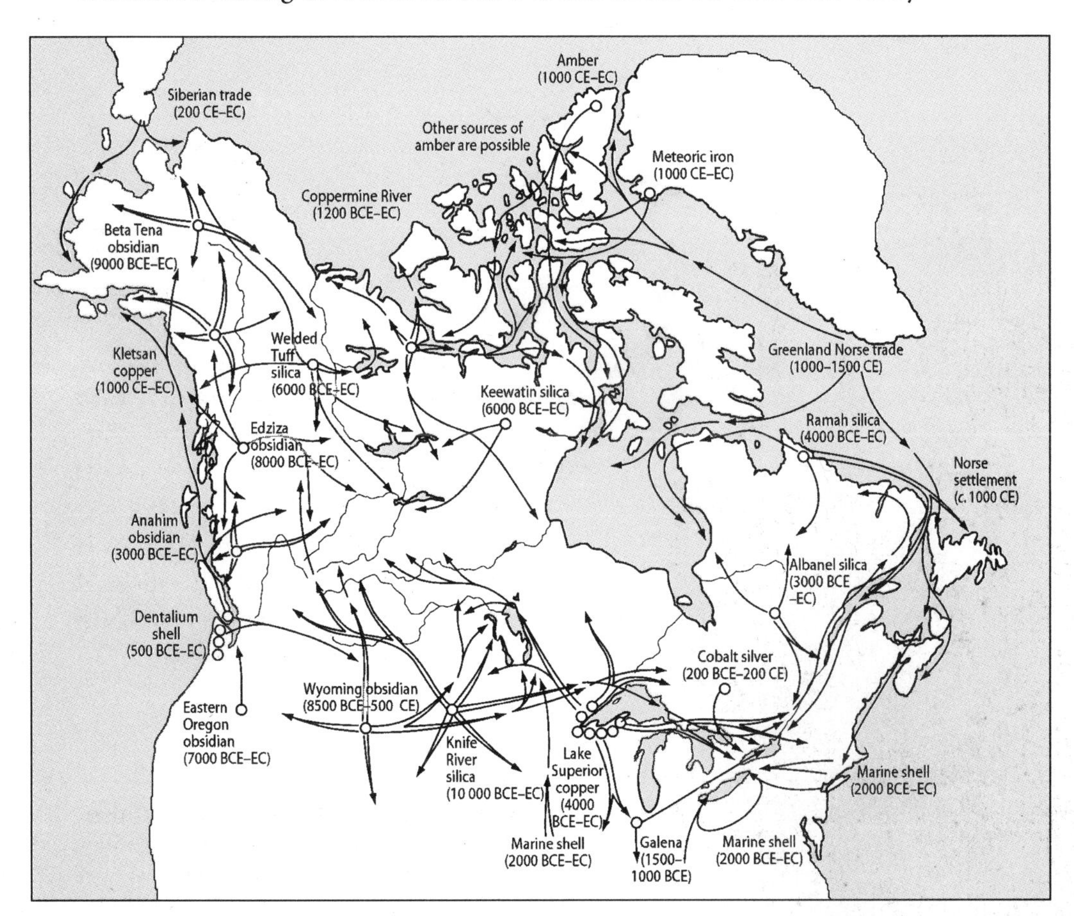

Figure 2.4 Trade Patterns Prior to European Contact The Haudenosaunee (Iroquois) of the Great Lakes region established themselves as intermediaries for trade. They facilitated the exchange and transfer of goods from one culture to another. *Source: Adapted from R.C. Harris (ed.),* Historical Atlas of Canada: Vol. 1—From the Beginning to 1800 *(Toronto: University of Toronto Press, 1987), plate 14.* *EC = European Contact*

include tools made from copper found north of Lake Superior, projectile points made from minerals found in Labrador, and tools made from shells found along the Gulf of Mexico. This and similar evidence confirms that trade took place over long distances all across North America.

1. a) What are some of the spiritually significant aspects of your culture? Why are they significant?

   b) Do some research to identify sites in your province that are spiritually significant to a particular Aboriginal culture. Choose five sites. Create a chart describing each site: its location, the culture for which it is spiritually significant, and why.

2. Compare the attitudes toward children in First Nations and Inuit cultures with attitudes in your own culture. In what ways are they similar? In what ways are they different? How do you think children should be treated?

3. Read the following quotation and answer the questions that follow:

   When I was young, my grandfather and I, almost every evening we would sit on the west side of the summer house and watch the sun set or we would sit on the east side and watch the colours cover the mountains. My grandmother would join us. Then they would tell me about the mountain, about the evening sounds, my grandfather would sing a particular song and tell me "remember it." I would try. Sometimes I would ask my grandmother to help me remember. She would only tell me that that was between my grandfather and me. She would not interfere and it was the same with what my grandmother was teaching—my grandfather did not interfere. And these things they were advising me, their thoughts were the same.

   —Source: P.V. Beck, A.L. Walters, and N. Francisco, *The Sacred Ways of Knowledge, Sources of Life* (Tsaile, AZ: Navaho Community College Press, 1992).

   a) How did the child learn from his grandparents?

   b) What were the roles of the grandparents? How were they different?

   c) In what ways do you learn things from your family?

4. a) Review the code of ethics of First Nations cultures on page 29. What things do you agree with? What things do you disagree with? Give reasons to explain your responses.

   b) Do you think good citizenship requires people to follow a code of ethics? Explain your answer.

LANGUAGE FAMILIES

Linguistics is the method of identifying cultural groups based on language. In Canada, there are 11 First Nations and Inuit language families, although none of these are confined exclusively to Canada. Figure 2.5 shows where these language families were traditionally located in Canada.

The language spoken by each culture shaped the thoughts and identity of the people. It was an important element in each group's survival as a distinct culture. Since First Nations and Inuit cultures relied heavily on the oral tradition to pass on their stories, songs, histories, and traditions, language was particularly important to them.

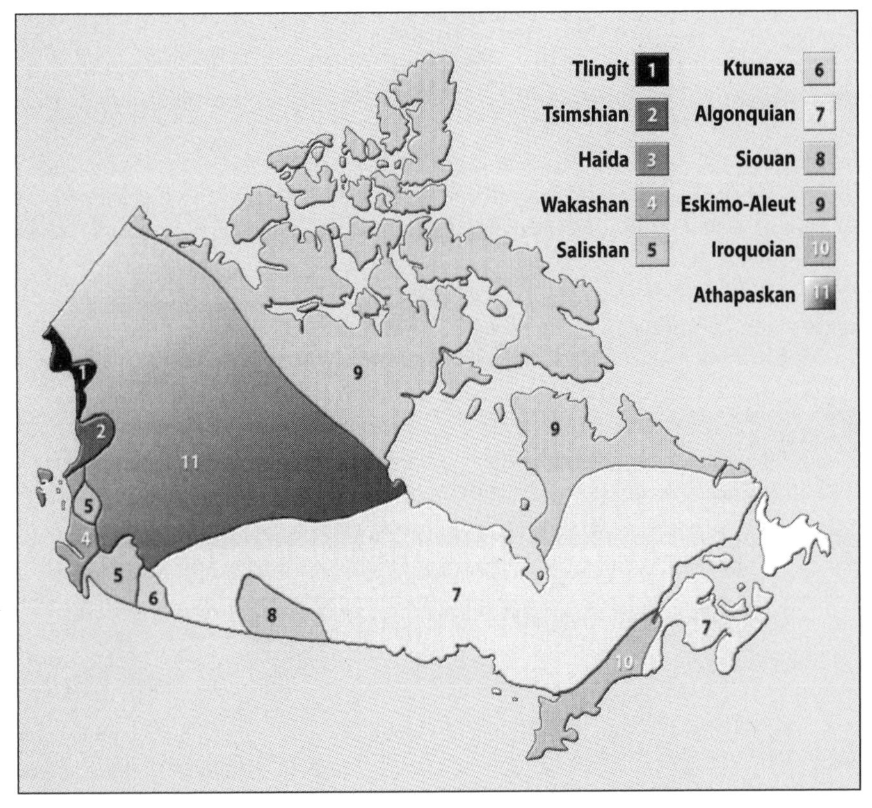

Figure 2.5 Language Families in Canada Environment played a role in shaping language groups. Cultures living in the mountainous regions of the West Coast, for example, were isolated. They had little contact with other linguistic groups. Therefore, their languages developed with minimum influence from outside language families and they retained highly distinctive speech patterns.

Word Origins

More than 1,000 words used in English today have their origins in First Nations and Inuit languages.

Innu: kayak, parka

Nehiyaw (Cree): pemmican, persimmon

Mi'kmaq: toboggan

Algonquian: caucus, chipmunk, hickory, moccasin, moose, muskrat, opossum, pecan, persimmon, raccoon, skunk, squash, succotash, woodchuck

1. **Tlingit:** Tlingit is an isolated linguistic group located in the northwestern corner of British Columbia and in Yukon and Alaska. It has only one language in its family.

2. **Tsimshian:** There are three language groups in the Tsimshian culture. They are located along the coastal inlets of northern British Columbia, the Alaskan Panhandle, and the inland areas of British Columbia along the Nass and Skeena rivers. Because of their geographic location, the Tsimshian, like many other linguistic groups in British Columbia, maintained their distinctiveness. Like all west coast languages, the Tsimshian languages are highly complex and distinct.

3. **Haida:** This is a unique language family found on the Pacific coast. Today, only a few hundred people—mostly of the older generation—speak the Haida language.

4. **Wakashan:** This linguistic family is located on the western and northeastern parts of Vancouver Island and on the adjacent British Columbia coastline. There are six languages within this group, five of which appear in Canada.

5. **Salishan:** The Salishan language family is also located along the eastern and southern coast of Vancouver Island and in inlets along the adjacent mainland. Pockets of this group are found along the Fraser and Okanagan rivers as well.

6. **Ktunaxa:** The Ktunaxa language family is represented by a single language group located on the Pacific coast. Its distinct forms of speech have no connections with any other language families in North America. This suggests that the Ktunaxa once lived in relative isolation.

7. **Algonquian:** There are 20 languages spoken in the Algonquian language family, with many more dialects. The Algonquian language family stretches from the Rockies to Labrador. (Note that the term *Algonquin* refers to an Aboriginal group that lived in the eastern Woodlands. It is often confused with the term *Algonquian*, which refers to the language family.)

8. **Siouan:** The Siouan language family is located in the central prairies. As a linguistic group, it is connected to the Iroquoian family.

9. **Eskimo–Aleut:** The Eskimo–Aleut (also known as Inuktitut) language family is located across northern Canada from coast to coast. It is the only language family in North America with probable linguistic ties with the indigenous peoples of Siberia.

10. **Iroquoian:** The Iroquoian language family thrived along the Great Lakes–St. Lawrence Valley. Some of the languages in this family, such as the Wendat (Huron), are extinct today. However, many members of the Six Nations Confederacy (the Kanien'Kehaka [Mohawk], Oneida, Onondaga, Cayuga, Seneca, and Tuscarora) have maintained their languages.

11. **Athapaskan:** The Athapaskan languages are found primarily in central Canada to the edge of the Rocky Mountains. Fifteen of the 24 languages in this family are spoken in Canada.

Figure 2.6 Characteristics of Language Families The numbers in the table correspond to the numbered regions in the map in Figure 2.5.

1. Today, many First Nations and Inuit languages are disappearing. Do you think it is important that languages be preserved? Why or why not? How could language preservation be encouraged in Aboriginal communities? Why is this so difficult?
2. Brainstorm a list of other words that you know of that have their roots in a First Nations or Inuit language.

DISTINCTIONS AMONG CULTURAL GROUPS

The six main First Nations and Inuit cultural groups in what is now Canada were defined by the environments in which they lived. Climate, terrain, plants, and wildlife influenced the development of each culture. The map in Figure 2.7 identifies these six cultural groups.

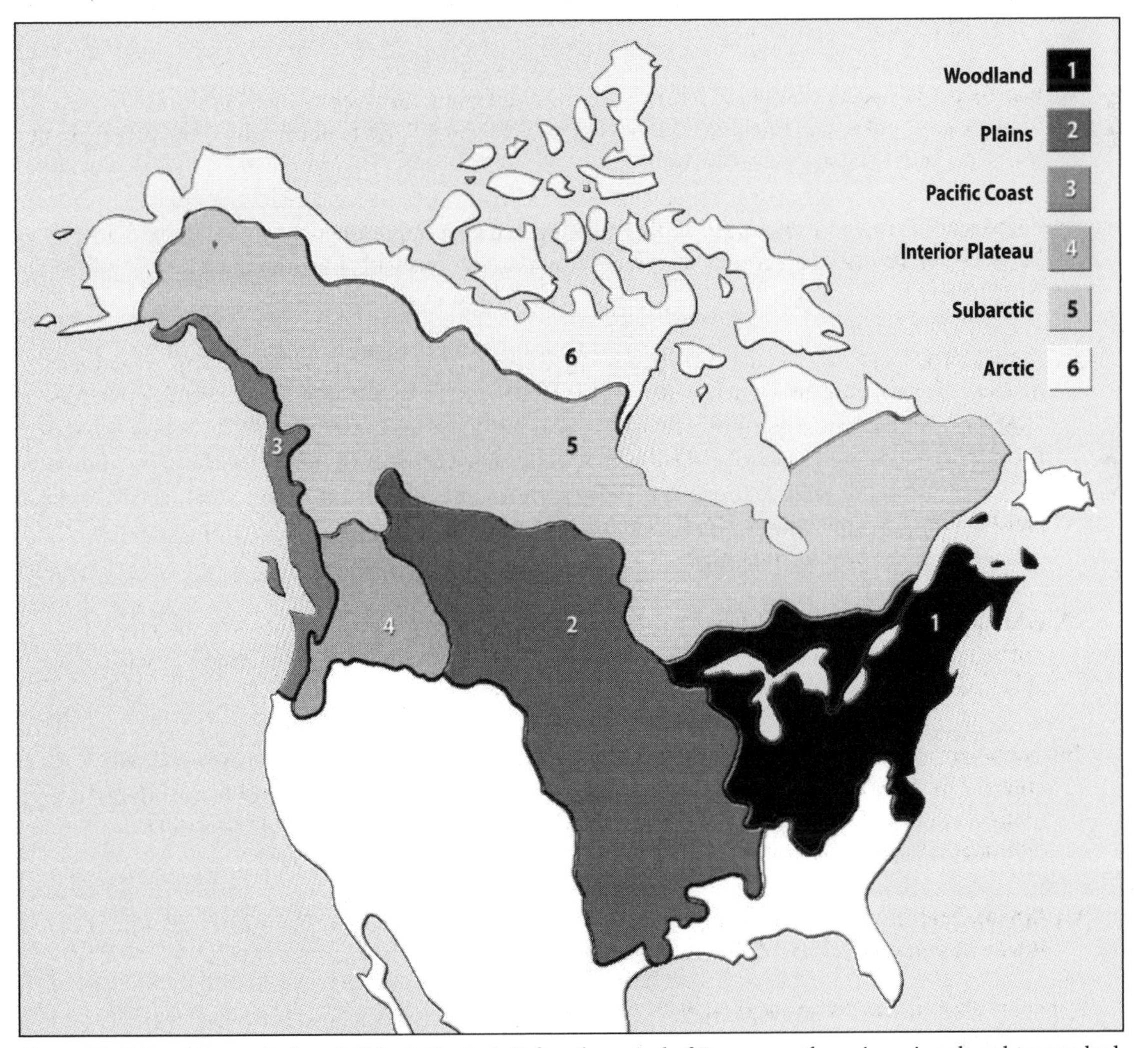

Figure 2.7 Cultural Groups in Canada Prior to Contact Before the arrival of Europeans, these six main cultural groups had developed thriving societies in all regions of a diverse land.

Specific characteristics, such as tools, clothing, and methods of transportation, reflected the ways in which the people adapted to their environments. However, within each culture there were many subcultures. These subcultures did not always share common characteristics. In addition, many subcultures blended characteristics of neighbouring subcultures.

The Peoples of the Woodland

In Canada, the deciduous forests of southern Ontario, the St. Lawrence Lowlands, the coastal Atlantic region, the southern Canadian Shield, and the Appalachians were all part of the Woodland region. This region also extended into the United States southwest to Illinois and east to coastal North Carolina.

In the eastern Woodland, there were two subcultures: the migratory, or nomadic, cultures and the agricultural cultures. The migratory cultures lived in an environment of extensive forests, mountainous or rocky terrain, and numerous lakes and rivers. They travelled from place to place in search of wild game such as deer, moose, and beaver, fish such as perch, pickerel, and pike, wild fruits such as blueberries, strawberries, and chokecherries, and natural vegetation such as roots, plants, and wild rice. Because the winters were long and cold, the Woodland peoples ate meat for most of the year. They also had well-developed methods of transportation, such as canoes, snowshoes, and toboggans. Their homes were wigwams or tipis. These dwellings were easy to dismantle, so the people could take them with them as they followed the migrating herds of big game. All these technologies enabled them to live successfully in their environment.

Six Nations Confederacy an alliance of the Kanien'Kehaka (Mohawk), Oneida, Onondaga, Cayuga, Seneca, and Tuscarora nations

Three Sisters corn, beans, and squash, which were planted together in the same mound so that the corn stalks supported the climbing beans and the leaves of the squash discouraged weeds

The southern Woodland peoples were mainly the Haudenosaunee of the **Six Nations Confederacy** and the Tionantati (Tobacco), the Wendat (Huron), and the Attiwandaron (Neutral). Like the eastern Woodland peoples, they hunted wild game for food. However, because the area in which they lived had fertile soils and a milder climate than other parts of the region, they were able to farm as well. Although the growing season was short, the people were able to grow many of their own foods. Their main crops were the **Three Sisters**—corn, beans, and squash—and tobacco. Because they were farmers, the southern Woodland peoples were more sedentary than the nomadic cultures. They lived in semi-permanent communities for up to 10 years, moving only when the soil's nutrients were depleted.

The homes of the southern Woodland peoples were rectangular longhouses that accommodated up to 10 families. (See Figure 2.8.) They had a highly developed political system, in part because of the permanency of their home base. In addition, the southern Woodland peoples were skilled pottery makers. They made their clothing and footwear from animal skins, but they also wove such items as cloaks, sandals, and mats from grass.

Figure 2.8 A Longhouse The Woodland peoples built wooden palisades around their villages to protect them from enemies.

People	Have Been Called	Language Family
Beothuk	Beothuk	Beothuk
Mi'kmaq	Micmac	Algonquian
Wuastukwiuk	Maliseet	Algonquian
Abenaki	Abenaki	Algonquian
Odawa	Ottawa	Algonquian
Haudenosaunee	Iroquois	Iroquoian
Wendat	Huron	Iroquoian
Attiwandaron	Neutral	Iroquoian
Tionantati	Tobacco	Iroquoian

Figure 2.9 The Peoples of the Woodland

The Peoples of the Plains

The Plains cultures extended from southern Manitoba and the Mississippi River west to the Rocky Mountains, and from the North Saskatchewan River south into Texas. About 10,000 years ago, small bands of nomadic hunters roamed the plains. By about 200 CE, First Nations cultures from the Mississippi Valley settled in the southern part of what is now Alberta and Saskatchewan. There they established semi-permanent villages along the rivers, where they farmed and hunted.

CLOSE-UP

Figure 2.10 A Dog Travois A travois was an effective method of transportation—travois dogs carried more freight than the large pack animals used by mountain cultures.

THE TRAVOIS

All cultures invented forms of transportation that were suited to their environment. Because they migrated in pursuit of the buffalo herds, the Plains people needed a method of transportation that could carry their possessions, including their tipis. They invented the travois—two poles made of long sticks held together by criss-crossed rawhide straps that created a sturdy platform. One end of the poles was attached to a dog. The other end trailed along behind the dog. The people strapped their goods onto the carrying platform in between the poles.

The travois became an even better mode of transportation after horses arrived on the plains. Now the people built larger carrying platforms, made with sturdier shafts. The travois could move the lodge poles the people needed to erect their tipis: the heavy bundles of poles were attached to both sides of the horse so that they dragged along the ground. The travois also came in handy as a ladder when a woman had to adjust the flaps of a tipi or make any repairs that were out of reach.

The Plains people were a product of their environment—a vast expanse of open plains, with long prairie grasses and few trees and lakes. They followed the seasonal migration of the buffalo, carrying their dwellings and possessions with them. Initially, they transported their goods using travois pulled by dogs. Later, when horses came to the prairies around 1720, the people adapted their technology to create a better form of transportation.

Figure 2.11 A Tsuu T'ina Camp Because the Plains peoples were nomadic, their dwellings had to be easy to pack and transport. They made tipis out of buffalo hides.

People	Have Been Called	Language Family
Tsuu T'ina	Sarsi	Athapaskan
Anishnaabe	Saulteaux; Ojibwe	Siouian
Nakoda	Assiniboine; Stoney	Siouian; Algonquian
Piikunii	Peigan	Algonquian
Kainai	Blood	Algonquian
Nehiyaw	Cree	Algonquian
Mushkegowuk	Swampy Cree	Algonquian
Ah-ah-nee-nin	Gros Ventre	Algonquian
Siksika	Blackfoot	Algonquian

Figure 2.12 The Peoples of the Plains *Source: Based on "Legends of Our Times," http://www.civilization.ca and the Department of Indian Affairs and Northern Development.*

The Buffalo Culture

The buffalo culture flourished across the prairies for thousands of years. The buffalo, or bison, was the single most important food source for the Plains peoples. Their economies and societies revolved around the seasonal migration of the great herds of buffalo. With as many as 60 million buffalo roaming the prairies before European contact, the food supply was plentiful.

Traditionally, groups of extended families travelled together on foot across the prairies. Scouts travelled ahead to search out a herd of buffalo. Once they sighted one, the entire hunting party moved toward the herd. The hunter's cunning was essential in approaching the herd unobserved.

The hunter approached an individual buffalo to within range of his bow and arrow. Then he shot his arrow, aiming to strike the buffalo in the chest. The arrow was marked to identify the hunter and allow him to claim his kill when the hunt was over.

Following the hunt, the buffalo was skinned. Then the women prepared the meat to eat. Although some meat was consumed immediately, most was sun-dried and preserved for winter. The choice portions of the meat, including the hump and tongue, belonged to the hunter who killed the animal. The rest was shared by the band. All parts of the buffalo were harvested, including the sinew (tendons), fat, and hooves. The people used these body parts to make everything from moccasins, mittens, and robes to knives, toboggans, and scrapers.

The Horse Comes to the Plains

The introduction of the horse to the Plains cultures made it easier and faster to hunt the buffalo. The speed of the horses allowed the hunters to approach the herd quickly and to keep up with the animals when they ran. The Plains people became skilled riders and experts at training their horses for the hunt. A good hunting horse was ridden only for the hunt—the people did not even use them to ride to the hunting grounds.

In their hunting camps, once the work was done the people played games and gambled. Men and women formed secret societies that reflected the importance of hunting and warfare in their culture. Men joined warrior societies to decide on military strategies. Women joined dancing societies to oversee dancing and religious ceremonies. Young girls and women sought the guidance of the wise and respected Elder women of the community. The leaders of the camps were chosen by consent of the group based on their skills as hunters and their esteem among their peers.

The smoking of ceremonial pipes finalized bonds and decisions. Pipes were part of a special ritual of blowing smoke in each of the four cardinal directions, then skyward, and finally toward the Earth. The Pipe ceremony was more than an important part of Plains cultures; it was the central aspect of all the sacred traditions of the Plains Peoples.

Social Practices

Survival dictated that all members of the community work together. Different bands frequently cooperated with one another. They established social networks with their neighbours. Sometimes they arranged marriages

MAKING PEMMICAN

The term *pemmican* comes from the Nehiyaw (Cree) word *pimiokan*, meaning "a kind of fat." Pemmican was a mainstay in the diet of the Plains peoples. To prepare it, they dried the best cuts of the buffalo on racks. (Sometimes they boiled the meat first to soften it.) Then they pounded the strips of meat into a powder and mixed the powder with fat from the buffalo's back. (This fat in itself was a delicacy in Plains cultures.) Next, they added dried and crushed berries to the mixture. Sometimes, they added peppermint leaves, too. Then they placed the pemmican in bags of green hide (that is, with the hair left on). Finally, they stored the pemmican bags for winter.

with people from a neighbouring band. Girls usually married as young teenagers. However, boys were young adults before they married. First, they had to earn the right to marry. They had to show that they could support a family by becoming skilled hunters, by demonstrating their prowess in war, or by becoming leaders in the community. Often, it was the chief or the Elders who decided when a young man had earned this right.

The Elders, who were known for their wisdom and good judgment, maintained discipline in the community. They supervised the use of natural resources and presided over family matters and local government. The Elders reprimanded anyone who broke the rules. When a serious infraction took place, though, the punishment was more severe. The community either shunned the offender or banished the person altogether.

The Peoples of the Interior Plateau

The Interior Plateau extends from the coastal mountains of British Columbia in the west across the Rocky Mountains in the east, ending at the central plains. The cultures of the Interior Plateau lived in a land of extremes. In the south, the climate is extremely dry and the land is desert-like. In the north, the climate is moist and the land is lush and fertile. However, the peoples of the plateau shared many common characteristics. They ate similar foods, such as salmon, game, roots, and berries, and made similar clothing, utensils, and tools. They also had similar methods of preparing and cooking foods, such as nutritious fish pemmican. They developed unique tools and technologies for catching salmon. At waterfalls, the fishers perched along the edge of the river and used hooks, spears, nets, and baskets to catch fish. On shallow rivers, they built wooden weirs to trap the fish as they swam upstream.

The Plateau peoples had highly skilled techniques for weaving baskets and clothing. They wove their clothes from bark fibres or sewed them from animal skins. They lived in different types of dwellings depending on their environment. These included tents made from animal skins or reeds, semi-subterranean houses known as pithouses, and rectangular log and bark huts. Unlike the Pacific Coast peoples, they did not have sophisticated dugout canoes.

Figure 2.13 A Pithouse Some of the peoples of the Interior Plateau lived in pithouses similar to this one.

People	Have Been Called	Language Family
Secwepemc	Shuswap	Interior Salish
Stl'atl'imx	Lillooet	Interior Salish
Nlaka'pamux	Thompson/Couteau	Interior Salish
Okanagan	Okanagan	Interior Salish
Ktunaxa	Kootenay	Ktunaxa
Tsilhqot'in	Chilcotin	Athapaskan
Dene-thah	Slavey	Athapaskan

Figure 2.14 The Peoples of the Interior Plateau *Source: Adapted from Cheryl Coull,* A Traveller's Guide to Aboriginal BC *(Vancouver: Whitecap Books, 1996), based on a map from the British Columbia Ministry of Education, Department of Aboriginal Studies.*

The Peoples of the Pacific Coast

The cultures of the Pacific Coast occupied the coastal areas from southern British Columbia to Alaska. These complex and highly individualized cultures lived in a region of imposing mountains and lush vegetation. Most of

Figure 2.15 A Cedar Plank House The large cedar trees of the coastal rainforest allowed the Pacific Coast peoples to build sturdy plank houses and carve beautiful totem poles.

People	Have Been Called	Language Family
Haida	Haida	Haida
Tsimshian	Tsimshian	Tsimshian
Nisga'a	Tsimshian	Tsimshian
Haisla	Kitimat	Wakashan
Heiltsuk	Bella Bella	Wakashan
Oweekeno	Kwakiutl	Wakashan
Kwakwaka'wakw	Kwakiutl	Wakashan
Nuu-chah-nulth	Nootka	Wakashan
Tsilhqot'in	Chilcotin	Athapaskan
Tutchone	Tuchone	Athapaskan
Nuxalk	Bella Coola	Coast Salish
Coast Salish	Coast Salish	Coast Salish
Tlingit	Tlingit	Tlingit

Figure 2.16 The Peoples of the Pacific Coast *Source: Adapted from Cheryl Coull,* A Traveller's Guide to Aboriginal BC *(Vancouver: Whitecap Books, 1996), based on a map from the British Columbia Ministry of Education, Department of Aboriginal Studies.*

the land was accessible only via the ocean and rivers. The people depended on the bounty of the sea for their survival. They ate fresh, smoked, and dried fish, particularly salmon, hunted game, and picked wild fruits and berries. They made extensive use of the large cedar trees of the dense forests to build elaborate dugout canoes. They also used these trees to make wooden trays and boxes and tree bark to make clothing. In addition, the Pacific Coast peoples carved elaborate totem poles that were both ceremonial and spiritual in nature. They also had highly developed trade relationships among themselves and with the peoples of the Interior Plateau.

The Peoples of the Subarctic

The Subarctic cultural groups lived in a region covering the vast northern interior, or Subarctic. The landscape is dotted with many lakes and rivers. In the south, there are dense forests of spruce and fir. These gradually give way to patches of smaller trees and shrubs until the Subarctic turns into open tundra. Winters in this region are long and cold.

The people of the Subarctic were nomadic hunters and fishers. Their traditional economy was based on both large game such as caribou and moose and small game such as beaver and lynx. The many lakes and rivers provided an abundant supply of fish such as trout and pickerel.

Figure 2.17 A Tipi of a Northern First Nation In summer, the people built hide tipis that they could transport easily.

People	Have Been Called	Language Family
Innu	Naskapi; Montagnais	Algonquian
Nehiyaw	Cree	Algonquian
Dene	Chipewyan	Athapaskan
Dunne-za	Beaver	Athapaskan
Dakelh	Carrier	Athapaskan
Wet'suwet'en	Carrier	Athapaskan
Sekani	Sekani	Athapaskan
Dene-thah	Slavey	Athapaskan
Dogrib	Dogrib	Athapaskan
Kaska	Kaska	Athapaskan
Tahltan	Tahltan	Tlingit
Tagish	Tagish	Tlingit
Tutchone	Tuchone	Athapaskan
Han	Han	Athapaskan
Hare	North Slave	Athapaskan
Gwich'in	Kuchin	Athapaskan

Figure 2.18 The Peoples of the Subarctic *Source: Adapted from Cheryl Coull,* A Traveller's Guide to Aboriginal BC *(Vancouver: Whitecap Books, 1996), based on a map from the British Columbia Ministry of Education, Department of Aboriginal Studies.*

The people wore clothing made from animal hides. Their summer dwellings were made of hides that the people could take with them as they followed the migrating herds. Their winter homes were rectangular huts made of bark or logs or lean-tos made of logs, hides, or bark. For transportation, they built lightweight birch-bark canoes, which enabled them to travel long distances quickly and easily. In winter, they made snowshoes and built toboggans to transport their food and supplies.

The Peoples of the Arctic

The Arctic or Inuit peoples lived on the fringe of the inhabitable world. Their territory included the western Subarctic from the Alaskan interior across Hudson Bay to northern Quebec and Labrador. The environment consists of treeless tundra, mountains, frozen lakes and rivers, and days of 24-hour darkness. The people hunted for land and sea mammals, such as

Figure 2.19 An Inuit Igloo Igloos were built in different sizes. Some were simple one-room dwellings, while others contained several rooms and passageways.

People	Have Been Called	Language Family
Inuvialuit	Eskimos	Inuktitut
Inuit	Eskimos	Inuktitut

Figure 2.20 The Peoples of the Arctic

caribou, seals, walrus, whales, musk oxen, and polar bears. They fished for Arctic char, cod, and trout. They used animal hides to make warm clothing, boots, tents, harpoon lines, dog harnesses, and boat covers.

In winter, the Arctic peoples lived in igloos made from blocks of ice. In summer, they lived in dwellings made from animal hides. The Arctic diet consisted of blubber, raw meat, and animal organs. The people used snowshoes to walk on the icy terrain. They built **kayaks** and **umiaks** to navigate the frigid waters. They relied on dogs to carry their belongings.

kayak
a traditional Inuit sea vessel used for hunting

umiak
a large, flat-bottomed boat used by the Inuit to hunt and carry freight

1. In Canada today, people are encouraged to maintain their cultural identity. How do different cultures in your community preserve their languages, traditions, and culture? What factors might contribute to the lessening of a cultural identity?
2. Do some research on an Aboriginal culture from another part of the world. Compare the ways in which this culture is similar to and different from First Nations and Inuit cultures in Canada.

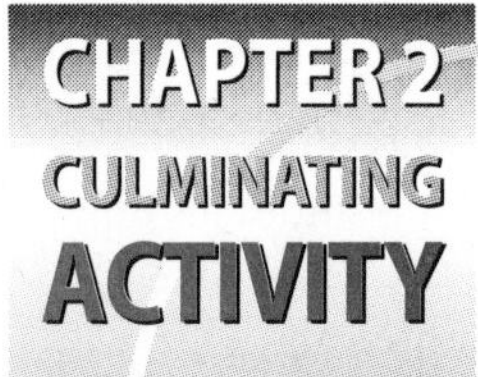

First Nations and Inuit Cultures and the Influence of Geography

All societies are influenced by the environments in which they live. Our environment determines the types of housing we live in, the types of clothing we wear, the kinds of foods we eat, and how our economies develop. This is true today, and it was certainly true thousands of years ago as the societies of the First Peoples flourished all across North America.

In this chapter, you learned about the different First Nations and Inuit cultures that lived in what is now Canada prior to European contact. This activity gives you the opportunity to discover how the physical geography of the environment influenced the lifestyles of two of these cultural groups. Then you can compare and contrast this information to gain a greater understanding of how First Nations and Inuit peoples built successful economies by using the resources that were available to them.

Begin by referring to the map in Figure 2.7 and reviewing the text on pages 35–47. Choose two cultures to be the subjects of your investigation. Then, using the Internet, library resources, or both, find information about each culture under the following categories:

- Name of the culture
- Characteristics of the physical environment
- Climate
- Available resources
- Housing
- Food
- Clothing
- Tools and technologies
- Trade relations
- Government.

As you do your research, record your findings in a comparison organizer. Then create a visual presentation such as a web diagram or a poster showing the main characteristics of each culture.

Effects of European Arrival on Aboriginal Peoples and Cultures

The Impact of Colonization on Aboriginal Peoples

LEARNING OBJECTIVES

In this chapter, you will

- discover the effects of European colonization on Aboriginal peoples and their traditional ways of living
- examine the impact of the French and British governments on Aboriginal peoples
- explore the cultures of the Plains peoples before and after contact with Europeans
- investigate the origins of the Métis people, their involvement in the fur trade, and their quest for nationhood
- recognize the effects of contact with religious groups on Aboriginal peoples
- consider other socioeconomic and spiritual issues for Aboriginal peoples that resulted from contact with Europeans

INTRODUCTION

The arrival of Columbus in the New World in 1492 permanently changed the lives of Aboriginal peoples. Their cultures, described later in this chapter, were greatly affected by contact with Europeans.

From the beginning of contact, Aboriginal nations were at a disadvantage. They faced social changes, new technologies, and imported diseases, as well as the Europeans' quest for new lands. As a result, cultural and traditional changes and the erosion of Aboriginal **sovereignty** were inevitable.

sovereignty
having independence and freedom from external control; the right to self-government

In this chapter, you will explore the key European groups who contributed to these changes. You will also examine the beginnings of conflicts, especially those concerning land.

THE FIRST EUROPEANS

Historians consider Columbus's arrival in 1492 as a benchmark in terms of contact with the New World. However, previous contacts between North American Aboriginal peoples and Europeans had no doubt been made. Although written records are scarce, pre-1492 European records that describe North American Aboriginal peoples do exist. Aboriginal oral tradition also indicates contact before 1492.

Here are some examples of possible European contact with the New World before 1492:

- Claims have been made that the Irish monk Saint Brendan caught sight of Canada's Atlantic coastline in the 6th century CE.
- According to archaeological evidence, Norse settlements existed in Newfoundland as early as 1000 CE.
- It's possible that sailors from Bristol, England, reached Canada's east coast in the 1480s.

The first reliable written evidence of English contact with North America is from 1497, when John Cabot reached the shores of Maine and the Maritime provinces.

The Métis

The first Métis were the children of First Nations women and European traders on the Atlantic seaboard. Métis legend has it that the first Métis appeared on Canada's east coast nine months after Portuguese fishers came ashore in the late 1480s. The Métis were identifiable as a group on the Atlantic seaboard in the early 1600s, and soon after in New France.

Contact with the Beothuk

There are written records of contact with Aboriginal peoples after 1497. At the time, European fishers used Newfoundland as a supply base while fishing off the Grand Banks. In 1932, Diamond Jenness described contact between the Beothuk of Newfoundland and Europeans:

> The word "Beothuk" meant probably "man" or "human being," but early European visitors to Newfoundland considered it the tribal name of the aborigines who were inhabiting the island. They gave them also another name, "Red Indians," because they smeared their bodies and clothing with red ochre, partly for religious reasons, apparently, partly as a protection against insects. They may have been lighter in colour than the Indians of the Maritime Provinces, from whom they differed in several ways. Thus, they had no dogs, and did not make pottery, but cooked their food in vessels of birch bark. For sleeping places within their bark wigwams they dug trenches which they lined with branches of fir or pine. Their canoes, though made of birch bark like those of other eastern tribes, were very peculiar in shape, each gunwale presenting the outline of a pair of crescent

> moons; and they speared seals with harpoons modelled on an archaic Eskimo [Inuit] type. Many of their graves contain bone ornaments of curious shapes and etched with strange designs. We know nothing of their political organization except that they were divided into small bands of closely related families, each with its nominal leader. Some meagre vocabularies of their language suggest that they spoke two or three dialects of common tongue, although the entire tribe could hardly have numbered more than five hundred individuals ... in 1497.
>
> *From Diamond Jenness,* The Indians of Canada *(Ottawa: National Museum of Canada, 1932).*

The Beothuk

The Beothuk were an Aboriginal people of Newfoundland. It was difficult for them to adapt to contact with European fishers and settlers, and they were driven to extinction in the early 19th century. The last known Beothuk, Shanawdithit, died in 1829.

Jacques Cartier

In 1534, Jacques Cartier explored the Gulf of St. Lawrence. This was the first true European voyage of discovery into Canada. Cartier's journals describe a trading session (likely with the Mi'kmaq) in the Bay of Chaleur in that same year:

> The next day part of the saide wilde men [wild men encountered earlier] with nine of their boates came to the point and entrance to the Creeke, where we with our ships were at road. We being advertised of their comming, went to the point where they were with our boates: but so soone as they saw us, they began to flee, making signs that they came to trafique with us, shewing us such skinnes as they cloth themselves withall, which are of small value. We likewise made signes unto them, that we wished them no evill: and in signe thereof two of our men ventured to go on land to them, and carry them knives with other Iron wares, and a red hat to give unto their Captaine. Which when they saw, they also came on land, and brought some of their skinnes, and so began to deale with us, deeming to be very glad to have our iron ware and other things, stil dancing with many other ceremonies, as with their hands to cast Sea water on their heads. They gave us whatsoever they had, not keeping any thing, so that they were constrained to go back againe naked, and made signes that the next day they would come againe, and bring more skinnes with them.

On his second voyage in 1535–1536, Cartier reached Stadacona (Quebec City) and Hochelaga (Montreal). His journals describe a close but uneasy relationship with the Aboriginal peoples there, particularly the Haudenosaunee (Iroquois). They told Cartier that the St. Lawrence River provided a pathway to the interior of the continent. They also pointed out that, along with the fisheries of the east, the furs of the interior offered unlimited opportunities for wealth.

Opportunities in the New World

More Europeans began to come to North America in search of fish and furs. But they were convinced that there were also vast resources of gold somewhere in the unexplored interior. These explorers and opportunists did not care that they were invaders and that the land was occupied by Aboriginal peoples. Nor were they concerned that they were becoming a foreign occupying power.

The first Europeans who came to the Americas saw possibilities in the new land. Over time, many Europeans were drawn to the New World because of the opportunities it offered:

- the chance to become wealthy or to acquire land
- freedom from social, religious, political, and economic difficulties within their own countries
- freedom from the restrictions that were imposed on different groups within their own countries.

These factors are still the main reasons that immigrants come to North America.

At first, there were many more Aboriginal people than there were non-Aboriginal people. The European governments—particularly those of Britain and France—established diplomatic ties with Aboriginal leaders. However, as European immigrants began to arrive in increasing numbers, the British and French changed their approach to Aboriginal leaders and became more insistent in their claims to the land.

The Growth of European Settlements

Some of the earlier European communities eventually disappeared. Because of their lack of knowledge and experience in an often-hostile and unfamiliar environment, these early settlers likely could not cope with the severe weather or were killed by the Aboriginal peoples on whose territory they had settled.

One of the first New World colonies, La Navidad, was founded by Christopher Columbus. For political reasons—to reinforce the land claim for Spain—a fort had been quickly erected there during his first voyage to the New World. When Columbus returned on his next voyage, the fort had been burned to the ground. All of the 39 men he had left to guard the fort had either disappeared or had been killed by Aboriginal people or diseases. Columbus started more settlements, but they did not last because of epidemics, in-fighting among the colonists, and the severity of the climate.

Over the next few centuries, settlements and colonies of various European groups sprang up in North America, mostly along the Atlantic coast.

(See Figure 3.1.) In some colonies, the newcomers and their settlements thrived partly because they were able to adapt to the harsh new environment. After coming into contact with Aboriginal peoples, the newcomers adopted some of the tools, hunting methods, and clothing that were used by Aboriginal groups.

Living Together

To some extent, all the European people who chose to settle in the Americas incorporated some Aboriginal practices into their ways of living. Likewise,

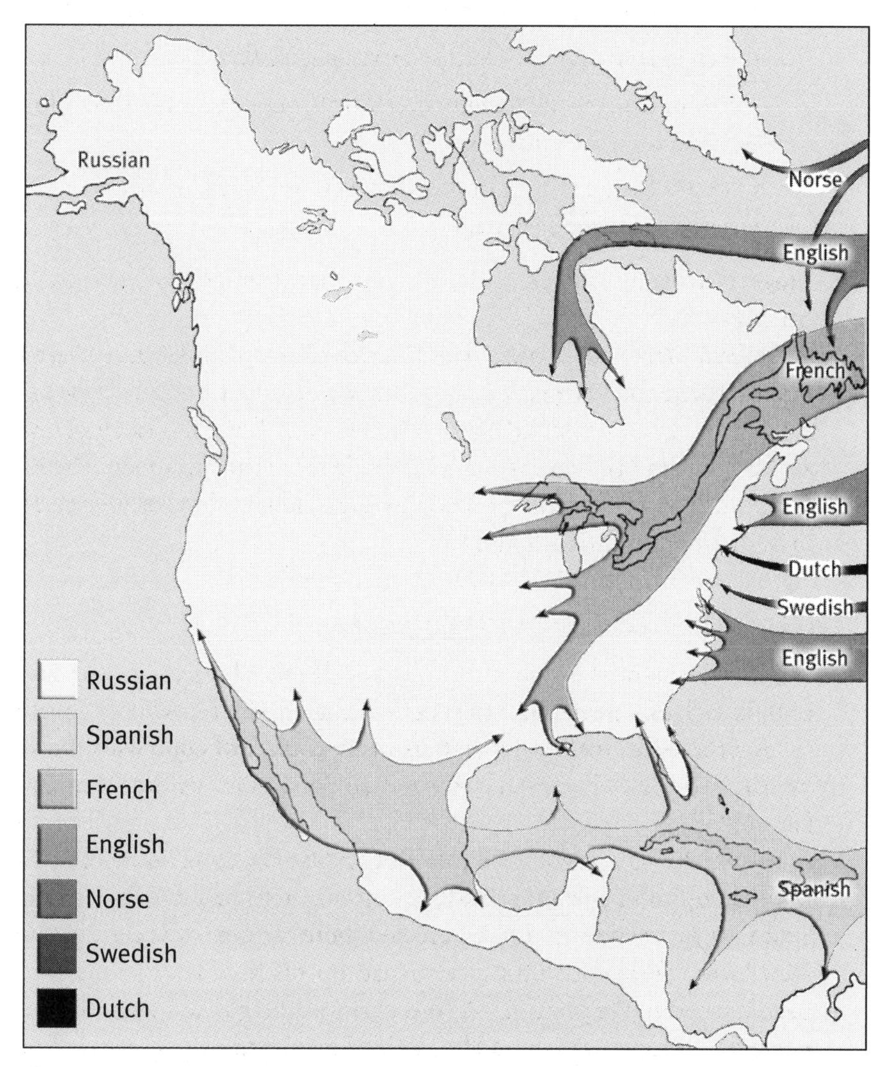

Figure 3.1 European Penetration of North America In its exploration of North America, France made incursions between those of Britain. This situation was certain to lead to war over supremacy on the continent and to conflict with Aboriginal peoples. *Sources: C. Waldman,* Atlas of the North American Indian *(n.d.); G. Barraclough (ed.),* The Times Atlas of World History *(Toronto: Fitzhenry & Whiteside, 1978), p. 161.*

acculturation the modification of the culture of a group or an individual as a result of prolonged contact with a different culture

Aboriginal peoples adopted some of the ways of the Europeans. This is known as **acculturation**—a natural process that occurs when individuals from different backgrounds get acquainted and share their cultures. As a result, each side may choose to incorporate some aspects of the other group into its own ways of being. This explains why cultures remain dynamic and ever-changing.

COUREURS DE BOIS

One of the earliest groups to become acculturated were men known as *coureurs de bois* (runners of the woods). They were fur traders from New France who travelled north and west to buy furs directly from the Aboriginal peoples in the interior. They made friends with Aboriginal peoples and adopted Aboriginal modes of transportation and ways of dressing for the climate. They learned to speak Aboriginal languages, and sometimes married and raised families with Aboriginal women. In this way, they were able to survive in a difficult environment, develop commercial contacts, and be accepted by Aboriginal groups. As a result of these intermarriages, the Métis as a group continued to increase.

Eventually, the governor of New France passed a law forcing all traders to obtain permits, but only a limited number were issued. Traders who managed to get permits were known as *voyageurs.* Those who didn't get permits often ignored the law and continued to travel to the interior and trade with Aboriginal peoples.

Acculturation was not the only influence on Aboriginal ways of living and Aboriginal–European relations. The majority of the European groups that encountered Aboriginal peoples had their own worldviews. These were quite different from the worldviews of the indigenous cultures described in Chapter 1. The Europeans came to the New World to acquire land or goods. In the process, they brought about changes to the lives and cultures of Aboriginal peoples. European cultures, traditions, and ways of living were imposed on them, often by force. This process is referred to as **assimilation**—a concept that will be examined further in Chapter 5.

assimilation a process in which a cultural group is absorbed by another and takes on its distinctive cultural traditions

This chapter explores the key groups of Europeans who exerted the most influence on Aboriginal peoples—first the European governments, then the Canadian government, the fur traders, the settlers, and various religious groups.

TALKING CIRCLE

1. Although Europeans began arriving in Canada in more significant numbers after Jacques Cartier's voyage in 1534, they could not adapt to conditions in North America, despite European technology. Discuss some of the ways that Aboriginal peoples helped the early European arrivals become accustomed to life in the New World.
2. Why did some of the original European settlements not survive?
3. Acculturation offered both Aboriginal peoples and Europeans an opportunity to take advantage of the best of both cultures. What were some advantages of acculturation for Aboriginal peoples? For Europeans?

IMPACT OF THE FRENCH AND BRITISH GOVERNMENTS ON ABORIGINAL PEOPLES

The French and the British were the main European influences in North America. They competed for dominance by establishing settlements. These powers also helped establish two companies that competed with each other: La Compagnie du Nord (French) and the Hudson's Bay Company (British). Each company fought for the rights to purchase furs from specific Aboriginal groups and to claim specific territory for trade and hunting purposes. Legal documents were drawn up to reinforce these rights. The charter granted to the Hudson's Bay Company (HBC) by the king of England in 1670 gave the company complete control over the territory drained by the rivers flowing into Hudson Bay. This charter is just one example of a European government's claim to territories and the natural resources located within those territories.

The two fur-trading companies competed for control of trade—first in Hudson Bay and the surrounding area, and then inland. They each formed a loose association with hunters and trappers from various Aboriginal groups. Both companies built forts to establish their claim to specific fur-trading routes and lands.

Britain and France at War

Britain and France were fierce rivals. A conflict broke out between them in 1702 and lasted until 1713. Now known as Queen Anne's War, it was one of several wars fought between Britain and France for control of North America. The two countries fought battles with each other on both sides of the ocean. During the Seven Years' War (1756–1763), the French and the British enlisted Aboriginal groups as allies, based on their historical relationships with these groups. In 1763, the French were defeated in both Europe and North America. They had to give up their claims to North American lands, in addition to their official right to trade within specific waterways. After 1763, British and American fur traders began to assume control over canoe routes previously held by the French. They competed with the HBC by offering more goods to the Aboriginal peoples in exchange for furs. After a number of power struggles, the British and American traders joined together to form the North West Company (NWC). This company became a strong influence on the more northern Aboriginal peoples.

In 1763, Britain drew up an important piece of legislation called the Royal Proclamation. One of the intents of this document was to reserve a large piece of land for Aboriginal occupation and use only. You will learn more about the Royal Proclamation in Chapter 4.

The Hudson's Bay Company is one of the oldest corporations in the world still in existence. For several centuries, it controlled much of the fur trade throughout British North America and functioned as the government in many areas of the continent prior to large-scale settlement. In 1670, the company was granted a monopoly over fur trade with First Nations. Do research on the founding of the HBC and on its charter. Describe the impact of the HBC and its charter on First Nations in the late 1600s.

THE FUR TRADE ON THE PLAINS

The fur trade began in earnest on the Great Plains and in the Subarctic around the middle of the 1700s. It was in full swing by 1750, when some French posts were established to handle furs brought in by First Nations of the Plains. This profitable trade led to rivalries between the English and the French, and between the Hudson's Bay Company and the North West Company. As a result, many Aboriginal peoples were forced to choose sides. In some cases, however, there were economic advantages to these conflicts. For example, the Nehiyaw (Cree) and the Nakoda (Assiniboine) acted as middlemen for both French and English trappers, and supplied provisions to both sides.

Life in the Northwest

Marriage and family life were important to the early European men in the Northwest because they were lonely and because marriage tended to create

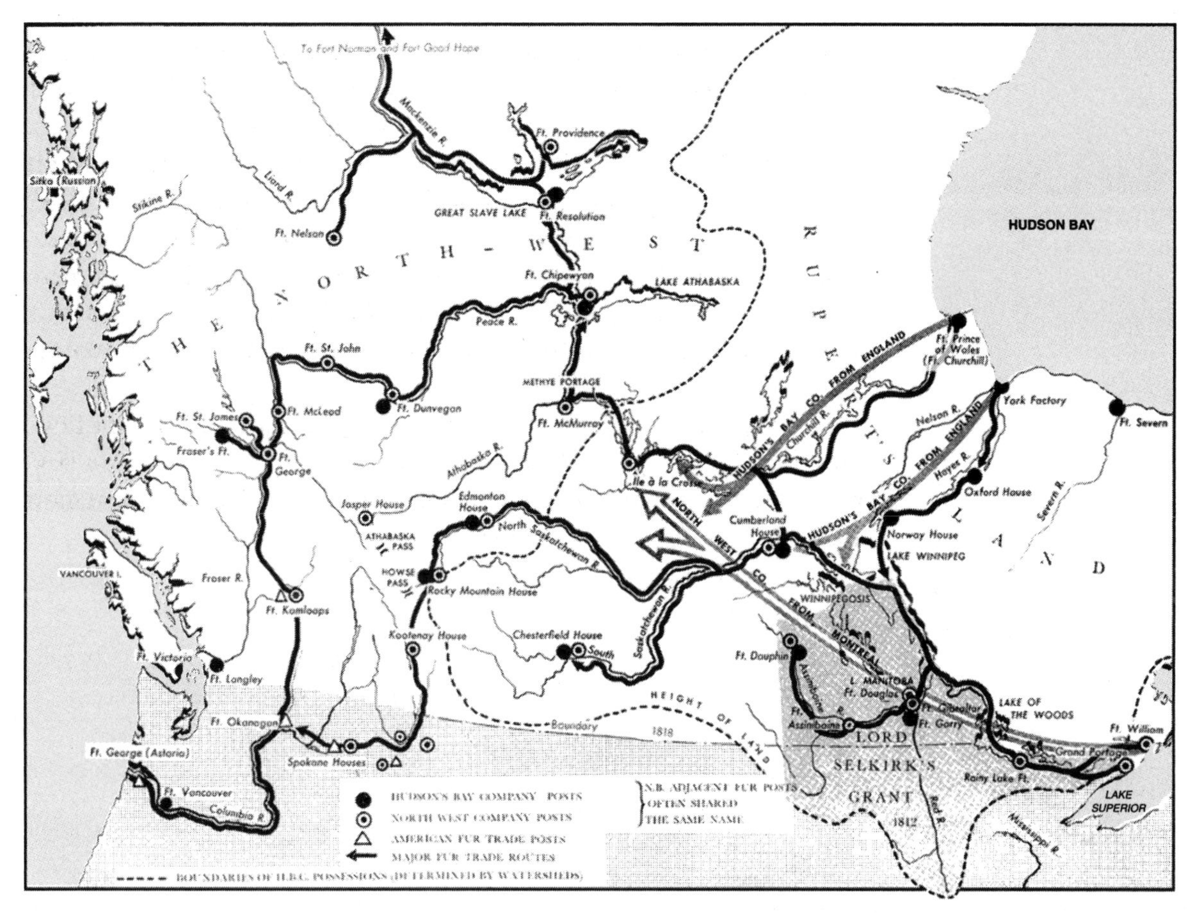

Figure 3.2 The Fur Trade in the West Fur-trading companies competed with each other by establishing trading posts where First Nations could exchange furs for European goods.

THE SIKSIKA AND THE FUR TRADE

Anthony Henday was likely the first European to contact the Siksika (Blackfoot). In 1754, he came across their main camp south of the Red Deer River, and tried to persuade them to travel to Hudson Bay to trade furs. They didn't go to Hudson Bay, but Henday did trade with the Siksika in later years. According to E.E. Rich in *The Fur Trade and the Northwest to 1857*, this was the start of the fur trade with the Siksika—and it would continue for well over a century.

social and economic bonds with First Nations. Trading loyalties were established when a European trader married into a First Nation. All members of the nation would be expected to trade with their kin. They could expect access to trading posts and provisions, and a certain amount of economic security. In fact, many families in First Nations, such as the Nehiyaw (Cree) and Chinook, planned to have at least one daughter marry a European.

European traders also married to survive. It was next to impossible to last in the Northwest without First Nations women because they did most of the work necessary to ensure survival. As D.B. Sealey points out in *The Métis: Canada's Forgotten People*, while the men hunted, trapped, and traded, the women

- dried the meat from the hunt
- gathered berries
- dug roots
- cared for garden plots
- dried and smoked fish
- tanned hides
- made clothing
- cooked
- collected firewood
- cared for the children.

Women also acted as interpreters and settled disputes between their communities and the traders.

When the Hudson's Bay Company and the North West Company merged in 1821, the roles of First Nations men changed. Some areas of the Northwest were trapped out, so middlemen were no longer needed. Some First Nations men began joining the Siksika (Blackfoot) in hunting buffalo to supply the Europeans. Because the buffalo were becoming scarce, conflict resulted as First Nations trespassed on one another's hunting grounds. In the end, the loss of the buffalo and the fur trade drove First Nations to sign the Numbered Treaties and retreat to reserves. You will examine the Numbered Treaties in detail in Chapter 4.

Things also changed for First Nations women. Most traders hadn't actually settled in the Northwest, so when their terms of employment were up, or when furs and buffalo became too scarce to make hunting and trapping worthwhile, the traders often returned to Europe without their wives. Europeans would not have accepted Aboriginal peoples because of the cultural differences between the Northwest and Europe.

There were few options open to the First Nations women who were left behind. The trading companies didn't want to be responsible for the women and their families. By 1835, the HBC had ordered its employees to

Figure 3.3 Nehiyaw Women in Prince Albert, Saskatchewan, c. 1900 Many First Nations women in the Northwest married European traders. These women had an important role in the fur trade—both at the trading posts and within their own cultures. The Métis in the Northwest would later emerge as a distinct group with a unique culture and history.

provide for their wives and children when they left the pay of the company. However, this did not always happen, and many abandoned families had to depend on the goodwill of the company or on their relatives. Some traders did remain in the Northwest with their families, but they were few.

What responsibility, if any, do you think trading companies such as the HBC had for families who had been abandoned by employees of the companies? Give reasons for your answer.

THE PLAINS AND WESTERN SUBARCTIC PEOPLES

In his journal, Anthony Henday described the Plains peoples' way of life in the mid-1700s. "Buffalo were so numerous [on the Plains] that we were obliged to make them sheer out of our way." He also reported that Plains peoples were skilled at the hunt, food was plentiful, and the horses were an impressive sight. The First Nations who are portrayed on television and in movies are based on the Plains peoples. In fact, what many people today know about the history of First Nations is based on what they know about the Plains peoples.

Stuart Fiedel analyzed the impact of contact on the Plains peoples in *Prehistory of the Americas*:

> ... it is not often realized to what extent the historic Plains cultures had developed in response to contacts with Europeans. Certainly, bison herds had been hunted successfully by Indians on foot. However, when Indians learned to ride horses, which the Spanish had reintroduced to the Americas, it became much easier to follow the migrating herds. Rifles, which the Indians began to acquire by the 18th century, also aided bison hunting. The acquisition of horses must have encouraged some tribes, who had formerly supplemented their farming with seasonal bison hunting, to rely increasingly on hunting, so that ultimately they stopped farming altogether and abandoned their villages. ... The Blackfoot [Siksika], Arapaho [Inuana-ina], and Assiniboine [Nakoda] were descended from bison hunters. Farming had been a largely female occupation, so as it was de-emphasized, women's economic role was devalued, and their social status diminished accordingly.

From Stuart Fiedel, Prehistory of the Americas
(Cambridge, UK: Cambridge University Press, 1987).

Profiles of the Plains and Western Subarctic Cultures

The Soyi-tapix Nation

The territory of the Soyi-tapix ("prairie people") stretched from the foothills of the Rockies to the Alberta–Saskatchewan border, and from northern Alberta to Montana in the United States. The Soyi-tapix consisted of three groups: the Siksika (Blackfoot), the Kainai (Blood), and the Piikunii (Peigan). They formed an alliance with the Tsuu T'ina (Sarsi) and the Ah-ah-nee-nin (Gros Ventre) to form what historians call the Blackfoot Confederacy. However, they were constantly at war with their many enemies, including the Nehiyaw (Cree), the Nakoda (Assiniboine), the Ktunaxa (Kootenay), and the So-sonreh (Shoshoni).

Like most Plains cultures, the Soyi-tapix were part of the buffalo cultures that occupied the vast prairies for thousands of years. After European contact and the introduction of guns and horses to the prairies in the 1700s, they began to dominate both the buffalo hunt and other Plains nations. The first contact with Europeans came by way of traders on the North Saskatchewan River. At the time, the population of the Soyi-tapix was about 12,000. Although they traded with both the HBC and the NWC, the Soyi-tapix fought with American traders until they made peace in 1831.

In 1877, the Soyi-tapix signed Treaty 7 with the government of Canada. As a result of the treaty, most of the Piikunii Nation moved to Montana, while the Siksika, Kainai, and northern Piikunii peoples settled on reserves in southern Alberta. There, they became ranchers and farmers, but they preserved their language and culture. Today, there are approximately 20,000 members of the Soyi-tapix Nation living in Alberta and Montana.

The Siksika

The Siksika (Blackfoot) was the smallest of the three Soyi-tapix nations. These people lived in the northern reaches of the Confederacy's territory. Their population ranged between 2,000 and 3,000 people in the 19th century. Today, it is between 3,000 and 4,000 people.

Like all Plains cultures, the Siksika were a self-reliant and self-sufficient society. Their traditional territory was rich in natural resources, which provided for all of their needs. The most important resource, however, was the buffalo. To honour the spirit of the buffalo, the Siksika held a four-day ritual each summer called the Sun Dance. A highly esteemed holy woman presided over the annual gathering. Offerings to the Great Spirit were hung on a pole. A buffalo skull was placed at the base of the pole to symbolize the animal's position as the junction between humans and the Creator.

After signing Treaty 7 with the Canadian government in 1876, the Siksika settled on a reserve. They adapted their lifestyle to become farmers and ranchers. In 1912 and 1918, they sold half the reserve for $1.2 million. For a time, the Siksika reserve was the wealthiest in Canada.

Figure 3.4 Siksika Crossing at the Bow River, Southern Alberta, c. 1885 The Siksika settled on a reserve at Blackfoot Crossing, east of Calgary.

BIOGRAPHY

ISAPO-MUXIKA (CROWFOOT) (1830–1890)

Figure 3.5 Isapo-muxika As chief, Isapo-muxika established peace with his people's traditional enemy, the Nehiyaw.

Isapo-muxika (also known as Crowfoot) was a great leader of the Siksika Nation. Although he was born into the Kainai Nation, he grew up among the Siksika. As a teenager, he showed great courage. He was wounded six times in 19 battles. For one of his daring raids, he was given an ancestor's name—Isapo-muxika, meaning "Crow Indian's Big Foot." Interpreters shortened this to "Crowfoot."

A wise and perceptive diplomat, Isapo-muxika became one of the three main chiefs of the Siksika Nation in 1870. He welcomed the North West Mounted Police when they arrived to put an end to the whiskey trade in 1874. In 1877, he signed Treaty 7 with the Canadian government and, in 1881, he led his people onto the reserve at Blackfoot Crossing. Although Isapo-muxika became disillusioned with the government's unfulfilled promises, he refused to allow his people to join the Northwest Rebellion in 1885. When he died in 1890, Isapo-muxika was widely mourned by his people.

The Kainai

Like the other nations of the Soyi-tapix, the Kainai (Blood) were fierce warriors. They counted the Nehiyaw (Cree), Ktunaxa (Kootenay), and So-sonreh (Shoshoni) among their enemies. As with all Plains cultures, they had a well-developed social structure, with established political and cultural systems. And like other buffalo cultures, the Kainai had many sacred sites at buffalo pounds and jumps, where they honoured the spirits of the buffalo.

They originally occupied the hunting grounds from the North Saskatchewan River across Alberta, west to the Rocky Mountains, and south to Yellowstone River in Montana. However, in the mid-19th century, they moved south into Montana, where they traded with both the HBC and the American Fur Company. At the time of European contact, the Kainai numbered between 2,500 and 3,500 people. However, this figure fell to around 1,500 following the smallpox epidemic of 1837.

Like the Siksika, the Kainai signed Treaty 7, which gave them a reserve next to the Siksika. They later relocated to the largest reserve in Canada, between the St. Mary and Belly rivers, where they became farmers.

BIOGRAPHY

RED CROW (1830–1900)

Red Crow became one of the head chiefs of the Kainai Nation in 1870. He wielded great power and influence. The Canadian government understood that in order to ensure the peaceful settlement of the West, it needed Red Crow's support.

In 1874, Red Crow welcomed the North West Mounted Police to the West. His trust of the NWMP led him to sign Treaty 7 in 1877. On the Kainai reserve, Red Crow encouraged his people to become self-sufficient through ranching and education. At the same time, he taught them the importance of preserving their customs and religion.

Figure 3.6 Red Crow Red Crow was a noted warrior who came from a long line of chiefs.

The Piikunii

The Piikunii (Peigan) was the largest of the Soyi-tapix Nations. Like the Kainai, the Piikunii were a warrior nation. The people were migratory hunters who travelled from the Rockies across the Great Plains and south into Montana. Because of its large size, the Piikunii Nation split into two: the Apatohsi Piikunii (North Peigan) and the Amoskapi Piikunii (South Peigan). The northern group lived in Alberta as far north as Edmonton. The southern group lived in Montana.

The Piikunii shared in the summer celebrations of the buffalo spirits during the annual Sun Dance. This sacred ceremony was the most important celebration of the buffalo cultures of the Plains.

The Apatohsi Piikunii signed Treaty 7 in 1877 and moved to a reserve near Pincher Creek, Alberta. Before European contact, the population of the Piikunii Nation was between 3,000 and 5,000 people. Today, there are between 2,000 and 3,000 Piikunii living in Canada.

The Nehiyaw

The Nehiyaw (Cree) territory ranged from Alberta to Quebec. It was the largest geographic territory of any First Nations or Inuit group in Canada. As a result, the Nehiyaw formed three distinct groups: the Plains peoples who lived in Alberta and Saskatchewan, the Woods peoples who lived in Saskatchewan and Manitoba, and the Swampy peoples who lived in Manitoba, Ontario, and Quebec.

The Nehiyaw lived in nomadic hunting bands for most of the year. In summer, they gathered in villages to socialize and hold spiritual ceremonies. They spoke or sang prayers to the Creator and participated in **vision quests**. They believed in spirit intermediaries who granted individuals a vision through teachings and prophecies.

vision quest
a sacred ceremony in which a person goes to a secluded place to communicate with the spirit world

With the introduction of the horse into their culture, the Nehiyaw evolved from nomadic hunters and trappers to buffalo hunters and warriors. As the fur trade grew, many Nehiyaw migrated to trading posts. However, the ravages of disease and the destruction of the buffalo herds forced them onto reserves. There, they adapted their lifestyle to become farmers and ranchers but succeeded in preserving their language and culture.

The Tsuu T'ina

There were five bands in the Tsuu T'ina (Sarsi) Nation. Their territory was in central Alberta along the foothills of the Rocky Mountains. They lived in tipis and camped along the edge of the forest in winter. In summer, the bands came together for the buffalo hunt and to hold special ceremonies.

Figure 3.7 A Nehiyaw Encampment This encampment in 1871, near present-day Vermilion, Alberta, predated Treaty 6.

BIOGRAPHY

PITIKWAHANAPIWIYIN (POUNDMAKER) (1842–1886)

Pitikwahanapiwiyin (also known as Poundmaker) was a Nehiyaw chief. In 1876, he opposed the signing of Treaty 6. He eventually signed it, but soon became disillusioned by the government's inaction in meeting the needs of his people.

During the Northwest Rebellion in 1885, Pitikwahanapiwiyin's followers launched a siege against the abandoned fort at Battleford. The warriors then defeated Canadian troops at Cut Knife Hill. Pitikwahanapiwiyin did not take part in the battle. In fact, he prevented his warriors from chasing after the retreating soldiers. Although he protested his innocence, Pitikwahanapiwiyin was tried for treason and sentenced to three years in prison. The experience proved too much for the proud chief. He died a broken man following his early release in 1886.

Figure 3.8 Pitikwahanapiwiyin Although he was born into the Nakoda Nation, Pitikwahanapiwiyin gained power and influence after he was adopted by Isapo-muxika in 1873.

The Tsuu T'ina gave thanks to the supernatural spirits when game was plentiful. When it was not, the spirits were appeased with special offerings. Holy men and women foretold the weather and the location of game. The people used special decorations and amulets to keep evil spirits away.

At the time of European contact, there were about 1,500 people in the Tsuu T'ina Nation. This number dropped dramatically to between 400 and 450 by 1877 as smallpox, scarlet fever, and other diseases claimed many lives. Today, about 1,000 members of the Tsuu T'ina Nation live on a reserve southwest of Calgary.

The Nakoda

The Nakoda (Assiniboine; also known as the Stoney in Alberta) migrated north from the United States to the Lake of the Woods and Lake Winnipeg. At the height of their power, they ranged from the Saskatchewan and Assiniboine rivers in Canada to north of the Missouri River in the United States.

BIOGRAPHY

MISTAHIMASKWA (BIG BEAR) (1825–1888)

Mistahimaskwa (also known as Big Bear) was the chief of the Plains Nehiyaw. In 1876, he refused to sign Treaty 6 because he believed that the terms of the treaty would destroy his people's way of life and sentence them to perpetual poverty. After the buffalo disappeared from the prairies, he reluctantly signed the treaty in 1882.

Still, Mistahimaskwa wanted to gain some concessions from the government. He held a series of meetings at Battleford. The largest of these was in 1884, when over 2,000 First Nations people came to a meeting. But Mistahimaskwa lost most of his supporters after the government refused to negotiate. Violence followed. During the Northwest Rebellion, a group of radicals attacked Frog Lake, killing nine settlers. Then they burned down Fort Pitt before they were finally defeated at Loon Lake. Although Mistahimaskwa did not take part in the attacks, he surrendered to authorities in 1885. He was tried and found guilty of treason and sentenced to three years in prison. He died in 1888.

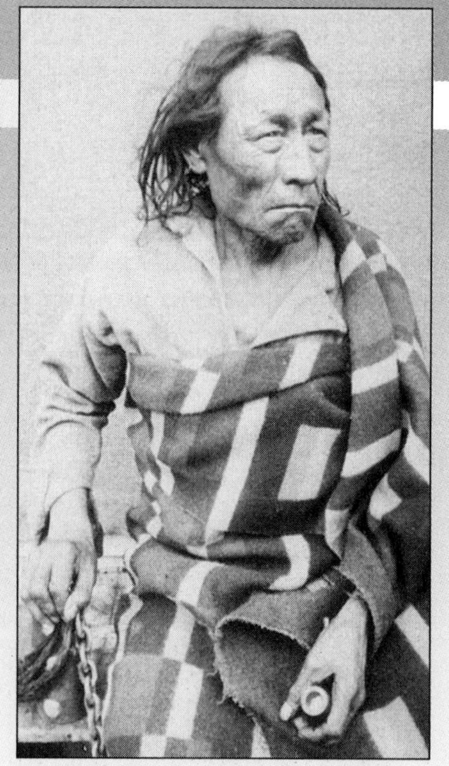

Figure 3.9 Mistahimaskwa Independent and strong-willed, Mistahimaskwa was determined that his people would live where they wanted to live.

In Nakoda culture, young people went on a quest to find their spiritual identity. Girls isolated themselves until they envisioned a spirit or song. Boys' initiation rites involved spending time in the wilderness to prove their worthiness as protectors of their people. During this time, they received a vision from a guardian spirit who granted them power.

The Nakoda were experts in building buffalo pounds for trapping and killing these great beasts. They had fewer horses than other cultures had, so they were more likely to use dogs as their work animals. From the late 17th century, the Nakoda traded with the HBC.

As with all First Nations, the Nakoda's numbers were greatly reduced by disease after European contact. Their population declined from 10,000 in 1800 to about 2,500 a century later. In 1874, some of the Nakoda bands signed Treaty 4. In 1876, other bands signed Treaty 6. The Nakoda then settled on three reserves in Saskatchewan.

The Ah-ah-nee-nin

The Ah-ah-nee-nin (Gros Ventre) migrated north into Montana and as far as the Saskatchewan River. Like the other Plains cultures, they were nomadic. They lived in movable tipis made from buffalo hides as they followed the buffalo herds that were their primary source of food and clothing. The Ah-ah-nee-nin were known for their clothing and leatherwork and for their elaborate decorative beading and quill work. They used these designs to create pictographs on clothing, tipis, and other items.

At the time of European contact, there were 3,000 Ah-ah-nee-nin living on the northern plains. However, war and diseases reduced the population to 500 by the 20th century. Today, estimates suggest there are around 2,500 people living on the reserve.

The Dunne-za

The Dunne-za (Beaver) were a nomadic people who lived in the Peace River area until their territory was invaded by a rival nation, who took over part of the territory. Traditionally, they lived in small hunting bands of 25 to 30 people. They came together in the summer to hunt large game animals and to hold special ceremonies. During this time, young people embarked on vision quests to establish their identity and gain supernatural powers from the animals.

The Dunne-za established fur-trading posts along the Peace River in the late 18th century. The missionaries who arrived in the area in the mid-1800s converted many of the Dunne-za to Christianity. However, while many Dunne-za today are Roman Catholic, most have kept some of their traditional beliefs.

The introduction of guns to the Plains in the 1800s had a devastating effect on the buffalo hunt. By 1870, the Plains buffalo was almost extinct. No longer able to practise their traditional lifestyle, the Dunne-za moved onto reserves after signing Treaty 8 in 1899, 1900, and 1910. Today, they live on reserves in British Columbia and Alberta, where farming and petroleum production are their main economic activities. In the North, however, the Dunne-za still hunt and trap.

The Dene-thah

The Dene-thah (Slavey) were a major cultural group who lived in the boreal forests of the western Canadian Subarctic. These people occupied a vast area extending along the Slave, Athabasca, and Mackenzie rivers south from Fort Nelson, British Columbia, on the west and from the Hay Lake region of Alberta on the east, north to Fort Norman in the Northwest Territories, and along the south shores of Great Bear Lake.

The Dene-thah formed several regional bands that moved within specific territories. Because they lived in a harsh environment, the people needed to move frequently to find the resources they needed. As a result, they maintained a simple social structure in their communities. They harvested fish, small game, moose, caribou, and berries. In winter, they camped in groups of 10 to 30 related people.

Their first contact with Europeans was with Alexander Mackenzie's expedition in 1789. As the fur trade expanded into their territory, their contact with Europeans increased. By the 1900s, western expansion and their changing lifestyle led the Dene-thah to sign treaties with the federal government. In British Columbia, Alberta, and parts of the Northwest Territories, they signed Treaty 8 between 1900 and 1911. Bands living in the rest of the Northwest Territories signed Treaty 11 in 1921–1922.

The Dene-thah continued to practise their traditional lifestyle until the mid-1940s. At that time, government programs and the collapse of the fur trade forced many people off the land and into urban areas. Today, however, traditional harvesting has regained its economic importance for many of the 5,000 Dene-thah.

The Dene

The Dene (Chipewyan), the largest of the northern Athapaskan-speaking peoples, are closely related to the Dene-thah (Slavey) and the Dogrib. Originally, they occupied the northern fringes of the boreal forest. By the 19th century, their territory had extended into northern Manitoba, Saskatchewan, and Alberta and the southern Northwest Territories.

Like the Dene-thah, the Dene lived in a harsh environment that required them to move in search of migratory game such as caribou and moose.

Therefore, their spirituality was closely linked to hunting and gathering and the struggle to survive in a harsh land. The Dene hunted in groups of two or more related nuclear families. They joined with other groups to form local or regional bands.

In 1717, the HBC founded Fort Churchill in present-day Manitoba to establish a fur-trading relationship with the Dene. Later, the HBC and the NWC established competing trading posts as each tried to control the Dene fur trade. Many Dene hunters and trappers travelled to the posts to trade their furs. However, in 1871, a smallpox epidemic forced them to seek refuge in the forests. They remained there until the 1960s, when they were forced onto reserves in order to receive government benefits. This disrupted their social and traditional ways of life. Today, however, many Dene are reviving their traditional lifestyle.

At the time of European contact, the Dene population was about 4,000. Since then, it has increased slightly.

The people of the Siksika (Blackfoot), Kainai (Blood), Piikunii (Peigan), Nehiyaw (Cree), and Tsuu T'ina (Sarsi) all considered themselves citizens of nations, such as the Sarsi Nation.

1. Why did these western peoples consider themselves nations?
2. What were some of the duties and responsibilities of the citizens of these nations?

SETTLEMENT IN THE WEST

The Métis

The first settlers in the West were the eastern Métis, who arrived there 100 years before the first permanent European settlers—and 200 years before the first white woman settled on the Plains. During the fur trade in the Northwest, both the French and the English intermarried with First Nations women. The French Métis worked for the North West Company as clerks, labourers, and provisioners. By the early 1800s, they were usually hiring out their services as independent workers, often providing buffalo meat and pemmican to the trading posts. The English Métis lived near and worked at Hudson's Bay Company posts.

Unlike the Métis in New France, who tended to assimilate, both the English and French Métis in the West developed their own distinct identities, based on their history and culture. They often spoke several languages—French, English, at least one First Nations language, and Michif (a combination of French and Nehinawe). Métis of French heritage were usually

Roman Catholic, while Métis of English or Scottish heritage were usually Protestant. The Métis were sometimes known as *bois-brûlé* (French for "burnt wood")—a reference to their complexion. Métis of British heritage were often called "the country-born."

The Buffalo Hunt

Each year, hundreds of Métis gathered in the spring and fall for the buffalo hunt. It was well organized and democratic—a governor of the hunt and 10 captains were elected to lead groups of hunters. There were strict rules:

- No buffalo to be run on the Sabbath.
- No party to fork off, lag behind, or go before without permission.
- No person or party to run buffalo before the general order.
- Every captain with his men, in turn, to patrol the camp and keep order.
- Any person convicted of theft to be brought to the middle of the camp and the crier to call out his or her name, adding the word "thief" each time.

After the hunt, the women would skin the carcasses and cut up the meat to dry in the sun. Clothing was made from the buffalo hides and pemmican from the meat. Pemmican was an important trade good for the Métis. Fur traders and voyageurs depended on it for their long journeys.

"The Métis, or *bois-brûlé*, became a well-marked type in Rupert's Land. At the beginning of the 19th century, so decided had become the feeling of kinship and common interest that the *bois-brûlé* spoke of themselves as 'The New Nation.'"

G. Bryce, 1903, in D.B. Sealey and A.S. Lussier, The Métis: Canada's Forgotten People *(Winnipeg: Métis Federation Press, 1975), p. 15.*

The Red River Settlement

provisioning station a place where necessary goods, especially food, can be obtained

The first significant European colony in the West was the Red River Settlement (also known as the Selkirk Settlement). It was founded by Thomas Douglas, Earl of Selkirk, a Scot who had established other settlements in eastern Canada. In 1811, Selkirk bought land from the HBC in order to set up a settlement of Scots at Red River (now Winnipeg) in Manitoba. (See Figure 3.2.) Settlers began arriving in 1812. The settlement was supposed to act as a **provisioning station** for HBC trading posts in the Northwest. This created clashes with the NWC and with the First Nations and Métis in the

Figure 3.10 A Nehiyaw (Cree) Woman by a Red River Cart, c. 1910 One of the Métis' greatest contributions to the development of the West was their adaptation of European technology to life on the Northwest frontier. The Red River cart was just one example. First developed in the Red River Settlement, it was based on the iron and wood carts in Quebec. Usually pulled by oxen, these carts could be disassembled, floated across rivers, and reassembled to continue the journey.

area, who were provisioners to the traders, trappers, and explorers. There were many armed conflicts, especially between the Selkirk settlers and the Métis, but the colony survived.

Annexing the West

The Canadian government did little to encourage settlement in the West until the late 1800s. The Red River Settlement was small, and the region was considered too remote and expensive to manage from the power centres in the East. Even though Confederation had occurred in 1867, the people who lived on the land mass from British Columbia to the Maritimes were hardly united. However, American settlement was starting to threaten the western territories (what is now western Canada), especially after the first transcontinental railway was built in the United States.

To deal with this threat from the Americans, the British government sent John Palliser to explore, map, and report on the lands of the West between the Red River and the Rocky Mountains. He decided that a large area, later known as the Palliser Triangle, was unsuitable for settlement. This area covered the southern part of Manitoba, all of southern Saskatchewan, and the southeastern part of Alberta. An area across the top of the triangle, however, would be suitable for agriculture. Despite the report, Canada purchased Rupert's Land from the HBC in January 1869. This territory stretched from Hudson Bay west to the Rockies. Canada would officially take over title to the land in December 1869.

The Red River Rebellion

The terms of the Rupert's Land purchase did not mention the rights of the First Nations and Métis who lived in the area. The Métis feared for their land, their culture, and their rights. They suspected that government policies would favour English-speaking Protestants from Ontario. In August 1869, surveyors from Canada arrived in Red River. They started marking off the land to prepare for the arrival of settlers once title to the land was transferred to Canada. A group of Métis, led by Louis Riel, told them to stop. With his foot on the surveyors' chain, Riel ordered, "You go no farther!" The surveyors left the area, and the Métis set out to ensure that their rights would be protected:

- In October 1869, the Métis formed the National Committee of the Métis to stop Canada's takeover of Red River until Métis lands and rights had been guaranteed. Louis Riel stepped forward to help lead the committee.
- In early November, William McDougall, the new lieutenant governor of the North-West Territories, arrived to take over the Red River Settlement before Rupert's Land officially became part of Canada in December. A group of Métis stopped McDougall from entering Fort Garry (now Winnipeg) and then took it over.
- The Métis wanted to ensure that they would be given the same rights that all the colonies had received on joining Confederation. They set up a **provisional government** at Red River, with Louis Riel as leader. In February 1870, this government drew up a Bill of Rights and sent it to Ottawa.
- Not everyone in Red River agreed with the provisional government. When a group of more-recent settlers from Ontario plotted to attack the government, Riel had them jailed. One of these settlers, Thomas Scott, was the most outspoken against the Riel government. He finally antagonized the Métis to such an extent that he was found guilty of insubordination and disloyalty and executed in March 1870.
- The Canadian government met most of the Métis' demands in an agreement called the *Manitoba Act*. On July 15, 1870, the province of Manitoba was created on a parcel of land that is today the southern part of the province.
- Prime Minister John A. Macdonald decided to send troops to Red River to keep the peace and to assert Canada's control of the area. Fearing that he would be arrested for the death of Thomas Scott, Riel fled to the United States.

provisional government
a government that is serving temporarily until a permanent government comes into power

Métis Bill of Rights

Key points:

- the right to elect an official government in Red River
- the right to elect members of Parliament to Ottawa
- the right to use both French and English as official languages in the Métis government, schools, and courts
- the right to keep existing customs, privileges, and practices

Dominion Lands Act

John A. Macdonald wanted to open the land to settlement. To encourage this, his government passed the *Dominion Lands Act* in 1872. The Act offered settlers in the West a quarter section (approximately 65 hectares) of farming land, and an adjoining quarter after three years of settlement, at low cost. Macdonald also planned to build a railway to link Canada to the Pacific.

Once again, the Métis in the West, particularly in Manitoba and Saskatchewan, rebelled against the Canadian government in 1885 (the Northwest Rebellion) because the government did not respect their land rights. The rebellion both hindered and helped Macdonald's settlement plans. The construction of the Canadian Pacific Railway had begun in 1882 but had stopped because of lack of funding. During the rebellion, the Canadian government used the railway to transport troops to put down the rebellion. The Métis, led by Louis Riel, were defeated at Batoche, Saskatchewan, ending the revolt. Macdonald was then able to justify more government spending to complete the railway.

Growth of European Settlements

By 1885, the West was finally open for European settlement. Settlement became significant after 1874, when the North West Mounted Police were sent west to enforce Canadian law. By the late 1880s, there were more settlers than Aboriginal people in the West.

There were no pitched battles with Aboriginal peoples as there were in the United States. (The Northwest Rebellion had resulted in about 100 deaths on both sides.) But First Nations had been hit hard by epidemics, and casualties were enormous, often wiping out entire groups. The buffalo were depleted, threatening the Plains peoples with starvation. And there was one significant problem between First Nations and the Canadian government. This problem had its origins in the United States. Sitting Bull (Ta-tanka I-yotank) was the Lakota (Sioux) chief who had defeated the American general, George Custer, at the Battle of Little Bighorn in 1876. To escape the wrath of the American army, he led his group of 5,000 people to Canada. They settled in the Wood Mountain area of southern Saskatchewan. For four years, Sitting Bull petitioned the Canadian government for a reserve, but the Canadian government refused his request. Facing starvation, Sitting Bull and his followers returned to the United States.

After Wilfrid Laurier was elected prime minister in 1896, his government encouraged immigration from Europe. When their populations had grown large enough, both Saskatchewan and Alberta became Canadian provinces in 1905. By 1911, there was a growing population base in the West. Wheat and other grain farming was encouraging the establishment of towns, and immigrants were beginning to outnumber the Aboriginal people on the Plains by a significant margin.

BIOGRAPHY

LOUIS RIEL (1844–1885)

Louis Riel was born in St. Boniface, across from the Red River Settlement. The eldest of 11 children, he spent several years training to become a priest, but withdrew from his studies and went to work as a clerk in a Montreal law firm. After a 10-year absence, he returned to St. Boniface, where he would soon become the protector of Métis rights during the Red River Rebellion.

After Riel fled to the United States, he became a schoolteacher and married. He also became an American citizen in 1883. However, he was still a Métis, so he returned to Canada in 1884 when Gabriel Dumont, leader of the Métis in the District of Saskatchewan, requested his help. In December 1884, Riel helped draft a petition to the Canadian government asking for

- legal title to land already occupied by Métis families
- provincial status for the districts of Saskatchewan, Assiniboia, and Alberta
- laws to encourage First Nations and Métis to settle on farms
- better treatment of First Nations.

Figure 3.11 Louis Riel This portrait was reproduced and sold by a Montreal newspaper right after Riel's execution. The paper said it had sold more than 50,000 copies of the portrait within six days of Riel's death. More than 100 years after his death, Riel is still Canada's most famous Aboriginal person and a messiah in the hearts of many Métis today.

The government's response was not satisfactory. The result was the Northwest Rebellion, which was over in two months. On May 12, 1885, 150 Métis were defeated at Batoche by 8,000 Canadian soldiers. Riel was captured, tried for treason, and executed at the North West Mounted Police barracks in Regina on November 16, 1885. There was a public outcry in the West against Riel's trial. In some cases, the media, such as the *Manitoba Free Press*, strongly supported Riel's cause:

> Wherever it is known that the half-breeds [Métis] and Indians are in rebellion, it is known that they were first deceived and wronged, then neglected, finally allowed to prepare openly for an appeal to arms without a step being taken to hinder them.

Louis Riel was and still is the archetypal Métis: proud, zealous, and willing to fight for justice as he saw it. He was in the right place at the right time to lead the Métis in a struggle against those who would deny them their heritage.

1. How did the Métis attempt to establish an identity in the West?
2. Research the life of Louis Riel.
   a) What qualities did he have that made him a leader of the Métis people?
   b) Describe efforts made to have Riel pardoned for his act of treason against the Canadian government.

THE IMPACT OF EUROPEAN SETTLEMENT ON ABORIGINAL CULTURES

Changes in the Barter System

The fur trade with non-Aboriginal peoples led to major changes in the traditional trading relations that Aboriginal groups had with one another. Although Aboriginal hunters and trappers continued to barter in the traditional manner, the types of goods they bartered changed. As a result, their immediate quality of life improved. On a long-term basis, however, the barter system did not help economic prosperity in their communities. The profits earned by the foreign traders were taken back to their home countries. From the Aboriginal peoples' viewpoint, the trading system was unfair because the trading posts received more benefits from the trading arrangements than Aboriginal peoples did.

The Notion of Wealth

Traditionally, northern Ontario First Nations did not consider furs to be a sign of wealth. The animals were killed for food, shelter, clothing, and tools. Anything that a family did not need was given to other community members. In fact, when a deer or moose was killed by a hunter, the whole community or the Elders were given a share of the meat or other parts of the animal. Because of these groups' nomadic existence, collecting and storing the hides would have been impractical. Since the people travelled with what they could carry, the concept of wealth—that one person could have more material goods than another—was not important to their way of life.

After the fur companies were established in northern Ontario, the attitudes of First Nations toward wealth started to change. The accumulation of goods or wealth began to determine a person's position in society. As some individuals in the community became wealthier than others, disputes and violence broke out over hunting and trapping territories.

However, the distribution of wealth is still a part of many First Nations' cultural practices today. Material goods are given to other community members in a number of ways. One of these practices is known as "giveaways." At a powwow—a social event where people gather to share their songs and dance—giveaways are always held at the end of the celebration. Gifts are first given to the Elders, drummers, and dancers, then to other community members and guests. Giveaway items include crafts and linen.

Another example of the distribution of wealth is the sharing of wild meat. In northern communities, it is still not uncommon for a hunter to give meat to neighbours. In fact, some First Nations are trying to return to this practice. For example, hunters and fishers in Wikwemikong, Manitoulin Island, are encouraged to give meat and fish to the Elders in the community.

Disappearance of the Clan System

Another change that occurred in First Nations cultures was the gradual disappearance of the **clan** system in many First Nations cultures (though it remained strong among the Pacific Coast peoples). Before contact with Europeans, this system kept communities together and gave them clear roles and responsibilities. According to the teachings that author Edward Benton-Benai received, the Creator gave the Earth's people the clan system to form a framework for strength and order.

clan
the basic social and political organization of Aboriginal societies, consisting of related groups and families

The Salteaux (Ojibwe) clan system included seven original clans, each with a specific role:

- the Crane (Ah-ji-jawk')—chieftains or leaders
- the Loon (Mahng)—chieftains or leaders
- the Fish (Gi-Goon')—intellectuals or teachers
- the Bear (Mu-kwa')—police, protectors, or herbal medicine people
- the Marten (Wa-bi-zha-shi')—warriors
- the Deer (We-we-shesh'-she)—gentle people
- the Bird (Be-nays')—spiritual leaders.

Each clan member served as a representative of the clan.

The clans had strict rules and customs. For instance, clan **lineage** was passed down paternally (on the father's side of the family). In other words, a child was part of his or her father's clan, while the mother remained part of her own clan. (In most First Nations, clan lineage was passed down matrilineally, or on the mother's side of the family.) Clan members did not always know all their relatives. Their lineage had never been recorded, so the only way of keeping track of their relatives was by maintaining the clan system. A clan included cousins, aunts, uncles, grandparents, and even distant relatives.

lineage
direct descent from a particular ancestor

When clan members visited another First Nations community, they would be asked to identify their clan. If they belonged to a clan in the community, that clan had to receive them as family members and invite them to eat and stay with them. People from the same clan were not allowed to marry. This practice prevented the potential problems caused by inbreeding.

Throughout the year, ceremonies and celebrations brought together many First Nations from various clans. However, after First Nations hunters and their families settled in permanent dwellings, the different clans did not have as much contact. There were now fewer opportunities to meet and marry people from other clans. The clan system eventually lost its influence and became ineffective. Although a number of First Nations people today may know their clan identity, many do not.

Selection of Leaders

Traditionally, leaders were chosen based on their clan. For example, many Salteaux leaders came from the Loon (Mahng) clan or the Crane (Ah-ji-jawk') clan because of these clans' leadership qualities. Leaders were not selected for their admired qualities or for any social standing that they had gained—social classes did not exist in the traditional Salteaux (Ojibwe) and Nehiyaw (Cree) cultures. However, as wealth became more important in the communities, the selection of a leader became influenced by the individual's material wealth.

Dependence on Europeans

Another change that affected Aboriginal peoples was their growing dependence on European traders. Aboriginal peoples were skillful hunters. They survived in a harsh environment, hunting animals for food and shelter. If they needed other goods, they bartered among themselves and with other Aboriginal nations. For example, tobacco was considered a sacred medicine and was used by the Salteaux and the Nehiyaw. Since few people within these two nations grew tobacco, they usually bartered for it with the Haudenosaunee (Iroquois), who did grow tobacco.

When the fur-trading posts were set up, Aboriginal peoples could trade furs for items they had never had before. Sewing needles, ceramic or glass beads (trimming for their clothing and moccasins), guns, axes, iron pots, tea, flour, and cloth were some of the goods they could get from the European traders. These items made hunting, cooking, and sewing clothes easier.

For some years, this arrangement worked well for both sides: the traders received the hides and then sold them in Europe, and the standard of living improved for Aboriginal peoples. Later, however, the shift from relying on the environment to depending on European goods led to problems for Aboriginal communities. It also affected their ability to govern themselves and make decisions about their ways of living.

CLOSE-UP

ABORIGINAL PEOPLES AND THE TRADING POSTS

At trading posts, Aboriginal peoples bought goods that they could not manufacture themselves. One example is the musket, along with the pellets, flint, and gunpowder that were needed to use it. In the 17th century, Aboriginal peoples did not have the skills or technology to melt ore, remove the impurities, and pour the metal into moulds to make guns. Nor could they make the pellets or gunpowder to fire them.

In Europe and elsewhere, inventions and ideas developed by people in different countries led to technological advances. Unlike the Europeans, Aboriginal peoples had not been exposed to other cultures or any developments within these cultures.

As Aboriginal peoples became more involved with the fur trade, they no longer had time to make their own tools and hunt for food. They came to rely totally on the European goods that they received in exchange for furs. Each trading post was in a position of strength because it had a **monopoly** in the surrounding area. Consequently, it is easy to see how Aboriginal peoples' dependence on the trading posts became so deeply rooted.

monopoly
exclusive control of the trade in a product or service in a certain market

Collapse of the Fur Trade

Fur prices varied because of the changing demands of the fashion market. For example, beaver pelt would be in fashion one season, and mink would replace it the next. To respond to these shifts in the market, the fur companies would change the monetary value of the furs they bought from Aboriginal trappers. As a result, the trappers did not receive the same amount of goods or money each time they brought furs to the trading post.

The environment also played a key role in the livelihood of Aboriginal trappers. When animal populations were scarce because of overtrapping or natural causes (for example, disease, fire, overpopulation of predators), there were fewer furs to sell to the traders. This meant a drop in income for the trappers.

Eventually, the fur trade collapsed in the late 1800s, and other types of economic activity, such as agriculture and forestry, began to make inroads on its territory.

Dependence on Government

Over time, Aboriginal trappers and hunters learned to use guns almost exclusively. They relied less and less on their traditional hunting skills. The demand for furs, overhunting, and the use of new weapons caused near-extinction of some animals, for example, the beaver in the 1800s. As a result, many trading posts closed. In 1870, the government of Canada took control of Hudson's Bay Company lands. Aboriginal peoples who had settled and developed ties with HBC posts began to experience hardships. Some died from starvation and related diseases. The government decided to intervene, providing food and other goods to Aboriginal peoples.

Many Aboriginal peoples saw the government's assistance as **paternalism**. They were being looked after as dependants, leaving their guardian, the government, to control their future. In many treaties and correspondence with Aboriginal groups in the 1800s, Queen Victoria was referred to as "Your Queen Mother." Aboriginal peoples resented this treatment because it implied that they could not care for themselves and make their own decisions. Another complaint was that the government often helped or intervened only because of political or public pressure—and only when situations were desperate or extreme. When help did come, it was often without Aboriginal input or with little consideration of what Aboriginal peoples wanted or needed.

paternalism
a policy or practice of treating or governing people in a fatherly manner, especially by providing for their needs without giving them rights or responsibilities

As you continue to study the relationship between Aboriginal peoples and the government, you'll see this theme of **ward** and guardian repeated in various government actions and legislation regarding Aboriginal peoples.

ward
a person under the protection or care of another

Missionaries

Among the European settlers in northern Ontario, English Protestants and French Roman Catholics were the two most dominant religious groups. Several religious orders also came to the New World to convert the Aboriginal peoples. These Christian **missionaries** thought of non-Christians as "lost souls" who needed to be saved. In New France, the first missionaries were Roman Catholic priests from the Récollet and Jesuit orders. They travelled and lived among the various Aboriginal groups, looking for converts. In the English-speaking colonies, most of the missionaries were Protestant.

missionary
a person sent to another country to spread a religious faith and to engage in charitable work

As you saw in Chapter 1, Aboriginal peoples had their own spiritual beliefs. Protestant and Catholic missionaries, however, saw these beliefs as "evil." They restricted or banned many Aboriginal ceremonies, teachings, and practices. For example, they discouraged the smudging ceremony (the burning of certain plants and herbs to cleanse the body and spirit)

Figure 3.12 A Missionary with Members of the Piikunii Nation, Rocky Mountain House, Alberta, 1871 Although the Piikunii had their own complex religious structure, missionaries tried to convert them to Christianity.

and any type of drumming. The missionaries also tried to impose restrictions on the Aboriginal way of living, including the type of clothing Aboriginal peoples wore. These restrictions had very little to do with biblical teachings.

At first, the Aboriginal peoples did not welcome the missionaries as openly as they had the traders. Unlike the value of guns, iron pots, and other implements, the value of new spiritual beliefs was not clear. However, northern Aboriginal groups generally respected the spiritual beliefs of European traders and settlers. Gradually, they began to accept the missionaries into their communities and adopted some or all aspects of the new religions. The missionaries had good intentions and contributed to some positive changes in Aboriginal communities. By providing basic health services and introducing health awareness, they helped to reduce deaths among Aboriginal peoples.

Unfortunately, the missionaries were also responsible for a number of rifts among community members and families. Sometimes the various religious orders would become rivals for "Aboriginal souls" and would compete with one another to see who could convert the most Aboriginal people. At times, they undermined one another's efforts. Today, there is still evidence of these religious orders' competitive nature. Most reserves have more than one Christian church, and some reserves, particularly in the North, have one dominant church that make other religions unwelcome in the community.

In K.J. Crowe's *The History of the Original Peoples of Northern Canada*, a non-Aboriginal woman from Manitoulin Island describes a time when the churches in her town would compete to see who could provide the most or best baked goods at Christmas. Each church wanted the Aboriginal people from a nearby reserve to come to its Christmas festivities and not those of its rivals.

Residential schools were one of the outcomes of this religious zeal and the Canadian government's assimilation policies. These schools were funded by the federal government and run by religious groups. You will examine them more closely in Chapter 5.

1. As European settlements grew, changes occurred rapidly in Aboriginal peoples' way of life. What were some of the changes that occurred?
2. How did the Aboriginal peoples' dependence on the government alter their sense of nationalism and sovereignty?
3. a) How did the introduction of Christianity benefit Aboriginal peoples?
   b) What were some of the damaging aspects of the introduction of Christianity?
   c) How might the adoption of Christianity have affected Aboriginal concepts of ethics, acculturation, nationalism, and sovereignty?

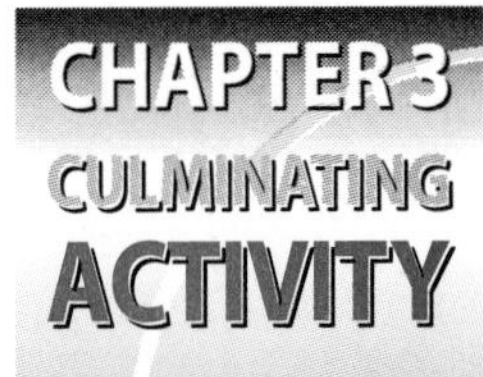

The Plains Peoples: European Contact and Change

When a cultural group comes in contact with other cultures, it often borrows or adapts ideas and practices from those cultures. In this chapter, you learned how First Nations of the Plains saw the advantage of using European firearms to hunt buffalo. By the late 1700s, they were trading furs in exchange for these new hunting weapons.

Cultures that have emerged over a long period of time have tended to develop practices and institutions in tune with their surroundings; abrupt cultural changes, even ones that appear to be beneficial at first, may lead to long-range, unforeseen consequences. For example, the fact that European firearms allowed the Plains peoples to kill buffalo more easily was a short-term advantage. In the long term, however, the use of firearms, as well as hunting by traders and US government policies regarding settlement of the prairies, contributed to the drastic decline of the buffalo herds, which had harmful effects on the lives of the Plains peoples.

This activity gives you the opportunity to identify and categorize the different ways in which contact with European fur traders and settlers changed the Plains peoples' cultures during the 1700s and 1800s. There are three parts to this activity:

1. Make a list of examples that show how contact with Europeans affected the Plains peoples; for example, the use of firearms to hunt buffalo or the epidemics of diseases such as smallpox that resulted in many deaths among First Nations. Some of these examples will be negative, others will be positive, and many will probably be a combination of both. Review Chapter 3 to find at least 10 examples of changes to First Nations' way of life as a result of contact with Europeans.

2. The following organizer divides the changes to First Nations cultures into three categories: Economic, Social, and Political. In many cases, these categories overlap somewhat; for example, the use of firearms affected the political balance among First Nations, increased the numbers of buffalo killed, and changed the way First Nations people lived. However, you need to decide which aspect of First Nations cultures was *most* affected by each of the changes. For example, in the organizer below, *use of firearms* appears in the Economic category. Find four examples of change for each category.

CHANGES TO ABORIGINAL CULTURE

Type of Change	*Examples of Change*
Economic	1. use of firearms 2. 3. 4.
Social	1. huge loss of life from disease 2. 3. 4.
Political	1. 2. 3. 4.

3. Finally, choose three of your examples of change from the column on the right. For each example, describe in one or two sentences how that change affected the lives of the Plains peoples. As a model, refer to the example in the introduction to this activity that explains how the use of firearms affected the Plains peoples' way of life.

Treaty Making and the Loss of First Nations' Lands and Autonomy

LEARNING OBJECTIVES

In this chapter, you will

- explore the various types of treaties between First Nations and European and Canadian governments
- understand why First Nations and Europeans established treaties
- examine specific treaties that the Crown made with various First Nations before and after Confederation
- recognize the significance of treaties in the loss of First Nations' traditional lands and autonomy
- consider the current process of land claims by Aboriginal nations in an effort to regain their right to traditional lands

INTRODUCTION

In this chapter, you will explore treaty making between Europeans and First Nations in Canada. You'll learn about the different types of treaties that were made before and after Confederation and the reasons why both Europeans and First Nations decided to establish treaties. You'll discover how treaties resulted in the loss of First Nations' traditional lands and **autonomy**. You'll also learn about treaty promises that were not fulfilled by the **Crown** and the actions First Nations took to protest this plight. Finally, you'll ex-

autonomy önrendelkezés
the right of self-government; personal freedom

Crown
the government under a constitutional monarchy

amine the process of present-day land claims to see how Aboriginal nations are trying to regain their rights and some control of their traditional lands.

EARLY TREATY MAKING BETWEEN FIRST NATIONS AND EUROPEANS

Before European explorers arrived in North America, First Nations and Inuit peoples lived within their traditional territories. As you learned in previous chapters, their cultures and traditions ranged from nomadic lifestyles, such as those of the Plains peoples, to more permanent communities, such as the Haudenosaunee (Iroquois). First Nations and Inuit peoples felt a strong connection with nature, and their ways of living were closely linked to the land. Although Aboriginal societies did not have centralized, official governments in the way that European societies did, they were self-governing through unwritten customs and codes of conduct.

Soon after contact, Europeans began to approach various First Nations to enter into agreements. These early **treaties** were made to establish peace, trade, alliance, neutrality, and military support.

treaty an agreement between two states that has been formally concluded and ratified

Indian Treaties

Indian treaties are formal agreements between First Nations and the Crown involving promises of peace and friendship, land cessions, and other issues and benefits. Rights promised to First Nations peoples in these treaties are recognized and confirmed by the *Constitution Act, 1982*; those included in land claims settlements also have constitutional force.

Source: The Canadian Encyclopedia *(Edmonton: Hurtig, 1985), pp. 872–873.*

CLOSE-UP

THE GREAT PEACE TREATY OF 1701

The Great Peace Treaty of 1701 is one example of early treaty making between First Nations and Europeans. Negotiations were held in Montreal between the French and 1,300 representatives from more than 40 First Nations. The resulting treaty ended almost a century of war between the Five Nations Confederacy and New France. It also laid the groundwork for New France to expand south and west, and ensured that the Five Nations Confederacy would not take sides in any conflict between Britain and France in the New World.

The Fur Trade

During the fur trade, First Nations and Inuit entered into negotiations with European traders, with the Métis acting as intermediaries in many cases. For example, the Hudson's Bay Company made agreements with First Nations and Inuit to ensure that they would sell furs only to the HBC. In return, the HBC assured them that they would receive quality goods from its trading posts. These discussions took place in a spirit of mutual respect and equality. First Nations often held special ceremonies to help establish a friendly relationship with Europeans. As a result, when First Nations began negotiating with Europeans over land, they expected to have the same type of relationship based on respect and understanding. However, this was not often the case, as you'll discover later in the chapter.

Land and Resources

As European settlements grew, treaties began to focus more on arrangements for living together peacefully and the acquisition of First Nations lands and resources. Changes to the First Nations' way of living on the land began with these first land treaties. Most important, the loss of First Nations' sovereignty is strongly linked to these treaties. From the start, First Nations peoples expressed concern about disruption to their traditional cultures. This concern is reflected in the terms of the treaties, which are outlined later in this chapter.

Misunderstanding

The cultural differences between First Nations peoples and Europeans led to misunderstandings during land negotiations. First, Europeans had a tradition of private ownership of land, while First Nations peoples felt that no one could own the land. It was a gift from the Creator, and they were its guardians, not its owners. The land was their means of survival.

Second, language barriers meant that First Nations didn't fully understand the terms of the agreements. Both sides had translators, but it was impossible to translate the ideas behind decades of tradition. First Nations weren't aware that they were selling the land, since it wasn't theirs to sell, as far as they were concerned. They didn't realize that they were giving up anything.

In the First Nations' view, treaties were intended to lay out the terms of a mutual sharing of resources—and their compensation for sharing these resources. These and other factors put them at a strong disadvantage during negotiations. In many cases, it wasn't until the Europeans began the process of removing them from their land that First Nations fully understood what they had signed. However, in the government's view, a deal was a deal. Treaties were a form of land surrender, the first step in the assimilation process.

Treaties between First Nations

Treaties were not new to First Nations at the time of contact. They had been making treaties with one another long before the arrival of European fur traders and settlers in the New World. Oral treaties had been made to settle wars and land disputes, to set up trading agreements, and to arrange marriages.

One of the first recorded treaties between First Nations involved the Onodowohgah (Seneca), Kanien'Kehaka (Mohawk), Onundagaono (Onondaga), Onayotekaono (Oneida), and Guyohkohnyoh (Cayuga). This treaty was called the Great Law of Peace of the People of the Longhouse and predates the year 1450. It covered 117 articles, including the establishment of a code of law and form of government between the five nations. The treaty was passed on orally and was not recorded until 1880.

Why Treaties Were Established

Europeans' Motives

In the 17th century, both the French and the British started to make treaties with First Nations. The French needed First Nations as their allies in the fur trade. Treaties with the French were made as friendship agreements and were not written down.

The British started treaty making in order to "legally" take over First Nations lands and resources. In this way, the British government could make room for settlement and fulfill its nationalistic goals with a minimum of trouble from First Nations.

First Nations' Motives

Why would First Nations go along with the idea of treaties? As you've learned, they had a different concept of land ownership from that of the Europeans, and assumed that European settlers wanted to share the land, not own it. Most treaties were signed between the late 1700s and the early 1900s. At that time, First Nations were facing great upheaval. Their traditional lands were being taken over by settlers; they were also losing their main source of food, the buffalo, and their main source of income, trapping. European diseases such as smallpox were wiping out large numbers of First Nations peoples. Historians estimate that 10 percent of the First Nations population in the West died from starvation or disease in 1883–1884 alone. In northern Canada, the decline of the fur trade was also affecting the livelihood of First Nations. So it was to First Nations' advantage to sign agreements with the British and Canadian governments that defined their rights, as well as the rights and responsibilities of the European settlers who would be sharing the land.

1. Compare the First Nations and European views of treaties. How did these views lead to misunderstanding during negotiations?
2. In an organizer, summarize the advantages and disadvantages of treaties for both sides.
3. In this early stage of treaty making, was there any evidence that treaties would have a harmful impact on First Nations peoples in the future? Explain.

TREATIES BEFORE AND AFTER CONFEDERATION

Historians classify First Nations treaties into three major groups: pre-Confederation treaties, the Numbered Treaties, and modern treaties (commonly known as land claims). This section examines pre-Confederation treaties and the Numbered Treaties; the next section examines land claims.

Pre-Confederation Treaties and the *Royal Proclamation of 1763*

Peace and Friendship Treaties

Between 1725 and 1779, the British government and First Nations on the east coast entered into a number of agreements known as Peace and Friendship Treaties. These treaties were established during a period of continual conflict between Britain and France. Britain wanted to ensure that First Nations would remain neutral or side with Britain. In exchange, Britain would not prevent First Nations from following their traditional ways of life.

One of the first Peace and Friendship Treaties was reached in 1725 with the Mi'kmaq First Nation of present-day Nova Scotia. In return for the Mi'kmaq's neutrality or military assistance in any conflicts with the French, the British agreed to smooth the way for trade in the area and promised to prevent any European interference with traditional Mi'kmaq hunting, trapping, and fishing practices.

Royal Proclamation of 1763

When the Seven Years' War ended in 1763, Britain had become the supreme European colonial power. With New France now under Britain's control, the British government passed the *Royal Proclamation of 1763.* This Act created the colony of Quebec and outlined its system of government. It also set aside a large area of land for First Nations.

The Royal Proclamation outlined and formalized a treaty-making process with First Nations. It ensured that no one could approach First Nations to buy their land, with the exception of representatives of the Crown. The

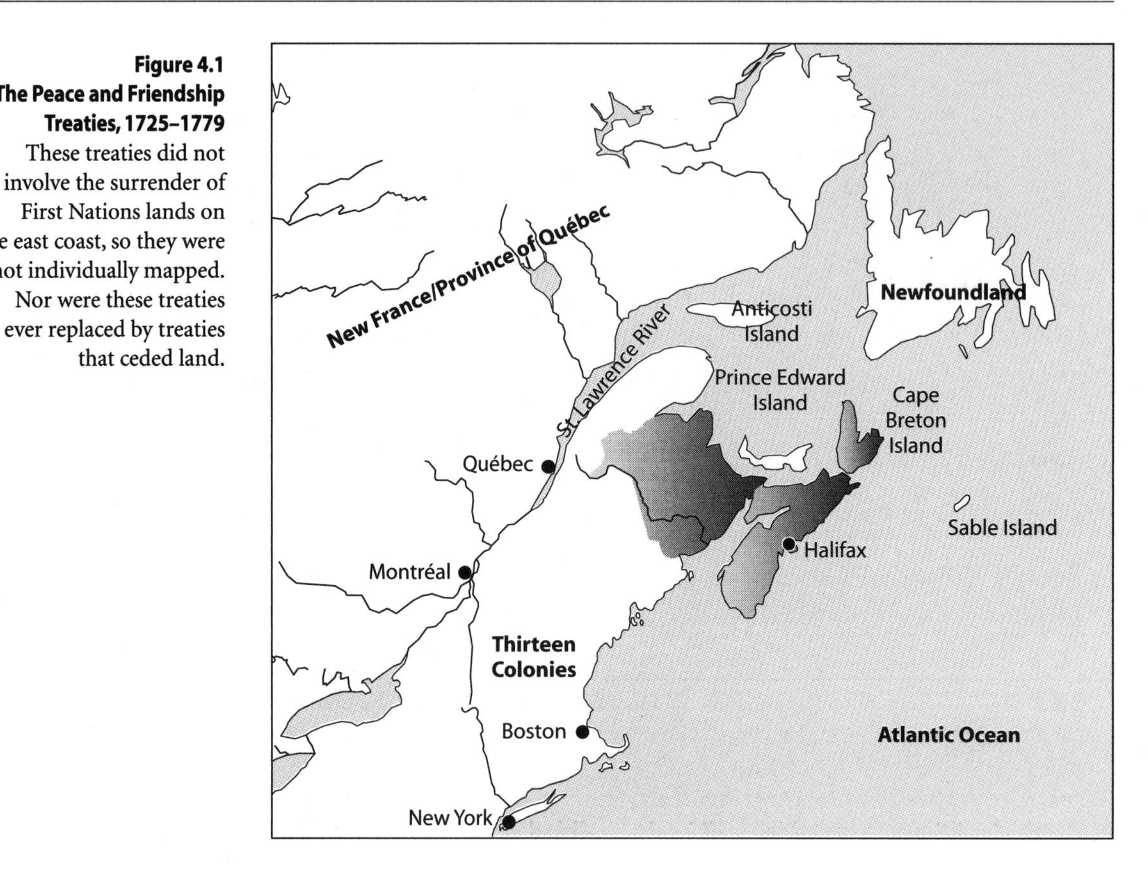

Figure 4.1
The Peace and Friendship Treaties, 1725–1779
These treaties did not involve the surrender of First Nations lands on the east coast, so they were not individually mapped. Nor were these treaties ever replaced by treaties that ceded land.

land could then be sold or given by the Crown to settlers and other Europeans. These laws prevented unscrupulous individuals from fraudulently obtaining First Nations lands.

Although the proclamation's terms did not extend to other settled colonies, it did set a precedent for treaty negotiations throughout the treaty-making era and continues to influence present-day land claims. For example, when the government of Canada purchased Rupert's Land and the North-Western Territory from the Hudson's Bay Company in 1869, it was required to follow Britain's treaty-making policy with First Nations:

> [U]pon the transference of the territories in question to the Canadian government, the claims of the Indian tribes to compensation for land required for the purposes of settlement will be considered and settled in conformity with the equitable principles which have uniformly governed the British Crown in its dealings with Aboriginal people.

Statutes Order 1870:264, quoted in Michael Asch, Home and Native Land: Aboriginal Rights and the Canadian Constitution *(Vancouver: University of British Columbia Press, 1993), p. 58.*

A Bill of Rights

The Royal Proclamation is an important acknowledgment of the rights of First Nations peoples and their status as nations. For this reason, it has often been called the "Indian Bill of Rights."

Sovereignty

Did the *Royal Proclamation of 1763* recognize the sovereignty of First Nations peoples? This question continues to be debated. First Nations state that their sovereignty as nations has never been **extinguished**. They argue that the Royal Proclamation, even though it placed boundaries on land reserved for First Nations peoples, continued to recognize their sovereignty. First Nations peoples were not seen or referred to as Crown subjects in this document, nor in any later Crown documents. They were recognized as separate and distinct peoples and nations. They were promised that their traditional ways, which included the right to their own laws, territories, and government, would not be violated.

extinguish to nullify a right, claim, etc.

The Indian Department

Between 1763 and 1830, the British government did not establish any other policies or pass any legislation that specifically addressed First Nations. However, the first Indian Department in Canada had been established in 1755 as a branch of the British military in North America. Its purpose was to maintain good relations with First Nations and to ensure their loyalty to Britain during times of war. The creation of this department reinforced the paternalistic attitude that the government had assumed in its dealings with First Nations. Despite this attitude, First Nations continued to be self-governing, looking after the needs of their communities at all levels—political, economic, and social.

Other Pre-Confederation Treaties

After 1763, the British Crown made a series of treaties mainly with First Nations in present-day Ontario. The purpose of these treaties was to open up areas for European settlement, farming, and mining.

Many treaties that were signed after the Royal Proclamation and before Confederation have never been found or were poorly documented. Examples of treaties that survived or were better documented include the following:

- **Upper Canada Treaties (1764–1862):** The first land treaties in present-day southern Ontario were made following the American Revolution in 1776. After Britain was defeated by American colonists, it needed land for its displaced Loyalist colonists and First Nations allies. They were in danger of losing their lives if they remained in the United States. Britain also needed land to reward military personnel who had fought in the revolution, including its First Nations allies who were primarily from the Six Nations Confederacy. Many of these refugees were resettled in Upper and Lower Canada. First Nations who were displaced in these early treaties to make room for the refugees received goods and lump-sum payments in exchange for land.

- **Province of Canada Treaties (1850–1862):** The three major Province of Canada Treaties are the two Robinson Treaties and the Manitoulin Island Treaty. With the discovery of minerals near the shores of lakes Huron and Superior, the government of the Province of Canada decided to extinguish First Nations' title to their lands. The two Robinson Treaties were signed in 1850 between the Anishnaabe (Ojibwe) and the Crown. The Anishnaabe gave up mining land in exchange for money and the creation of reserves. They were also given the right to hunt and fish on the land that they had surrendered. The Manitoulin Island Treaty was signed in 1862. It allowed European settlement on this island in Lake Huron.
- **Vancouver Island Treaties (1850–1854):** Also known as the Douglas Treaties, these 14 agreements gave First Nations cash, clothing, and blankets in exchange for nearly 570 square kilometres of land on the island. They also kept the right to use existing village lands and were allowed to hunt and fish on the surrendered lands. Although Governor James Douglas never used the word *treaty* in the negotiations, the Supreme Court of Canada later ruled that they were treaties because Douglas was representing the Crown. Treaty making on Vancouver Island ended in 1854 when the colony ran out of money for further expansion. Also, fewer Europeans were settling on the island, and industry was slow to develop.

Tecumseh was a Shawnee chief who wanted First Nations to unite in stopping non-Aboriginal settlement on First Nations lands:

"My heart is a stone. Heavy with sadness for my people; cold with the knowledge that no treaty will keep the whites out of our land; hard with determination to resist as long as I live and breathe. Now we are weak and many of our people are afraid. But hear me; a single twig breaks but the bundle of twigs is strong. Someday I will embrace our brother tribes and draw them into a bundle and together we will win our country back from the whites."

Tecumseh, c. 1795

The Numbered Treaties (1871–1921)

jurisdiction
the power or right to exercise authority

In 1867, the *British North America Act* (renamed the *Constitution Act, 1867* in 1982) created the Dominion of Canada, which included Nova Scotia, New Brunswick, Quebec, and Ontario. The Act also gave **jurisdiction** over the "Indians and Land reserved for Indians" to the government of Canada. The Inuit and Métis were not mentioned in the Act, but in 1939, the Inuit were also placed under federal jurisdiction. Chapter 5 explains the Métis' status as an Aboriginal people.

After Canada purchased Rupert's Land and the North-Western Territory from the Hudson's Bay Company in 1869, the entire area was renamed the North-West Territories. Prime Minister John A. Macdonald wanted to open the area to more settlement and complete the railway from the Atlantic to the Pacific. However, these lands were the traditional territories of First Nations; according to the terms of the *Royal Proclamation of 1763*, First Nations had to be compensated for surrendering their lands.

First Nations Ensure Their Survival

Between 1871 and 1921, 11 treaties were signed between the government of Canada and First Nations in present-day northern Ontario, Manitoba, Saskatchewan, Alberta, and portions of the Yukon Territory, the Northwest Territories, and British Columbia. They are commonly referred to as the "Numbered Treaties" because they are numbered 1 to 11.

Although some First Nations did not trust the Canadian government to honour the treaties, they had little choice. As you read earlier in the chapter, First Nations in the West were facing disease and starvation, as well as the loss of their culture and way of life in the face of European settlement. In order to survive, many First Nations agreed to surrender their lands in exchange for reserve lands, **annuities**, schools, hunting and fishing rights, agricultural implements, cattle, clothing, flags, medals, and annual cash distributions for ammunition and twine.

annuity
a sum of money paid yearly

WHO WAS INCLUDED IN THE TREATIES?

Under the terms of the *British North America Act*, First Nations peoples who were living on reserves in the new Dominion of Canada were registered by the federal government. First Nations peoples in the North-West Territories, or "Treaty Indians" as they were identified by the government, were also registered. When the *Indian Act* was passed in 1876, it set out three categories of "Indian status." (The *Indian Act* is explained in Chapter 5.)

Because the Numbered Treaties took these categories into account, families were often divided. First Nations peoples whom the government considered to be "troublemakers," or who had not accepted Christianity and its ideals of being "civilized," were not included in the treaties. The government did not approach a significant number of Aboriginal peoples for treaty negotiations—for example, First Nations in the James Bay area and most of British Columbia, as well as the Inuit.

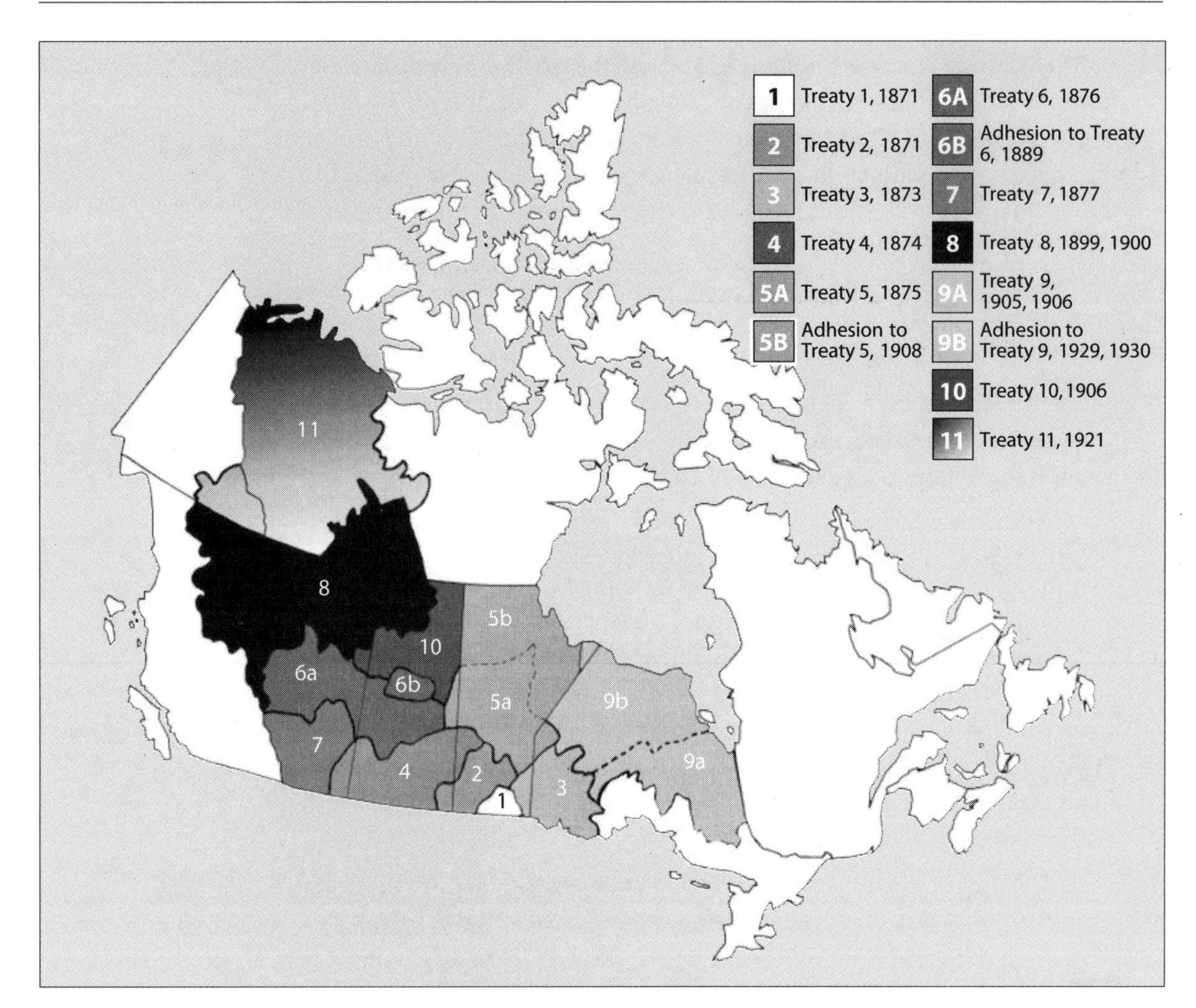

Figure 4.2 The Numbered Treaties, 1871–1921 Many of these treaties included cattle and farming implements as part of what First Nations would receive in return for their lands. The Canadian government thought that First Nations in the West should farm the land rather than hunt the rapidly disappearing buffalo. However, these First Nations were nomadic and had little experience of farming. They believed they had the right to preserve their own way of life and keep their independence.

Treaties 1 through 5 (1871–1875)

The first five Numbered Treaties covered lands in present-day northwestern Ontario, southern Manitoba, Saskatchewan, and Alberta. Treaties 1, 2, and 3 were negotiated with the Nehiyaw (Cree) and the Anishnaabe (Ojibwe) of Manitoba and northwestern Ontario. Treaty 4 primarily involved the Nehiyaw and the Anishnaabe of southern Saskatchewan, while Treaty 5 was signed by the Anishnaabe and the Mushkegowuk (Swampy Cree) in the area from the middle of Lake Winnipeg and Lake Manitoba to just below the southwestern quadrant of James Bay.

Treaty Adhesions

Some First Nations did not initially sign the treaties. However, at a later date, they decided to comply with the treaties and sign them. This is called a *treaty adhesion.*

The purpose of these treaties was to clear the way for European settlement and agricultural and industrial development. In exchange for giving up their land rights, First Nations were promised

- reserve lands—600 square metres per family of five (Treaties 1 and 2); 2.5 square kilometres per family of five (Treaties 3 and 4)
- cash—the amount differed from treaty to treaty but usually increased with each subsequent treaty
- an allowance for blankets and hunting and fishing implements
- farming assistance
- schools on reserve land
- a census to record the number of people in each band, mainly for financial compensation purposes
- the right to hunt and fish on all **ceded** land not used for settlement, lumbering, or mining (promised in writing from Treaty 3 onward)
- public buildings, roads, and other important infrastructure—to be built by the government.

cede
to surrender possession of, especially by treaty

In exchange for these items, First Nations promised they would keep the peace and maintain law and order on the reserves.

VOICES

Adams Archibald, the lieutenant governor of Manitoba and the North-West Territories, was the negotiator of Treaty 1. In a speech to the Anishnaabe, he described Queen Victoria's wish that First Nations adopt farming as a way of life and tried to explain the concept of reserves.

"Your Great Mother wishes the good of all races under her sway. She wishes her Red children to be happy and contented. She wishes them to live in comfort. She would like them to adopt the habits of the whites, to till land and raise food, and store it up against a time of want. ... Your Great Mother, therefore, will lay aside for you 'lots' of land to be used by you and your children forever. She will not allow the white man to intrude upon these lots. She will make rules to keep them for you, so that as long as the sun shall shine, there shall be no Indian who has not a place that he can call his home, where he can go and pitch his camp or if he chooses, build his house and till his land."

Adams G. Archibald, 1871

Treaty 6 (1876)

Treaty 6 was settled with the Plains and Woodland Nehiyaw. As explained in Chapter 3, the Nehiyaw chiefs Poundmaker and Big Bear at first refused to sign the treaty because they felt that the government was being unfair. However, they eventually relented because their people were dealing with starvation and disease. Treaty 6 is very similar to the five treaties that preceded it. In exchange for their land on the prairies in present-day Alberta and Saskatchewan, First Nations received reserve land, cash, farm animals and tools, and other items. Again, they had to promise to maintain law and order on the reserves.

The Métis

The Numbered Treaties encompassed lands where large numbers of Métis had lived for many years. However, their claims to these lands were largely ignored, and the Métis were not mentioned in the treaties. This treatment contributed to the Métis rebellions in the 1800s, which are discussed in Chapter 3.

Treaty 6 also guaranteed that a medicine chest would be kept in the home of the Indian agent for the use of First Nations. (Indian agents were government officials who lived within First Nations reserves.) Although this "medicine chest" clause does not appear in any of the other Numbered Treaties, it has become the basis of demands for free health care for First Nations peoples.

Treaty 7 (1877)

This treaty was signed by several First Nations, including the Siksika (Blackfoot) Confederacy, the Nakoda (Assiniboine), and the Dene (Chipewyan) in present-day southern Alberta. Although its provisions are much the same as those in the first six treaties, these First Nations negotiated for more money and supplies. No further Numbered Treaties were signed until 1899.

Treaties 8 through 11 (1899–1921)

The last four Numbered Treaties were signed over a period of two decades. Again, these treaties are similar to most of the Numbered Treaties that preceded them.

- Treaty 8 was negotiated with the Nehiyaw and Dene in 1899 so that the federal government could provide an overland route to the gold fields in the Yukon. The government acquired a vast area to the north of Treaty 6 that included lands in present-day northern British Columbia, Alberta, Saskatchewan, and the south-central Northwest

Territories. One provision new to Treaty 8 was the creation of small reserves for individual families to meet the needs of small band groupings such as the Woodland Nehiyaw and Dene.

- Treaty 9 was signed in 1905 and 1906 by the Anishnaabe and Nehiyaw in northern Ontario (the former Hudson's Bay Company land grant). The government wanted to open transportation routes and access to natural resources, such as timber, in this area.
- Treaty 10, signed in 1906, transferred land titles from the Anishnaabe and Nehiyaw to the newly created provinces of Saskatchewan and Alberta.
- Treaty 11 was negotiated in 1921 with the Dene-thah (Slavey), Dene (Dogrib), Gwich'in (Loucheux), and Hare (North Slavey) for land in the present-day Northwest Territories and Yukon Territory. It was the last of the Numbered Treaties and coincided with the discovery of oil at Norman Wells, on the Mackenzie River.

Figure 4.3 Treaty 1 with the First Nations of Manitoba In treaty negotiations, the Crown representative was initially a military officer and later an official from the Department of Indian Affairs. This individual would assemble chiefs of First Nations who inhabited the lands that the government wanted. The signing of a treaty was a solemn and formal event. The chiefs would dress in their finest regalia and the Crown's military negotiators would wear their uniforms. Many people from the First Nations communities would gather for the signing. Afterwards, First Nations would receive items and cash payments that were agreed on in the treaty. For First Nations peoples, treaty payments were very festive occasions.

Broken Promises

Many of the promises made in the Numbered Treaties were either broken or never completely fulfilled by the federal government. For example:

- In Treaties 1 and 2, First Nations were promised farming assistance and extra money, but these items were never provided.
- Some oral promises made by the federal government were not carried out.
- Promises made in earlier treaties—such as First Nations' right to hunt and fish on Crown land—were cut back or extinguished in later treaties.
- In Treaties 1 through 7, the government had agreed to take a census of First Nations people living on reserves in order to pay each person a lump sum of cash annually. However, by the time Treaty 8 was signed in 1899, the government had lost count of many First Nations people.
- The Williams Treaties of 1923 dealt with unresolved First Nations land claims in southern and central Ontario. Although First Nations in these areas received cash in exchange for ceding their lands, they lost the right to hunt, fish, or trap on these lands. As a result, First Nations in the West feared that the government was no longer interested in safeguarding their way of life, as promised in the Numbered Treaties.
- In 1925, the federal government banned some First Nations ceremonies, including powwows (Sun Dances had already been banned in 1896). Again, the government was interfering with First Nations cultural traditions.
- In 1930, new agreements with the federal government gave the prairie provinces greater control over their natural resources. Since these provincial governments now had the right to control fishing, hunting, and trapping on Crown land, yet another promise made in the Numbered Treaties had been broken.

First Nations Take Action

legislation
a law or series of laws passed by the federal or provincial governments

In the early 1900s, First Nations peoples started to protest these broken promises. A delegation of First Nations from the prairie provinces went to Ottawa in 1910 to lodge a complaint. In the 1920s and 1930s, further broken promises—and new **legislation** that contradicted these promises—spurred the growth of First Nations political activism. The League of Indians of Canada, a national political organization, was formed in 1919, the Indian Association of Alberta in 1939, and the Federation of Saskatchewan Indians in 1944. In the mid-1940s, when the Canadian government was considering amendments to the *Indian Act*, these organizations made recommendations to the government. Canada was planning on signing the

United Nations *Universal Declaration of Human Rights*, so it had to redress its treatment of Aboriginal peoples.

In Chapter 5, you'll examine Aboriginal political activism more closely.

Treaty Rights Today

Broken treaty promises, both before and after Confederation, have led to a number of disputes that are ongoing. Many First Nations are fighting to reclaim their rights or to receive some form of compensation. These disputes share a common theme—the land. As you'll discover in the next section, many cases are currently in the courts, where attempts are being made to resolve them. Canadian courts still uphold existing treaties, signed in those early years, as sound and legal documents. Unfortunately, a number of disputes over land have erupted outside the courts, resulting in tension between First Nations and non-Aboriginal people in several communities across Canada.

Figure 4.4 Lubicon Nehiyaw (Cree) Demonstrate Lubicon elder Reinie Jobin, from Peace River, Alberta, speaks to supporters at a demonstration in front of Daishowa Corporation in Montreal, 1997. The Lubicon have sought for years to get the forestry company to cease logging operations on their land.

Aboriginal rights special rights held by Aboriginal peoples of Canada based on their ancestors' long-standing use and occupancy of the land; for example, the rights of certain Aboriginal peoples to hunt, fish, and trap on ancestral lands

In recent years, the federal courts have been reluctant to recognize treaty rights to fish, hunt, or trap for commercial purposes, even though some treaties specifically mention these rights. For example, in regard to Treaty 9, the Ontario courts have maintained that First Nations cannot be regulated by provincial trapping legislation because the treaty protects their right to trap. However, this matter remains unsettled because federal government policies say that **Aboriginal rights** include only the traditional methods of hunting, trapping, and fishing that were used prior to European contact. This continues to be one of the more controversial issues between the federal government and First Nations.

VOICES

First Nations seemed to have had little control or influence over the treaty-making process—from their ceded lands, to the size of reserve lands, to the type and amount of other remuneration they received. Chief Buckquaquet of the Rice Lake Missisakis (Mississauga) expressed the vulnerability of First Nations peoples during negotiations for the Kawartha Lakes region of Ontario:

"Father: If I was to refuse what our Father has requested, our Women and Children would be more to be pitied. From our lands we receive scarcely anything and if your words are true we will get more by parting with them, than by keeping them—our hunting is destroyed and we must throw ourselves on the compassion of our Great Father the King.

"Father: Our Youth, People, and Chief have always thought of not refusing our Father any request he makes to us, and therefore do what he wishes."

Quoted in E.S. Rogers and D.B. Smith, Aboriginal Ontario: Historical Perspectives on the First Nations *(Toronto: Dundurn Press, 1994), p. 43.*

TALKING CIRCLE

1. In your opinion, did the *Royal Proclamation of 1763* recognize the sovereignty of First Nations? Explain.
2. Provide at least three reasons to support the statement that First Nations were not in a position of equal bargaining power with the Crown when the pre-Confederation and Numbered Treaties were negotiated.
3. During treaty negotiations, how did the misunderstandings created by language barriers, cultural differences, and First Nations' views of the land affect the issue of First Nations' sovereignty?

4. You first examined the policy of paternalism in Chapter 3. How was this policy reflected in the treaties that the Crown made with First Nations?
5. a) How were the promises that Queen Victoria made to First Nations in 1871 eventually broken or unfulfilled?
   b) Do you think these promises were feasible in the first place? Explain.
6. a) Compare Chief Tecumseh's and Chief Buckquaquet's statements on making treaties. What similar theme(s) do you notice? How do their attitudes toward non-Aboriginal authority differ?
   b) What would your attitude be if you were in the same situation?
7. Use a Venn diagram to identify the benefits and drawbacks of treaties for the Crown and for First Nations.

LAND CLAIMS

Usufructuary Right

Since early contact, various First Nations have attempted to regain some control of their traditional lands. First Nations land claims are based on the argument that they occupied and used the land long before the arrival of European settlers. Early court cases described Aboriginal people's legal right to the land as a personal and **usufructuary right**—that is, merely a right to use certain land for hunting, fishing, trapping, and gathering. More recent cases have recognized a more substantial right, known as Aboriginal title. Aboriginal title is unique in that it is less than full ownership but includes more than the right to engage in activities on the land. The meaning of Aboriginal title is still evolving.

usufructuary right the right to use and benefit from the land

Land Claims prior to 1973

Before 1969, land claims were addressed on an individual basis, either by the Department of Indian Affairs and Northern Development or by the Department of Justice. For the most part, the claims were held up because of the federal government's refusal to pass the necessary legislation to deal with First Nations' claims to the land. The government had not formally acknowledged that First Nations were entitled to the land and had a legal basis for making claims.

In 1969, an Indian Claims Commissioner was appointed to receive and study First Nations' grievances and claims, and to recommend measures that the government could take to resolve them. That same year, a claim launched by the Nisga'a Nation in British Columbia became a precedent-

fiduciary
holding something in trust for another

setting case for the recognition of First Nations' claim to the land. The Supreme Court of Canada formally recognized the **fiduciary** relationship between the Crown and First Nations peoples. The government was also now obligated to guarantee the rights and freedoms of all its citizens, which provided further support for land claims. In 1973, the Supreme Court of Canada finally recognized the Nisga'a as the historical inhabitants of the land and ruled that they had to be compensated for their loss. (The Nisga'a Final Agreement is profiled on page 109.)

Soon after the Nisga'a ruling, recognition of First Nations' land claims became a formal process. The federal government agreed to negotiate settlements in which First Nations' title had never been extinguished by treaty. In 1973, the government established the Office of Native Claims, which dealt with two main types of claims: comprehensive and specific.

Comprehensive Land Claims

Comprehensive land claims are based on the concept of continuing Aboriginal rights and title to land and natural resources that have not been dealt with by treaty or other legal means. These claims relate to the traditional use and occupancy of land by the Inuit, Métis, and First Nations who did not sign treaties. The claims involve the Northwest Territories, the Yukon Territory, and the northern parts of some provinces, and cover about half of Canada's total area. They are settled through negotiation, and compensation can include a range of terms: cash, land, protection of language and culture, local self-government, and so on.

The federal government's policy on comprehensive land claims requires Aboriginal peoples to extinguish their title to much of their traditional lands as a condition of settlement. This is an extremely controversial issue for Aboriginal peoples, and there has been much discussion about whether or not this requirement is appropriate.

In the provinces, most of the lands and resources addressed in the claims are under provincial jurisdiction. Consequently, the provinces must take part in the negotiations and contribute to compensation. The first comprehensive land claim was the James Bay and Northern Quebec Agreement, signed in 1975.

Comprehensive Claims as of 2005

Fifteen comprehensive land claims have been settled in Canada. The most recent are the eight Yukon First Nations Final Agreements (1995–2002) and the Nisga'a Final Agreement (2000).

Northern and Southern Land Claims

In *Native Peoples in Canada,* James Frideres describes two types of comprehensive land claims based on regions: northern and southern. Comprehensive claims in the more southern regions of Canada deal with lands in heavily populated areas. These claims are difficult to settle because the land is in use and is "owned." Comprehensive claims in the northern regions of Canada are easier to resolve because there are fewer communities and the land in question is usually Crown land.

Specific Land Claims

Specific land claims are based on issues arising from the following:

- the non-fulfillment of a treaty or other agreement
- a violation of the *Indian Act* or other laws
- a violation in the government's administration of First Nations funds or other assets
- an illegal sale or other transfer of First Nations lands by the government.

Specific Claims in Canada as of March 31, 2003

- 1,185 received
- 540 under review
- 112 in negotiation
- 251 settled

Whenever possible, specific land claims are resolved through negotiation; otherwise, they are settled through the courts. These claims are generally made by First Nations living in the provinces, rather than the territories, and the settlements usually include cash and land.

In both Quebec and the Maritimes, some First Nations claim that treaty terms have not been fulfilled. A number of reserve lands were lost through re-surveying, settlement of non-Aboriginal people on First Nations lands, formal surrenders, and government **expropriations**. First Nations maintain that verbal promises were not kept and that treaty terms were deficient. Language and cultural differences made it difficult for First Nations to understand the terms of the treaties, and the terms didn't provide adequately for a basic standard of living.

expropriation the takeover (especially by the government) of property from its owner

Examples of Specific Claims

Between 1970 and 2004, the Province of Manitoba dealt with 87 specific land claims, 46 of which have been concluded. The remainder are either under review or in negotiation. For the same period, Alberta had 119 specific land claims, 62 of which were concluded.

For example, the Kainai (Blood) Nation in Alberta launched two specific claims in 1995. The first stated that no compensation was ever received for land surrendered in 1889. The second stated that the same 1889 surrender was invalid because of irregularities in the surrender process and because an excessive amount of land was included. The first claim was settled in 1995, the second in 2004, nine years after the claim was launched.

Between 1980 and 1985, four specific claims launched by the Siksika (Blackfoot) Nation were settled. Like the Kainai's claims, two of these pertained to surrendered lands and were settled in 2000 and 2003.

Information on Specific Claims
For further information on specific claims, refer to the Web site of Indian and Northern Affairs Canada: http://www.ainc-inac.gc.ca.

Resolving Land Claims

The greatest difficulty in resolving land claims is the number of parties involved. Negotiations might involve both the federal and provincial governments. Other parties who have an interest—either political or economic—in the results of a specific land claim may also participate in negotiations. These parties might include regional and municipal governments, private corporations, and individuals.

For example, an area affected by a land claim might involve a variety of federal and provincial services, such as highways, pipelines, railways, policing, power generation stations, educational facilities, and provincial parks. An entire urban area might be located within the boundaries of the land claim. Businesses that operate within that area would also be affected. All these stakeholders must be involved in the negotiations; as a result, it often takes decades to reach an agreement.

Federal and Provincial Governments

Frequently, the greatest hurdle in the resolution of land claims is reaching an agreement with the government, both federal and provincial. First Nations negotiators can't simply ignore the government; under the *Constitution Act, 1982*, the federal government has exclusive jurisdiction over First Nations peoples who are registered and live on reserves. Therefore, the federal government must be involved in all land claims.

However, the constitution also states that the provinces have control over natural resources and Crown land, and responsibility for civil law, law enforcement, protection of property, and public works. Under the *Indian Act*, First Nations peoples are subject to all laws that fall under provincial jurisdiction, such as hunting and fishing laws. These laws take precedence over rights that were negotiated in treaties prior to the *Indian Act*. The federal government cannot deny provincial jurisdiction in the resolution of land claims.

Bill C-6

Between 1927 and 1951, it was illegal for Aboriginal peoples to bring a claim against the government without the federal government's permission. As you learned earlier, it was not until 1973 that the federal government began to consider specific land claims from First Nations. This process was not considered objective, however, because the government authorized and negotiated land claims against itself.

Indian Claims Commission

In 1991, after consultations with First Nations leaders, the government established the Indian Claims Commission, an independent advisory group. The commission held public inquiries into specific land claims that had been rejected by the government. But because the commission held only advisory powers, and could be disbanded by the government at any time, its powers were limited.

Specific Claims Resolution Act

In 2002, Bill C-6, the *Specific Claims Resolution Act*, was introduced in the House of Commons in order to overcome some of the difficulties in settling land claims. This legislation established the Canadian Centre for the Independent Resolution of First Nations Specific Claims, providing a process through which specific claims could be settled without **litigation**. The centre would offer information and expertise on the land claims process and would act as a mediator for specific claims.

litigation
legal proceedings

Bill C-6 established the new criteria under which a First Nation could launch a specific claim:

1. A breach of the Crown's legal obligations, including
   - fiduciary responsibilities to the First Nation
   - legislation affecting reserve lands
   - administration of reserve lands.
2. The illegal use or lease of Crown land.
3. The failure to provide adequate compensation for the use of reserve land.
4. Fraud or other white-collar crimes by employees of the government or its agents.

The exclusions under this legislation include the following:

1. No claim can be launched involving actions by the government after December 31, 1973.
2. No claim can be launched involving any government actions in the 15 years prior to the filing of a claim.
3. Acts of Parliament and previous land claim settlements are exempt.
4. No claims can be launched relating to law enforcement or policing.
5. No claims can be launched concerning issues that are being decided by other means.

Opposition to Bill C-6

Under Bill C-6, claims can be launched regarding treaties prior to 1850. First Nations, however, are opposed to Bill C-6, mostly because of the first exclusion. It means that no agreements made between the government and a First Nation after 1973 can be renegotiated, despite any irregularities or perceived unfairness regarding the negotiations.

First Nations have given other reasons why they want to see Bill C-6 withdrawn, including government control over appointments to the negotiating process, a lack of funding to address claims, and conflict of interest on the part of the government.

Despite these objections, Bill C-6 was passed by Parliament on November 4, 2003. It now must be officially proclaimed before it becomes law.

VOICES

The Assembly of First Nations is only one of several First Nations organizations that oppose Bill C-6. It has concluded that the *Specific Claims Resolution Act* is so seriously flawed that it cannot be fixed by amendments and must be withdrawn.

"The position of the Assembly of First Nations on the development of an independent claims body has been clear and consistent. The Assembly of First Nations wants to develop a truly fair, efficient, and effective independent claims body. The *Specific Claims Resolution Act* [Bill C-6] does not accomplish these objectives, and as a result the AFN is calling on the Government of Canada to withdraw the legislation and return to a joint table with First Nations. This cooperative approach produced a legislative framework for a truly independent Claims Body that was agreed to by all parties, and is described in the 1998 Joint Task Force Report on Claims."

http://www.afn.ca/legislation%20Info/billc6.htm.

1. In an organizer, compare the differences between a specific and a comprehensive land claim.
2. Create a web diagram that illustrates First Nations' main grievances concerning land claims.
3. Describe some possible reactions of non-Aboriginal people in Canada over the granting of First Nations land claims.
4. Given that First Nations agreed to extinguish certain rights during earlier treaties and negotiations, do you think land claims should now be reopened? Explain.
5. How are land claims and First Nations sovereignty connected?
6. There are a number of Aboriginal groups in the world today that are asserting their sovereignty and filing land claims against the governments of their countries. Do some research on Aboriginal groups in Australia, New Zealand, Mexico, and Africa. Find out why they are filing land claims and how the process is being handled by the various governments. How do these situations compare with that in Canada? Present your findings in a visual or written format of your choice.

Profile of a Land Claim: The Nisga'a Final Agreement

On May 11, 2000, the Nisga'a Final Agreement—British Columbia's first modern-day land claims agreement—came into effect. On that day, a number of Final Agreement provisions were fulfilled, including the transfer of nearly 2,000 square kilometres of Crown land to the Nisga'a Nation, the creation of Bear Glacial Provincial Park, the establishment of a 300,000 cubic decametre water reservation, and a $190 million cash settlement to be paid out over 15 years. The federal government, the government of British Columbia (BC), and the Nisga'a Nation are continuing to implement the Nisga'a Final Agreement, guided by an Implementation Plan and a tripartite Implementation Committee.

Prior to the conclusion of negotiations and the installing of the Nisga'a Final Agreement in August 1998, more than 400 meetings were held with advisory groups, local government, and the public. In 1991, the government of BC joined negotiations already under way between the Nisga'a and the federal government.

The following timeline, which extends over 113 years, shows the complexity of this land claim:

Figure 4.5 Signing of the Nisga'a Final Agreement "Today, the Nisga'a people become full-fledged Canadians as we step out from under the *Indian Act*—forever. Finally, after a struggle of more than 130 years, the government of this country clearly recognizes that the Nisga'a were a self-governing people since well before European contact. We remain self-governing today, and we are proud to say that this inherent right is now clearly recognized and protected in the Constitution of Canada." —*Chief Joseph Gosnell, April 13, 2000*

1887 Nisga'a chiefs travel to Victoria to demand recognition of title, negotiation of treaties, and provision for self-government.

1890 To start its campaign for recognition of territorial rights, the Nisga'a Nation establishes its first Land Committee.

1913 The Nisga'a Nation sends a petition to the British Privy Council seeking to resolve the land question.

1927 The Parliament of Canada holds hearings on Aboriginal title and passes legislation to prohibit First Nations organizations from discussing or spending money on land claims.

1951 Parliament repeals legislation that prohibits holding potlatches and organizing to pursue land claims.

1955 The Nisga'a Land Committee re-establishes itself as the Nisga'a Tribal Council.

1968 The Nisga'a Tribal Council initiates litigation in the BC Supreme Court on the land question, which later becomes known as the *Calder* case.

1973 In the *Calder* case, the Supreme Court of Canada unanimously recognizes the possible existence of Aboriginal rights to land and resources but splits on whether or not this title has been extinguished. This decision prompts the federal government to develop a new policy to address Aboriginal land claims.

1976 The federal government begins negotiating with the Nisga'a Tribal Council.

1989 The federal government and the Nisga'a Tribal Council sign a bilateral framework agreement that sets out the scope, process, and topics for bilateral negotiation.

1990 The BC government, recognizing that its involvement is necessary to resolve questions around lands and resources, formally joins Canada and the Nisga'a Tribal Council at the negotiating table.

1991 Canada, BC, and the Nisga'a Tribal Council sign a tripartite framework agreement that sets out the scope, process, and topics for negotiation.

1991 Federal and provincial negotiators hold close to 200 consultation and public information meetings in northwestern BC between 1991 and 1995.

1992 The three parties sign an interim protection measures agreement regarding resources and land use.

1996 Canada, BC, and the Nisga'a Tribal Council initial an agreement-in-principle that will form the basis for the first modern-day treaty in BC.

1997 The three parties initial the Nisga'a Final Agreement.

2000 The Nisga'a Final Agreement comes into effect.

Source: Adapted from Nisga'a Final Agreement, Treaty Negotiations. *Copyright © 2001, Province of British Columbia, http://www.gov.bc.ca/tno/negotiation/nisgaa/default.htm; and from "Chronology of Events Leading to the Final Agreement with the Nisga'a Tribal Council," Indian and Northern Affairs Canada, http://www.ainc-inac.gc.ca/pr/agr/nsga/chrono_e.html.*

Treaties with First Nations: Fair or Flawed?

In this chapter, you learned about specific treaties that the Crown made with various First Nations before and after Confederation. You also considered the significance of these treaties in the loss of First Nations' autonomy. Many people in Canada have strong opinions about the origin and nature of these treaties. This activity gives you the opportunity to discover the basic positions of different sides in this debate—and the arguments used to justify these positions.

The following is a debate between two students who are studying the nature of the treaties made between the Crown and First Nations over the past 150 years and the current issue of Aboriginal land claims. One of the students believes that the treaties were a fair and effective method of reaching agreement between Europeans and First Nations peoples, and that modern land claims are unjustified. The other student believes that the treaty system was flawed from the outset, and that action is needed today to redress the injustice of the treaties.

Participate in this debate by completing the dialogue below. Provide the evidence needed to support the statements started by each debater. Use this textbook, particularly the material in Chapter 4, to help you gather facts to support each position.

"The treaties signed between First Nations and the Crown were fair. Both sides wanted to reach an agreement, and they did. What is the problem with that? First Nations groups were usually eager to make an agreement because ... "

____

____

____

"The Crown wanted these treaties because ... "

"You are quite selective about the history you use. Yes, both sides wanted a deal to be reached, but did both sides know what they were getting into? There were huge differences between cultures that made a clear understanding impossible for First Nations peoples. For example ... "

"Speaking of being selective ... look at all the concessions that the Crown gave to First Nations peoples. For example ... "

"Yes, but has the Crown lived up to its commitments? Remember, these treaties were signed between sovereign nations, but the Crown tended to forget its obligations once First Nations were isolated and on the reserves. You seem to have forgotten about broken promises such as ... "

"But common sense must prevail. First Nations' land claims, if accepted, would create a great deal of harm by ... "

"Actually, in the name of justice, Canada must honour First Nations' land claims because ... "

"After all, the rights that are being sought, such as ...

are simply an attempt to regain traditional lands and autonomy."

CHAPTER 5

The Challenges to Aboriginal Sovereignty

LEARNING OBJECTIVES

In this chapter, you will

- identify the assimilation policies and legislation of the Canadian government toward First Nations after Confederation
- understand the factors that diminished First Nations' sovereignty and quality of life
- understand the emergence of Aboriginal political activism in Canada
- identify the events that led to the demand for Aboriginal self-determination and self-government
- understand the roles of key national Aboriginal organizations
- understand the effects of constitutional change in Canada upon Aboriginal peoples

INTRODUCTION

In this chapter, you have the opportunity to examine the policies and practices of the Canadian government in the years following Confederation as it attempted to assimilate First Nations peoples into Canadian society. You'll begin by looking at the *Indian Act* and the power it had over First Nations. You'll see how elements of the system of government that was imposed on First Nations bands persist today. You'll learn about the role of residential schools and discover the devastating impact that they had on First Nations children, families, and communities. You'll see what factors led to the Métis' becoming the forgotten Aboriginal nation in Canada for almost a century. Finally, you'll see how all Aboriginal nations today are challenging the government to assert their rights.

ASSIMILATION

In the *Constitution Act, 1867* (originally named the *British North America Act*), which created Confederation, responsibility for First Nations peoples was given to the federal government. For the first time, Canada had the power to assume extensive, arbitrary power and control over First Nations. The government ignored the diversity of their cultures and treated them as a single, homogeneous group. Although Confederation greatly affected the lives of First Nations peoples, they were never consulted about their place in the new nation.

Following Confederation, the government launched an aggressive campaign to assimilate First Nations peoples. To achieve this goal, during treaty negotiations the government promised to supply First Nations reserves with the tools and livestock necessary for farming. As you discovered in Chapter 4, however, this plan was unsuccessful. The government failed to live up to its promises. In turn, many First Nations peoples were reluctant to abandon their traditional way of life. Government officials could not understand why First Nations did not embrace the opportunity to become part of mainstream Euro-Canadian society. To combat this resistance, the government increased its efforts at assimilation.

Two Peoples Ignored

In 1867, many Métis people hoped that they would benefit from a new relationship with the Canadian government. They were bitterly disappointed. While the *Constitution Act, 1867* gave special status to First Nations, both the Métis and the Inuit peoples were not placed under federal jurisdiction. The Métis claimed that since the term "Indian" was not defined either in the *Royal Proclamation of 1763* or in the *Constitution Act, 1867*, they should be considered an Aboriginal people. The Inuit, too, were ignored by the new Act. However, the Inuit were placed under federal authority following a ruling by the Supreme Court of Canada in 1939. The Métis were not recognized as an Aboriginal people until the *Constitution Act, 1982.*

The *Gradual Enfranchisement Act* of 1869 was intended to remove special status for First Nations peoples. The Act provided that if they gave up their legal status as "Indians," First Nations peoples would be granted the

Prime Minister John A. Macdonald acknowledged the government's goal to have First Nations peoples adopt Euro-Canadian values and ways of life and become farmers:

"[The aim of the government is to] wean [First Nations peoples] by slow degree, from their nomadic habits, which have become almost an instinct, and by slow degrees absorb them on the land."

right to vote in provincial and federal elections. In addition, the government promised to compensate them financially and to provide them with 20 hectares of land—although the land being offered was not government land, but land that would be taken from each band's own reserve.

Opposition to the *Gradual Enfranchisement Act* was widespread. As a result, few people signed up to be enfranchised. When the Act failed to meet its objective, the government decided that more aggressive action was needed to assimilate First Nations.

TALKING CIRCLE

1. a) Why do you think the Canadian government wanted to assimilate First Nations peoples?
   b) What impact do you think assimilation would have had on the sovereignty of First Nations?
2. a) What other options might the federal government have taken in its relationship with First Nations?
   b) Why do you think the government did not choose these options?

THE *INDIAN ACT* OF 1876

In 1876, the Canadian Parliament passed the *Indian Act*. This Act gave the federal government exclusive power over First Nations and their land. In effect, the people became wards of the state.

Until the passage of the *Indian Act*, most bands still practised their own forms of government. However, the Act gave the federal government the power to change the ways in which chiefs and councils operated. It dictated their specific duties and responsibilities and regulated their decisions. It disregarded the traditional line of heredity that many First Nations followed in choosing their leaders. Instead, the Act decided when, where, and how all leaders were chosen and gave government officials the power to remove a chief for dishonesty, **intemperance**, **immorality**, or incompetence. To enforce these policies, the government refused to honour treaty payments or to provide services to any band that failed to obey.

intemperance
the making, selling, purchasing, or drinking of alcohol

immorality
under the *Indian Act*, living in a common-law relationship, having a child born out of wedlock, or conducting an extramarital affair

Indian Agents

Indian agents were government officials who lived within First Nations reserves. Their role was to enforce the government's policies and to manage the financial affairs of the reserve. The agents were the final authority on schools, health care, and social services provided by the federal government.

Periodically, the government amended the *Indian Act* to introduce policies to accelerate assimilation. These new regulations became increasingly

Defining First Nations Status

The *Indian Act* defined who was an Indian. It included

- Status Indians—those people who are entitled to have their names listed on the official Indian Register maintained by the federal government. Status Indians are entitled to certain rights and benefits under the law.
- Non-Status Indians—those people who consider themselves Indians or members of a First Nation but whom the government does not recognize as Indians under the *Indian Act*, either because they are unable to prove their status or have lost status rights. (Many women lost their status rights by marrying non-Aboriginal men.) Non-Status Indians do not have the same rights and benefits as Status Indians.
- Treaty Indians—Status Indians who belong to a First Nation that signed a treaty with the government.

Source: Words First: An Evolving Terminology Relating to Aboriginal Peoples *(Ottawa: Indian and Northern Affairs Canada, 2004).*

coercive. Indian agents were given the authority to spend money belonging to the reserves without the bands' permission. The agent could impose an elected system of government on bands and depose leaders he did not approve of. An amendment was passed that allowed Indian agents to become chiefs, even though they were not members of the band—a law that remains in effect today.

Prohibition
a period during the 1920s in North America when it was illegal to manufacture, sell, or consume alcohol

Prohibiting Alcohol

Under the terms of the *Indian Act*, First Nations peoples were forbidden from making, buying, selling, or consuming alcohol. Anyone found to be intoxicated could be arrested. Anyone who sold alcohol to First Nations peoples could face up to six months in jail. With the exception of **Prohibition**, such restrictions were never placed on other Canadians.

The Impact of the *Indian Act*

Inequality

Aboriginal cultures were not given the same rights as French Canadians, who were allowed to maintain their laws and language.

The *Indian Act* abolished the unspoken agreement between First Nations and the British government that had existed since the days of the *Royal Proclamation of 1763*, which respected First Nations' right to govern themselves. Now, First Nations peoples were marginalized in the new country of Canada. They were denied citizenship and were treated as minors who required the protection of the state. Their lives were controlled and restricted by a government that had little understanding of their needs, traditions, and cultures. They lost their autonomy, and were

CLOSE-UP

GOVERNMENT IN FIRST NATIONS COMMUNITIES

The *Indian Act* established a system of elected band councils to govern reserve communities. Today, there are 633 First Nations bands in Canada operating under band councils.

Bands must elect a chief and a council every two years, unless leaders are chosen by customary band elections. In this case, the band decides who will vote and when a term of office ends. However, any election held under the *Indian Act* can be overturned by the federal cabinet. Only residents of a reserve who are registered on a band list and who are 18 years of age or older may vote. Each band can elect one chief and one band councillor for every 100 band members, but there cannot be fewer than two, or more than 12, band councillors.

Band councils oversee local matters on reserves, such as law and order, road construction, local works projects, land surveying and zoning, public games and amusements, fish and game stocks, daycare and senior support services, and qualifications for band residency. The chief and the council pass bylaws concerning these matters, called band council resolutions. Before these resolutions can become law, however, they must be submitted to Indian and Northern Affairs Canada, which has the power to disallow any resolutions it sees fit.

Many First Nations peoples feel that this process restricts their rights and conflicts with their traditional methods of decision making. They believe that the councils were designed to serve as agents of the government to administer federal policies and programs that reflect mainstream Canadian culture rather than the cultural needs of First Nations. In so doing, the government has failed to address the uniqueness and diversity of First Nations societies and their long history of self-government.

Today, many chiefs and councils want to be accountable to their communities instead of to the federal government. They want greater independence in governing their people and in regulating the affairs of their community. They believe that the current role of band councils is equal to that of municipal governments, with the same limited local powers. Today, First Nations are demanding more. They want the power to govern, with the interests of their nation first and foremost.

First Nations versus Bands

The federal government does not recognize the term "First Nations" as a legal definition. For legal purposes, the *Indian Act* identifies these communities as "bands." In recognition of their rights, which were never formally extinguished by the British or Canadian governments, many bands today refer to their communities as First Nations.

denied the opportunity to maintain their unique cultures. As a result, many cultures and languages were weakened.

TALKING CIRCLE

1. a) What political terms commonly describe a government that dictates people's activities without their consultation or consent?
   b) Do you think it is appropriate to apply these terms to the government of Canada after Confederation? Give reasons for your answer.
2. What do you think would have happened if the government had imposed the types of restrictions it placed on First Nations peoples on other Canadians?
3. a) Do you agree that band councils should be sovereign governments? Give reasons for your answer.
   b) What would you recommend that the federal government do to address the needs and concerns of band chiefs and councils today?

RESIDENTIAL SCHOOLS

The federal government was responsible for financing the education of First Nations children, who—like Aboriginal adults—were considered wards of the state. First Nations peoples wanted to educate their children to ensure that their cultures survived in a changing world. They hoped the government would help them. However, when the government created residential schools, it sought to further its own objectives. As a result, the children became pawns in the government's plan to assimilate First Nations peoples and to eliminate what it perceived as an obstacle to building the Canadian nation.

The government wanted children to attend schools that were located far away from their reserves:

"If these schools are to succeed, we must not have them near the bands; in order to educate the children properly we must separate them from their families. Some people may say that this is hard, but if we want to civilize them we must do that."

A federal cabinet minister, 1883, in J.R. Miller, Skyscrapers Hide the Heavens: A History of Indian–White Relations in Canada *(Toronto: University of Toronto Press, 1989), p. 298.*

First Nations peoples were powerless to stop the government's plan. Under the terms of the *Indian Act*, children were legally required to attend these schools and were prohibited from attending any other educational institution. They could attend a public, separate, or private school only if their parents became enfranchised and gave up their official status.

The Structure of Residential Schools

Although the government financed the residential schools, it gave responsibility for their daily operations to the Catholic, Anglican, United, and Presbyterian churches. Although the schools were run by different religious organizations, they had many things in common:

- All aspects of First Nations culture were eliminated from the schools. Children were forbidden to speak their native language and were punished for doing so.
- Boys were segregated from girls, and siblings were intentionally separated in an effort to weaken family ties.
- Children were required to wear school uniforms instead of traditional clothing. Hairstyles were cut short in the European style. The children ate primarily Euro-Canadian foods.

Figure 5.1 Before and After Thomas More was a First Nations child who attended a residential school in Regina. The photo on the left shows Thomas in traditional clothing before he entered the school. The photo on the right shows him in his school uniform. Before-and-after photographs like these were commonly used by the government to illustrate the "benefits" of attending residential schools.

- Students celebrated Christian holidays, such as Christmas and Easter. They learned to play European sports, such as soccer and cricket.
- The school day was divided between religious instruction and training for manual labour. The children were taught practical skills, such as sewing, woodworking, reading, and writing, rather than academic subjects, such as history, geography, mathematics, and science.

The Impact of Residential Schools

Residential schools isolated the children. During the school year, they were prohibited from any contact with their families and communities. During school vacations, they were boarded in Euro-Canadian homes to prevent them from renewing their cultural connections with their families.

As a result, many children had little or no contact with their families and communities for many years. When they finally returned home, their family relationships were often distant. The children and their families had little in common. The children could no longer speak their native language. Their parents could not speak English, so they were unable to communicate with one another. The children no longer understood or practised their traditions and customs. They no longer shared their family's beliefs and values. Unaccustomed to the poor living conditions on the reserves, they often viewed their communities as backward. The children were caught between two cultures and did not fit into either one. Many people have used the term **cultural genocide** to describe the effect of residential schools on individuals and entire communities.

cultural genocide the mass extermination of a people's culture and way of life

The impact of residential schools is still evident today. Children who were deprived of the benefits of family life did not learn how to raise children themselves. Today, many First Nations leaders cite this as one of the causes

The experience at residential schools left many students searching for a cultural identity:

"When an Indian comes out of these places it is like being put between two walls in a room and left hanging in the middle. On one side are all the things he learned from his people and their way of life that was being wiped out, and on the other are the white man's way which he could never fully understand since he never had the right amount of education and could not be part of it. There he is, hanging in the middle of the two cultures and he is not a white man and he is not an Indian. They washed away practically everything an Indian needed to help himself, to think the way a human person should in order to survive."

John Tootoosis, late senator, political activist, and former student in a residential school, in Susan LeBel and Jeff Orr, Canada's History: Voices and Visions *(Toronto: Gage Learning, 2003), p. 174.*

of such problems as spousal and child abuse, violence, alcoholism, and suicide within their communities.

Abuse at Residential Schools

For some children, residential schools were an opportunity to experience a different world from the one in their own communities. Despite feelings of homesickness and loneliness, some of these students had positive experiences at the schools. For many others, however, life at the schools was brutal. As punishment, children were often deprived of food or were forced to spend long hours in isolation or performing back-breaking labour. Some children were physically beaten. Others were raped. For many, the cruelty they endured in residential schools created traumas that they carried with them throughout their lives.

CLOSE-UP

THE LEGACY OF RESIDENTIAL SCHOOLS

The legacy of residential schools lives on among the children of residential school survivors, and even among the children of their children. The following story describes how one child of a residential school student, Darlene Isaac-Downey, finally found peace in her troubled life:

> Abused by those who were supposed to protect her for most of her first 26 years, [Darlene] vividly recalls how her mother shoved a dirty cloth diaper down her throat because she hadn't cleaned her room properly. Some of her teeth were knocked out. Her mother took her into the bathroom and abruptly wiped away the blood that was dripping down her face. "I was screaming, mommy, mommy, my teeth are gone!" she said. "I couldn't breathe." During yet another incident, her mother stabbed her in the back for not putting enough water in a pot for spaghetti.
>
> Eventually, Downey grew so tired of her pain, she wanted to poison her mother's drink, hoping the abuse would stop. Although she suffered cruelty at the hands of her mother, Downey now understands her mother's behaviour. Her mother is a survivor of a British Columbia residential school, where she was beaten and abused. "She was only passing on what she was taught," states Downey.
>
> In 1999, Downey went back to her reserve in Fort St. James, B.C., to visit her mother's grave. "I left a yellow rose," she said. The next year she went to a sweat [lodge]. "It was there I prayed and asked the Creator to help me forgive." During the sweat, Downey saw a bright light and felt someone breathe on her. It was at that moment her prayers were answered. "I cried, knowing that at long last I had made peace with my mom."
>
> *Excerpted from Gord Atkinson, "Strong Woman Song,"* Windspeaker, *December 2004, p. 6.*

Making Amends

In the late 1990s, the churches and the federal government publicly apologized for the residential schools. In January 1998, the federal government acknowledged abuse at the schools and announced a $350-million program aimed at providing community healing initiatives to deal with the effects of physical and sexual abuse. However, many people believe the gesture did not go far enough in acknowledging the widespread impact that federal policies have had on First Nations communities and cultures. They argue that the initiative fails to recognize the cultural and social upheaval created by the schools in terms of the loss of family ties, languages, and cultures.

In a continuing effort to deal with the controversy, in June 2001 the government announced a new department to deal exclusively with the issues involving residential schools. It also created a process for handling lawsuits more quickly and efficiently. However, these efforts were denounced by some First Nations organizations because they required former students to waive any claims for loss of language and culture. The debate over righting the wrongs of residential schools continues, as do the finger-pointing, blame, shame, and guilt that characterize this long-running controversy.

Righting the Wrongs of Residential Schools

It was not until the 1990s that abuse at the schools became widely known. At the hearings of the Royal Commission on Aboriginal Peoples, many former students spoke publicly about their experiences. As a result, during the 1990s hundreds of lawsuits were filed against the churches and the federal government, including over 200 in Alberta and over 400 in Saskatchewan. In total, almost 3,500 lawsuits were filed across the country.

1. How would you feel if, as a child, you were forcibly separated from your family for an extended period of time? How do you think this would affect your relationship with your family? How do you think it would affect your life as an adult?
2. Read the following poem written by Mi'kmaq poet Rita Joe (1998), a former student of the Shubenacadie Residential School in Nova Scotia. Then discuss the questions that follow.

Hated Structure: The Indian Residential School

If you are on Highway 104
In a Shubenacadie town
There is a hill
Where a structure stands
A reminder to many senses
To respond like demented ones

I for one looked into the window
And there on the floor
Was a deluge of a misery
Of a building I held in awe
Since the day
I walked into the ornamented door.

There was grime everywhere
As in buildings left alone or unused
Maybe to the related tales of long ago
Where the children lived in laughter, or abused.

I had no wish to enter
Nor to walk the halls
I had no wish to feel the floors
Where I felt fear
A beating heart of episodes
I care not to recall.
The structure stands as if to say:
I was just a base for theory
To bend the will of children
I remind
Until I fall.

Source: Rita Joe, *We Are the Dreamers: Recent and Early Poetry* (Wreck Cove, NS: Breton Books, 1999).

a) What did Rita Joe dislike about her residential school?

b) How does her school experience compare with your own school experiences?

THE "LOST" MÉTIS NATION

Under federal policies, the Métis did not fare any better than First Nations peoples. They were not part of the Numbered Treaties, with the exception of Treaty 3 in 1873—and then only to extinguish any Métis claims in the area covered by the treaty. The government issued **scrip**, which was redeemable for land, but most Métis redeemed their scrip for cash because they were poverty stricken. The government then ruled that because the Métis had been offered scrip, they had no title to the land they had historically occupied.

scrip
a certificate issued to Métis people entitling the holder to land or money for the purchase of land, issued as compensation for lands lost by the Métis after the Northwest Rebellion

VOICES

For the most part, the Canadian government treated the Métis people with indifference:

"If they are Indians, they go with the tribe; if they are half-breeds, they are whites."

Sir John A. Macdonald, 1885, in The Canadian Encyclopedia *(Toronto: McClelland & Stewart, 1999), p. 1479.*

Scattered to the Wind

Following the Northwest Rebellion in 1885, those Métis who were either directly involved in the conflict or who feared persecution simply because they were Métis took refuge in unsettled parts of Saskatchewan, in the area around The Pas, Manitoba, in the Mackenzie River area, and in the southern Northwest Territories. The Métis were marginalized, forced to live on lands that had little potential for farming. They also had little opportunity to hunt and fish because of new game and fishing laws imposed by the federal government.

VOICES

For the Métis people, life was now full of hopelessness and despair:

"Many [Métis] were forced to abandon a life dependent upon hunting, but the only other lifestyle that they had the opportunity to pursue was that of chance employment in agricultural areas. This type of seasonal employment forced a condition of nomadism and developed a worse poverty-stricken existence. A common sight throughout the West was the Métis family ... that wandered the countryside, with all its worldly possessions piled in a rickety, horse-drawn cart. They looked for jobs repairing fences in late spring, cut and stacked hay in summer, stocked and worked on the threshing gangs in the fall, cut wood in the winter, and trapped muskrats in the early spring. During all seasons home was usually a [small] tent, heated, if at all, by a small tin stove. The children were undernourished, and rarely attended school."

D. Bruce Sealy and Antoine Lussier, The Métis: Canada's Forgotten People *(Winnipeg: Métis Federation Press, 1975).*

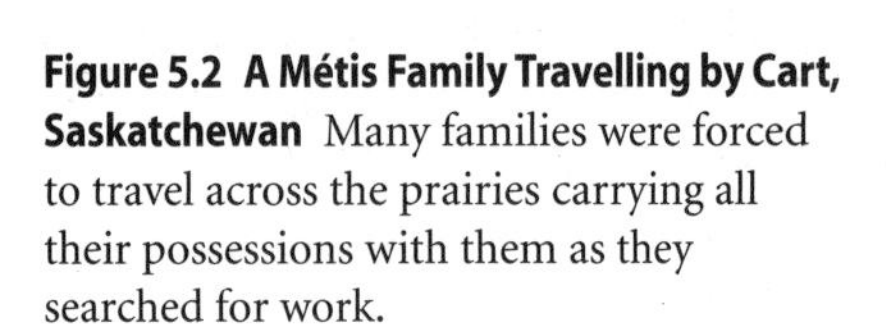

Figure 5.2 A Métis Family Travelling by Cart, Saskatchewan Many families were forced to travel across the prairies carrying all their possessions with them as they searched for work.

In 1896, the Catholic Church established the reserve of Saint-Paul-de-Métis, 100 kilometres northeast of Edmonton. The Church promised to provide the people with the things they needed to farm. However, it failed to make good on its promise, and over the next decade most of the Métis on the Saint-Paul reserve moved away.

In 1900, the Métis living in Batoche, Saskatchewan received a land settlement from the federal government that gave them individual parcels of land rather than a reserve. However, many of the Métis who received land sold it because they lacked the money to buy farm implements and livestock.

At the end of the 19th century, the Métis were chronically plagued by poverty and discrimination. They continued to attend First Nations gatherings, but they did not fit in as they had before. They were known as the "poor relatives," not only because they were different, but because the First Nations had land and security while the Métis had nothing. It seemed that First Nations and Métis were related by blood, but not by economics.

The Métis entered the 20th century a dispersed and forgotten people. To the government, they would remain so for almost a century. But the Métis people never lost their identity or their spirit. Nor did they lose their love of life and their hopes for a better future. In time, they would reassert their status as an Aboriginal people and lay claim to their land.

A Forgotten People
It was not until 1981 that the federal government recognized the Métis as a distinct cultural group in the Census of Canada.

You have read in this chapter that First Nations and Métis "were related by blood, but not by economics."

1. Why do you think the federal government refused to recognize Métis rights?
2. Why do you think First Nations groups discriminated against the Métis?

THE EMERGENCE OF ABORIGINAL POLITICAL ACTIVISM

Aboriginal peoples have faced many challenges and obstacles in their fight for political recognition in Canada. Since the days of Confederation, they have struggled for the right to have a say over laws such as the *Indian Act*, which control so much of their lives. For many years, Aboriginal peoples were excluded from the formal political process. The federal government expected that the question of Aboriginal rights would eventually disappear once people were assimilated into mainstream society.

However, Aboriginal peoples in Canada did not meet the government's expectations. Instead, they began forming political associations designed to lobby for their rights and to settle land claims.

THE ALLIED TRIBES OF BRITISH COLUMBIA

One of the earliest First Nations political organizations was the Allied Tribes of British Columbia. It was formed in 1916 to settle land claims in the province. In most provinces, governments had avoided land claims by signing treaties with First Nations. However, there were no such agreements in British Columbia. When a commission recommended reducing the size of reserves in the province, the Allied Tribes launched a land claim against the federal government.

Predictably, the government rejected the Allied Tribes' claim and proceeded to pass legislation reducing the size of BC reserves. It also stepped up its efforts to assimilate Aboriginal peoples by passing a law that automatically enfranchised all First Nations people who had served in World War I.

Canadian poet Duncan Campbell Scott, then deputy superintendent of the Department of Indian Affairs, made the government's objective clear:

> I want to get rid of the Indian problem. ... That is my whole point. Our objective is to continue until there is not a single Indian in Canada that has not been absorbed into the body politic, and there is no Indian question and no Indian Department and that is the whole objective of this bill.
>
> *Brian Tilley,* A Narrow Vision: Duncan Campbell Scott and the Administration of Indian Affairs in Canada *(Vancouver: University of British Columbia Press, 1986), p. 50.*

The Allied Tribes realized there was little hope of reaching a settlement. So, in 1926 they took their case to the Privy Council in London. They were met by the head of Canada's High Commission, who promised to deliver their petition. The delegates returned home. The government now seemed willing to negotiate, and a meeting was planned for the spring of 1927. However, these plans were short lived, as Scott dismissed the Allied Tribes' land claim.

Restricting Aboriginal Rights

As political activist groups such as the Allied Tribes lobbied for land claim settlements, the government became determined to prevent such activism in the future. In 1927, it passed an amendment to the *Indian Act* prohibiting First Nations from raising money to pursue land claims and restricting their right to assemble for political purposes. By 1930, the government's actions had succeeded in temporarily stifling First Nations' political activism in Canada.

The Union nationale Métisse Saint-Joseph du Manitoba

The Union nationale Métisse Saint-Joseph du Manitoba, the oldest Métis organization in Canada, began as a cultural and historical society created in 1887 to publicize the plight of the Métis nation. It marked the beginning of a long struggle to regain Métis lands and assert their Aboriginal rights.

During the 1920s and 1930s, two prairie social activists, Jim Brady and Malcolm Norris, began working through the Union nationale to build a political base to defend the interests of the Métis people. This cooperation produced the Association des Métis de l'Alberta in 1932, the first of many provincial Métis organizations. The association eventually pushed the government to pass the *Metis Population Betterment Act* in 1938, which set aside lands in Alberta for the Métis.

BIOGRAPHY

MALCOLM NORRIS (1900–1967)

Malcolm Norris was born into a prominent family in Edmonton. However, he rejected a life of privilege, devoting himself instead to the fight against racial discrimination against Métis and First Nations peoples. Norris was one of the leading figures in the Association des Métis de l'Alberta and in the Co-operative Commonwealth Federation (CCF), forerunner of today's New Democratic Party (NDP). He challenged the government in many battles to win rights for his people and urged Aboriginal leaders to avoid financial dependence on the government. Malcolm Norris is considered one of the most important and charismatic Métis leaders in Canada's history.

Figure 5.3 Malcolm Frederick Norris and His Family
Norris was a brilliant speaker and an extremely effective Métis politician.

The Renewal of Aboriginal Activism

When World War II broke out in 1939, over 3,000 Aboriginal people volunteered to serve in the armed forces. However, because they were not recognized as Canadian citizens, these volunteers had to obtain permission to enlist from the Department of Indian Affairs. They also had to become enfranchised, which forced them to give up their official status.

Figure 5.4 A Soldier from the Siksika Nation, 1916 Mike Foxhead (centre) served with the 191st Overseas Battalion in the Canadian Expeditionary Force. He was killed during battle in the trenches.

During the war, Aboriginal soldiers fought alongside Canadian soldiers in all major campaigns. After the war, however, the government failed to acknowledge their contributions. Aboriginal war veterans were denied the benefits granted to other veterans, such as pensions and the right to vote and own land. They were expected to return to the lives they had lived before the war. For most First Nations, this meant returning to the poverty of the reserves. Métis people were forced to move away from their traditional homes by unemployment, prejudice, and discrimination. They settled in urban centres, where they became unskilled labourers when they could find work, and welfare recipients when they could not. These injustices served as the spark to ignite a renewed campaign of Aboriginal political activism in Canada.

The Right to Vote

Aboriginal peoples were the last group in Canada to gain the franchise (right to vote). Under pressure from First Nations groups, in 1947 the government held hearings into the *Indian Act.* The committee recommended that First Nations peoples be allowed to vote in federal elections. The following year, British Columbia granted them the franchise in provincial elections. In 1950, the Inuit gained the right to vote in federal elections. Over the next two decades, the other provinces, one by one, followed British Columbia's lead. In 1969, Quebec became the last province to enfranchise First Nations peoples.

The National Indian Council

Aboriginal communities worked together to create a national lobby group to represent their collective interests. In 1961, the National Indian Council (NIC) was created to represent Treaty and Status Indians, Non-Status Indians, and Métis. The goal of the NIC was to promote unity among these groups. However, achieving this goal was a challenge because of the diversity of these cultures and their many different issues and priorities. Unable to create a united front, the NIC dispersed. Treaty and Status Indians then formed the National Indian Brotherhood, while Non-Status Indians and Métis formed the Native Council of Canada.

The National Indian Brotherhood/ The Assembly of First Nations

The National Indian Brotherhood (NIB) was formed in 1969. In 1982, it changed its name to the Assembly of First Nations (AFN). Today, the AFN acts as a watchdog for First Nations' interests in Canada and is a voice for positive change in both federal and provincial policies toward First Nations.

The AFN provides a forum for First Nations to express their views about such issues as treaty rights, land claims, economic development, education, housing, health care, social services, and the environment. It has succeeded in many of its efforts to focus public attention on First Nations issues, including

- gaining the right for First Nations to participate in federal–provincial constitutional talks
- increasing dialogue with the federal government over the **inherent** right to self-government
- increasing public awareness about First Nations issues today.

inherent
essential; e.g., as in a natural right

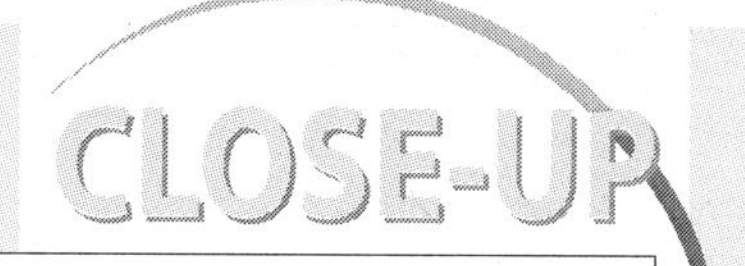

THE WHITE PAPER OF 1969

Soon after its inception, the National Indian Brotherhood was severely tested. In 1969, the federal government introduced a White Paper on Aboriginal issues. This non-binding policy proposal was drafted without consulting a single Aboriginal group in Canada. Among other things, the paper proposed

- abolishing the *Indian Act*
- eliminating the Department of Indian Affairs
- transferring responsibility for Aboriginal rights to the provinces
- eliminating reserves
- abolishing special status for First Nations peoples.

The ultimate goal of the policy was to create equality for Aboriginal peoples by assimilating them into mainstream Canadian society. This sparked a public outcry from Aboriginal groups. They argued that the plan removed all traces of laws and lands that recognized their presence as the indigenous peoples of Canada. The Alberta Indian Association launched a counter-proposal in a document known as the Red Paper. However, the federal government failed to respond to the paper, prompting an even louder outcry as Aboriginal peoples demanded that their views be heard. In the face of widespread opposition, the government withdrew the White Paper in 1971 and agreed to talk directly with Aboriginal leaders about its policies and practices.

VOICES

The 1969 White Paper prompted the emergence of many activist groups lobbying for the rights of Aboriginal peoples. In 1975, the Dene Nation issued a declaration that expressed the sentiments of many Aboriginal nations:

"We the Dene of the NWT insist on the right to be regarded by ourselves and the world as a nation . . . . As once Europe was the exclusive homeland of the European peoples, Africa the exclusive homeland of the African peoples . . . North and South America were the exclusive homeland of . . . the Amerindian and the Inuit. . . . As Europe is the place where you will find European countries with European governments for European peoples, now also you will find in Africa and Asia the existence of African and Asian countries with African and Asian governments for African and Asian peoples. . . . But [we] have not fared so well. . . . The Dene find themselves as part of a country. That country is Canada. But the government of Canada is not the government of the Dene. These governments were not the choice of the Dene, they were imposed on the Dene. . . . What we seek then is independence and self-determination within the country of Canada."

Rick Ponting and Roger Gibbins, Out of Irrelevance *(Toronto: Butterworths, 1980), p. 351.*

The Native Council of Canada/The Congress of Aboriginal Peoples

The Native Council of Canada (NCC) was formed in 1970 to speak on behalf of Métis and Non-Status Indians. However, following the emergence of the Métis National Council in 1984 as an alternative voice for Métis nationalism, the NCC began to redefine its goals and objectives. As a result, a new organization called the Congress of Aboriginal Peoples (CAP) emerged in 1994. Its objective is to focus on practical issues that face Aboriginal peoples living in urban communities, such as housing, health, justice, youth, and the environment, and to continue to seek special status for Métis and Non-Status Indians.

National Métis Organizations

The Métis are represented by three major groups: the Métis National Council (MNC), the Congress of Aboriginal Peoples, and the Canadian Métis Council (CMC). The MNC is the principal organization dealing with the federal government. However, while the MNC claims to represent Métis across Canada, there are serious disagreements over its definition of who is of Métis heritage and what constitutes Métis territory. As a result, many independent groups seeking federal recognition and funding for all Métis people have sprung up across Canada.

Constitutional Recognition for the Métis

The Métis were finally recognized as an Aboriginal people in the *Constitution Act, 1982.* Although the federal government still refused to consider their land claims, recognition under the constitution did afford the Métis some advantages. Government funding was directed toward two Métis organizations, the Métis National Council and the Congress of Aboriginal Peoples, for education, training, housing, and other benefits. However, this move was viewed by many Métis as a "divide and conquer" strategy designed to keep the Métis fighting among themselves over funding rather than focusing on the broader issues of common concern to all Métis people.

The *Constitution Act, 1982* also failed to confer Aboriginal rights on the Métis. However, a Supreme Court decision in 2003 ruled in favour of the Métis National Council, which had taken the government to court over Aboriginal harvesting rights after a Métis hunter was charged with hunting out of season. While the ruling was a victory for the Aboriginal rights of Métis people, it quickly degenerated into a political debate over the definition of the term "Métis." Only those Métis with an ancestral connection to the Red River colony could assume Aboriginal harvesting rights, and they could assume these rights only if they harvested in their traditional areas and had the permission of the present-day Métis who lived there. In the end, the ruling was a limited victory.

The Inuit Tapiriit Kanatami

The White Paper prompted Inuit groups in the far north to organize into a national alliance, or *tapirisat*, in 1971. Originally called the Inuit Tapirisat, today it is known as the Inuit Tapiriit Kanatami (ITK). Its goal is to provide a national voice for Inuit peoples and to promote their interests in Canada. The national organization consists of four regional associations representing Nunatsiavut (Labrador), Nunavik (Quebec), Nunavut, and the Inuvialuit Settlement Region of the Northwest Territories, as well as the National Inuit Women's Association.

The ITK works to preserve Inuit language and culture and improve their living conditions both economically and socially. It has also fought to gain comprehensive land claim settlements in the north, including the creation of Nunavut on April 1, 1999. (See page 183 in Chapter 7.) Today, the ITK's agenda includes an all-encompassing action plan with specific strategies and solutions designed to meet the needs of Inuit peoples in Canada.

1. Reread the Dene declaration on page 130.
   a) What are the declaration's main points?
   b) How would you define the relationship that the Dene are seeking with Canada?

c) Do you think the Dene's objective represents a fair and just relationship with the federal government? Give reasons for your answer.

2. In what ways are political organizations such as the Assembly of First Nations, the Métis National Council, and the Inuit Tapiriit Kanatami activist organizations?

THE ISSUE OF SELF-GOVERNMENT

Recognizing Rights

The *Constitution Act, 1982* states that "the existing Aboriginal and treaty rights of the Aboriginal peoples of Canada are hereby recognized and affirmed."

In 1985, the Supreme Court of Canada recognized that Aboriginal sovereignty was independent and separate from the federal government because First Nations and Inuit peoples had occupied the land since time immemorial. As a result, today the federal and some provincial governments are more willing to discuss the issue of sovereignty and self-government.

However, the issue of self-government is a contentious one. In fact, governments and First Nations cannot agree on its definition. To Aboriginal peoples, however, self-government equals self-determination. Aboriginal peoples believe that self-government would give them greater autonomy and would put an end to their dependence on government assistance. Self-government is a means of resolving community issues and addressing human rights inequalities. Aboriginal peoples believe that it would eliminate the debilitating social and economic experiences that many of their communities have endured.

VOICES

Former National Chief of the Assembly of First Nations, Ovide Mercredi, has expressed First Nations' point of view on self-government:

"The First Nations are not a threat to Canada. We do not preach separatism. This is our country, from north to south and east to west. It is the only homeland we have. We did not come from anywhere else; we have nowhere else to return to and we have no divided loyalties. ...

"In seeking explicit recognition of our self-government in the Canadian Constitution, we [are] not advocating the dismemberment of our country; rather we envisage the sharing of this land and its bountiful resources based on mutual respect and co-existence of jurisdictions, and based on the recognition of our inherent rights and our distinct societies in Canada."

Quoted in Susan LeBel and Jeff Orr, Canada's History: Voices and Visions *(Toronto: Gage Learning, 2003), p. 218.*

At the same time, Aboriginal peoples want to remain part of Canada. However, as diverse peoples with distinctive histories and cultures, they want acknowledgment that they are different from other Canadians. They believe this fact warrants the right to govern their own lives politically, economically, socially, and culturally. Through self-government, they hope to provide a better way of life for their people.

The Complexity of Self-Government

Under self-government, each First Nation would remain under the jurisdiction of the federal and provincial governments. However, each jurisdiction would have the power to create laws in those areas that directly affect its people, including education, citizenship, lands and resources, conservation, economic development, health care, and law enforcement.

A Third Order of Government

The Assembly of First Nations promotes the idea of a third order of government—that is, self-government with status equal to that of the provinces within the current Canadian federation.

The Royal Commission on Aboriginal Peoples

In 1991, the Canadian government created the Royal Commission on Aboriginal Peoples to examine the relationship between Aboriginal peoples, government, and society. After a five-year study, the commission issued its report in 1996. Among its more than 400 recommendations were several proposals that would fundamentally alter the relationship between Canada and Aboriginal peoples:

- restructuring the *Indian Act*
- self-determination through self-government
- the creation of an Aboriginal parliament
- dual citizenship as Aboriginal nations and Canadians
- self-determination through Aboriginal nations rather than smaller communities
- an Aboriginal system of taxation
- Aboriginal economic initiatives through the provision of more land
- the establishment of a national Aboriginal bank.

While very few of these recommendations have been implemented, including the creation of a national Aboriginal bank, negotiations continue over other recommendations.

Currently, the federal government recognizes First Nations' rights to administer the needs of individual communities in terms of education, health care, social services, and community and economic development. However, it does not recognize the collective rights of Aboriginal peoples to be fully self-governing, although self-government has been attained by some bands as part of land claim settlements. (See page 108 in Chapter 4.)

Self-Government for the Sechelt Nation

In 1986, the Sechelt Nation of British Columbia was the first band in Canada to achieve a degree of self-government. The Sechelt Government Indian District has the power to negotiate contracts and agreements, buy and sell property, and invest and borrow money. It also has the power to provide programs and services for its members and to implement economic development policies for the community.

Today, the lives of Aboriginal peoples, while still controlled by the federal government, are moving toward greater autonomy. Many Aboriginal people in Canada believe that as long as they remain united, they will continue to move toward self-determination to become strong, independent members of society.

1. Many francophones have tried to have Quebec defined as a "distinct society" in the Canadian constitution. Do you think the Aboriginal nations create a distinct society in Canada? Give reasons for your answer.
2. Do you think Aboriginal peoples should have dual citizenship—that is, should they be citizens of their Aboriginal nation as well as citizens of Canada? What would be the advantages of dual citizenship? What would be the disadvantages?
3. In 1996, the Canadian government proclaimed June 21 each year as National Aboriginal Day. Do some research to find out more about the purpose of National Aboriginal Day. Do you think this is a meaningful policy designed to celebrate the importance of Aboriginal peoples in Canada? Give reasons for your answer.

CHAPTER 5
CULMINATING
ACTIVITY

Analyzing Stereotypes in the Media

The mass media are a powerful tool in our society. Television, movies, newspapers, magazines, radio, advertising, and the Internet can influence the way we think and view events, situations, and cultures.

In this chapter, you have seen how misconceptions and misunderstandings have combined with European attitudes of cultural superiority to create a stereotype of Aboriginal peoples. For many years, the media perpetuated these historically inaccurate images as movies and television misrepresented Aboriginal peoples' values, traditions, and cultures. Despite the diversity of these cultures, a common image persisted of Aboriginal peoples as a single, homogeneous group in which all people shared common traits and characteristics. As well, mainstream North American culture held a one-sided view of history that ignored the important contributions of Aboriginal peoples.

Today, many Aboriginal historians, authors, politicians, and others are combating these stereotypes to eliminate them and to ensure that the images that the media portray accurately reflect Aboriginal peoples and cultures.

The following activity gives you an opportunity to explore these cultural stereotypes. Begin by brainstorming some of the common stereotypes and misconceptions about Aboriginal peoples that have been presented in the past. Discuss the factors that led to the creation of these stereotypes and the reasons why these images are inaccurate. Then, with a partner, view a recent movie or television program and an older movie or television program that both portray Aboriginal peoples. Compare and contrast these movies or TV programs in a graphic organizer similar to the one shown below. When you have completed your organizer, write a statement summarizing your findings. Then, present your results to the class.

	Title	Title
Type of program		
Year produced		
Setting and time period		
Presentation of Aboriginal peoples		
Evidence of bias		
Evidence of stereotyping		

Contemporary Aboriginal Issues

Aboriginal Peoples and Socioeconomic Issues

LEARNING OBJECTIVES

In this chapter, you will

- examine demographics relating to Aboriginal populations in Canada and compare them with those of the general population
- explore the social and economic issues relating to Aboriginal populations
- understand that many of the socioeconomic challenges facing Aboriginal peoples today are the result of past events and government policies
- investigate how poverty affects the health and well-being of Aboriginal populations and limits self-determination
- recognize that educational attainment is a key factor in improving quality of life for Aboriginal peoples
- identify strategies and programs initiated by Aboriginal peoples and by government to address the challenges facing Aboriginal populations

INTRODUCTION

In this chapter, you will look at the socioeconomic challenges that face Aboriginal peoples today. You'll see that many of these challenges are the result of past events and government policies that you investigated in previous chapters. You'll consider how income and educational attainment affect the well-being and self-determination of Aboriginal peoples. You'll also have the opportunity to explore several initiatives developed by Aboriginal peoples and government organizations that address Aboriginal concerns.

THE ABORIGINAL POPULATION

Before examining the social and economic issues relating to Aboriginal peoples in Canada, it is important to consider some **demographics** of this population—in particular, size, growth rate, and provincial and territorial distribution.

demographics statistics on population numbers, distribution, and trends

Aboriginal Ancestry and Identity

The 2001 census indicated that the percentage of Aboriginal people within Canada's total population is increasing. Slightly over 1.3 million people reported some Aboriginal ancestry in 2001. This figure represented 4.4 percent of the total Canadian population, compared with 3.8 percent in the 1996 census.

To be more precise, 1,319,890 persons claimed some Aboriginal ancestry in 2001. But not everyone identified him- or herself as an Aboriginal person (First Nations, Inuit, or Métis). A total of 976,305 people claimed Aboriginal identity; the remaining 343,585 people had some Aboriginal ancestry but did not identify themselves as Aboriginal. This total increased from 799,010 in 1996. People reported Aboriginal identity as follows:

- 608,850 First Nations (529,040 in 1996)
- 292,310 Métis (204,115 in 1996)
- 45,070 Inuit (40,220 in 1996).

Reinstatement of First Nations Status

As you learned in Chapter 5, some First Nations people lost their legal status as "Indians" through the *Indian Act* of 1876. Most affected were First Nations women who lost their Indian status when they married non-Aboriginal men or non-status Aboriginal men. As well, the children from these marriages did not have Indian status. In 1985, Bill C-31 was passed in Parliament as an amendment to the *Indian Act.* Among other things, Bill C-31 introduced a process by which Indian status would be restored to those who had lost it through discrimination or enfranchisement, and that would prevent anyone from gaining or losing status through marriage. The ratification of Bill C-31 was a key factor in the significant increase of people reporting Aboriginal identity.

Growth Rates

In the 2001 census, the number of people reporting an Aboriginal identity rose 22.2 percent from 1996, with a 15.1 percent increase in those identifying as First Nations people (see Figure 6.1). This figure marks a 10-fold increase in the number of people who claimed Aboriginal ancestry in 1901, while the total population of Canada increased only sixfold.

One of the main reasons for the higher population of Aboriginal people was improved access to health care, which considerably reduced the rate of infant deaths after 1960. Another important reason was the increased tendency for people to identify as Aboriginal, especially since the 1986 census. Before the 1960s, it was not "popular" to be Aboriginal; consequently, many people who could have claimed Aboriginal ancestry did not do so.

Statistics Canada suggests that this new tendency might be the result of increasing public awareness of Aboriginal issues. The reporting of events

The Métis Population

After the *Constitution Act, 1982* recognized the Métis as an Aboriginal people, the number of individuals claiming Métis ancestry grew dramatically—and continues to grow. Of the three Aboriginal groups, the Métis had the largest gain in population between 1996 and 2001. Their numbers increased by 43 percent—almost three times the gain in the First Nations population (15 percent) and almost four times that of the Inuit population (12 percent).

	2001	1996	Percentage growth 1996–2001
Total: Aboriginal ancestry[1]	1,319,890	1,101,960	19.8%
Total: Aboriginal identity	976,305	799,010	22.2%
First Nations[2]	608,850	529,040	15.1%
Métis[2]	292,310	204,115	43.2%
Inuit[2]	45,070	40,220	12.1%
Multiple and other Aboriginal responses[3]	30,080	25,650	17.3%

Notes:

1. Also known as Aboriginal origin.
2. Includes persons who reported a First Nations, Métis, or Inuit identity only.
3. Includes persons who reported more than one Aboriginal identity group (First Nations, Métis, or Inuit) and those who reported being a First Nations person without reporting an Aboriginal identity.

Source: Adapted from Statistics Canada, Aboriginal Peoples of Canada: A Demographic Profile, 2001 Census *(Analysis Series, 2001 Census), catalogue no. 96F0030, January 31, 2003, p. 20.*

Figure 6.1 Size and Growth of the Population Reporting Aboriginal Ancestry and Aboriginal Identity, Canada, 1996–2001
In 2001, the majority (62 percent) of Aboriginal people were First Nations, 30 percent were Métis, and 5 percent were Inuit. The remaining 3 percent were either persons who identified with more than one Aboriginal group or First Nations people who did not identify themselves as Aboriginal.

such as the Oka crisis in Quebec, the Royal Commission on Aboriginal Peoples, the creation of Nunavut, and court decisions on land claims, human rights issues, and residential schools have made Canadians more knowledgeable about Aboriginal matters—and may encourage them to acknowledge their Aboriginal ancestry.

Decrease in Birth Rate

birth rate
the number of live births per 1,000 population in a given year

Thirty years ago, Aboriginal women had 6.2 children on average. In 1986, this figure fell to 3.2 children, while non-Aboriginal women had 1.67 children on average. The Aboriginal **birth rate** remains above the overall Canadian birth rate, although it has declined from four times the overall rate in the 1960s to 1.5 times today.

The birth rate for First Nations has been steadily declining, from 30.1 births per 1,000 population in 1987 to 25 births per 1,000 in 2000. This trend is consistent with the declining birth rate of the general population of Canada. However, in 2000, the First Nations birth rate was still more than twice the general population rate of 10.7 births per 1,000. In 2003–2004, the Inuit birth rate was twice as high as the general population rate of 10.4 births per 1,000.

Increase in Life Expectancy

life expectancy
the average lifespan of an individual

From 1956 to 1986, **life expectancy** for Aboriginal people increased by 10 years. For an Aboriginal male, life expectancy increased from an average of 53.8 years to 63.8 years. In comparison, life expectancy for a non-Aboriginal male was 73 years. In this same period, Aboriginal women increased their life expectancy from 61 years to 71 years, compared with 79.7 years for non-Aboriginal females.

While life expectancy is still lower in the Aboriginal population than in the non-Aboriginal population, the gap is gradually decreasing. For example, life expectancy continues to improve among the First Nations population. In 2005, it rose to 71.1 years for males and 76.3 years for females, an increase from 1985 of 11.3 percent and 7.5 percent, respectively (see Figure 6.2).

Aboriginal Seniors

There is a trend toward a larger proportion of older people in the Aboriginal population, but this proportion is still lower than that in the total Canadian population. This trend is largely the result of a gradually improving life expectancy and a declining birth rate among Aboriginal people.

While the Aboriginal population is relatively young, there has been a significant increase in the number of people over 65 years of age. The 2001 census counted 39,700 Aboriginal people aged 65 and older, an increase of 40 percent since 1996. This figure was the biggest increase of all the age groups. In the same

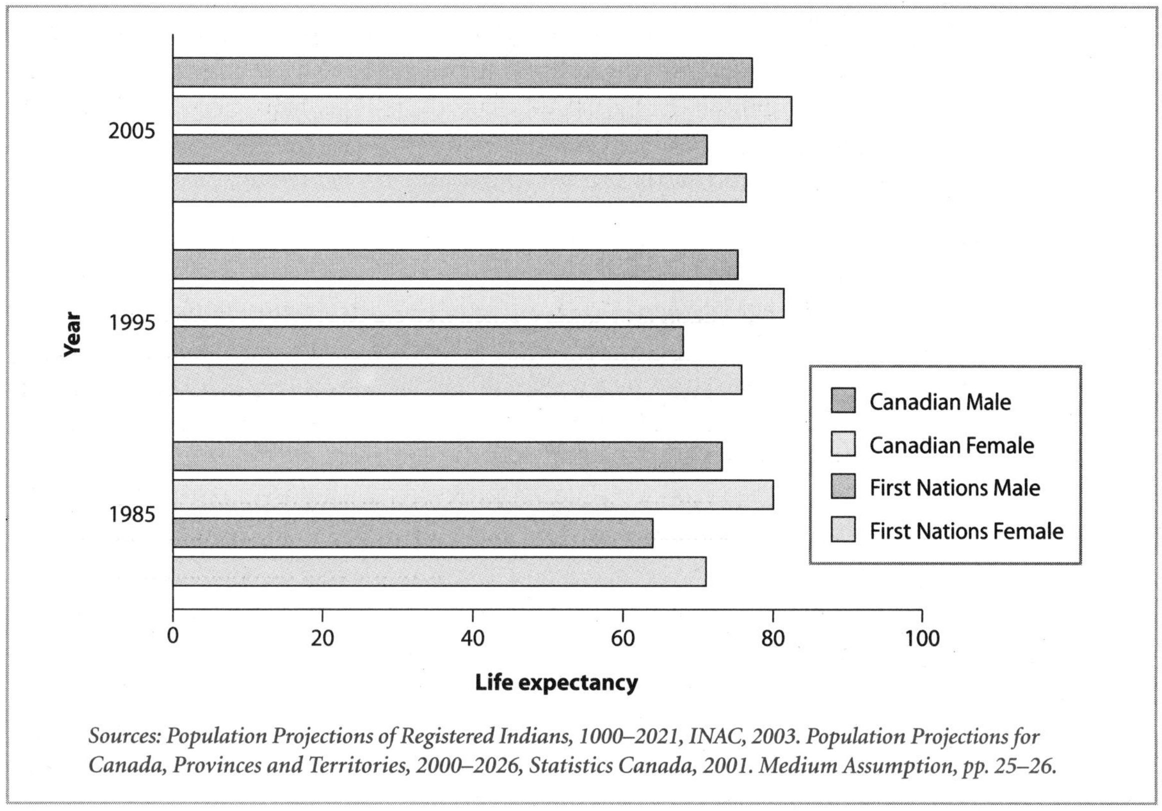

Figure 6.2 Life Expectancy at Birth by Gender, First Nations and General Population, Canada, 1985–2005 The increase in Aboriginal life expectancy over the last 25 years has resulted in the growth of the Aboriginal population aged 65 and older.

period, the number of seniors in the non-Aboriginal population grew by only 10 percent. However, because the overall Aboriginal population is young, Aboriginal seniors make up only about 4 percent of this population. Among non-Aboriginal people, seniors make up 13 percent of the population.

Provincial and Territorial Distribution of Aboriginal Populations

According to the 2001 census, the highest concentrations of Aboriginal people were in the North and the prairie provinces. Nunavut had Canada's highest concentration of Aboriginal people, numbering 22,720 and accounting for 85 percent of the territory's total population. Aboriginal people represented 51 percent of the population of the Northwest Territories and close to 25 percent of the population of Yukon Territory.

There were 150,040 Aboriginal people in Manitoba and 130,190 in Saskatchewan—about 14 percent of each province's population. In Alberta, only 5 percent of the population—156,220 people—reported an Aboriginal identity.

British Columbia had 170,025 Aboriginal people—4.4 percent of its population. While Ontario had the highest number (188,315) of Aboriginal people in 2001, they made up less than 2 percent of the province's total population.

Distribution of First Nations Populations

In 2001, Ontario had the highest First Nations population in Canada—131,560 people. This figure represented 21.6 percent of the total First Nations population in Canada, up from 17.7 percent in 1996. British Columbia followed at 19.4 percent, or 118,295 people. Figure 6.3 shows First Nations populations in each province and territory in 2001.

Migration to Cities

Increasingly, First Nations peoples are leaving the reserves, either for economic reasons or for better access to social services and education. In 2001, less than half (47 percent) of the First Nations population lived on reserves, while 24 percent lived in one of the 27 major census metropolitan areas (CMAs). Winnipeg had the largest First Nations population (22,955), followed by Vancouver (22,700), Edmonton (18,260), Toronto (13,785), and Saskatoon (11,290).

	Number	Percentage
Canada	608,850	100.0%
Newfoundland and Labrador	7,040	1.2%
Prince Edward Island	1,035	0.2%
Nova Scotia	12,920	2.1%
New Brunswick	11,490	1.9%
Quebec	51,125	8.4%
Ontario	131,560	21.6%
Manitoba	90,345	14.8%
Saskatchewan	83,745	13.8%
Alberta	84,990	14.0%
British Columbia	118,295	19.4%
Yukon Territory	5,600	0.9%
Northwest Territories	10,615	1.7%
Nunavut	95	0.0%

Source: Adapted from Statistics Canada, Aboriginal Peoples of Canada: A Demographic Profile, 2001 Census *(Analysis Series, 2001 Census), catalogue no. 96F0030, January 31, 2003.*

Figure 6.3 Population Reporting a First Nations Identity, Canada, Provinces and Territories, 2001 Nunavut has the smallest population of First Nations peoples (the vast majority reported an Inuit identity).

These figures mirror the overall population that identifies themselves as Aboriginal. Winnipeg had the highest numbers of self-identified Aboriginal people (First Nations, Métis, Inuit) at 55,755. Between 1996 and 2001, the city's Aboriginal population increased by over 10,000. This population formed 8 percent of Winnipeg's total population.

The 2001 census indicated a slow but steady growth among Aboriginal people living in Canada's cities. Almost one-half (49 percent) of people who identified themselves as Aboriginal lived in urban areas. The on-reserve Aboriginal population dropped from 33 percent in 1996 to 31 percent in 2001.

Mobility

The 2001 census indicated that Aboriginal people were more mobile than other Canadians. In the 12 months prior to the census, one in five Aboriginal people moved. Two-thirds moved within the same community, while one-third moved to a different community. **Net migration** was greatest in rural non-reserve areas (see Figure 6.4).

net migration
the effect of in-migration and out-migration on an area's population in a given period, expressed as an increase or decrease

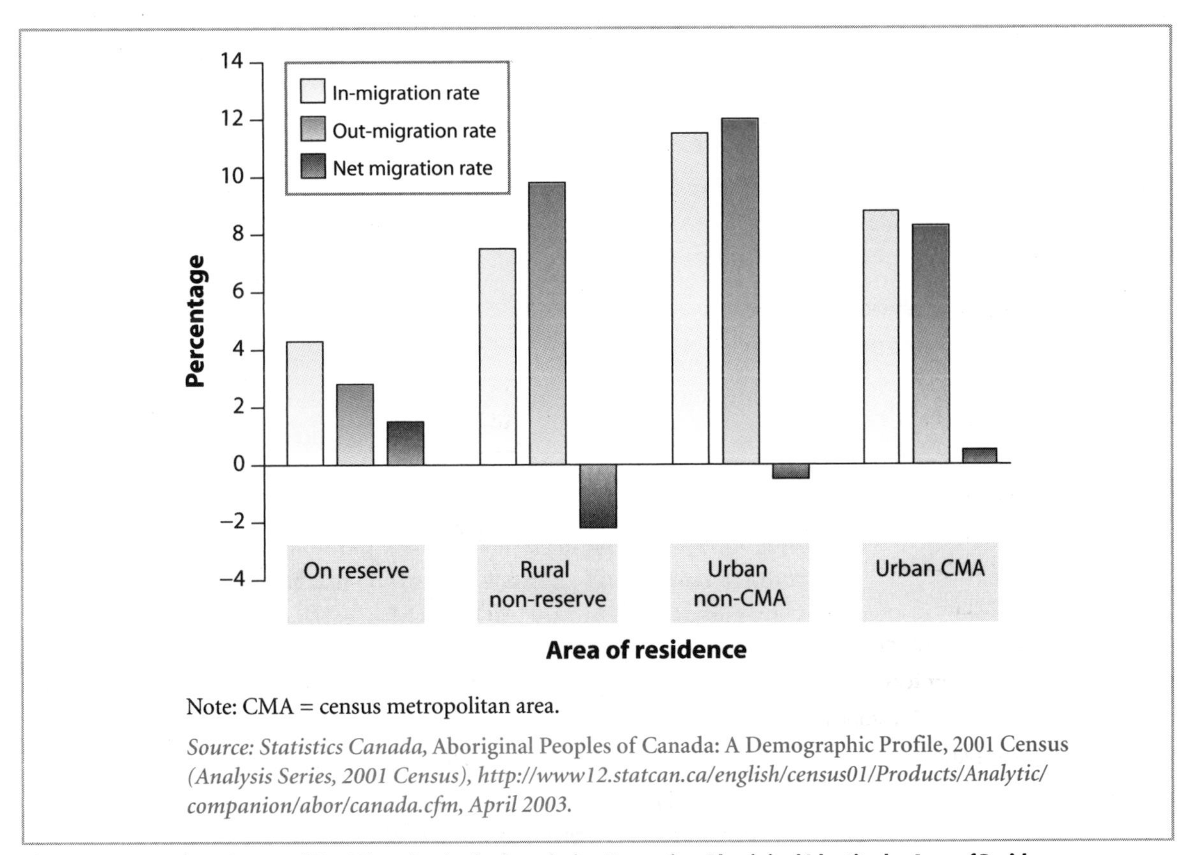

Note: CMA = census metropolitan area.

Source: Statistics Canada, Aboriginal Peoples of Canada: A Demographic Profile, 2001 Census *(Analysis Series, 2001 Census), http://www12.statcan.ca/english/census01/Products/Analytic/companion/abor/canada.cfm, April 2003.*

Figure 6.4 Rate of In-, Out-, and Net Migration in the Population Reporting Aboriginal Identity, by Area of Residence, Canada, 2000–2001 In this one-year period, 22 percent of Aboriginal people moved, compared with 14 percent of non-Aboriginal people.

1. Create a web diagram illustrating the reasons that the Aboriginal population in general has increased dramatically.
2. Why do you think there has been such a large increase in the number of people who have identified themselves as Métis?
3. What do you think are some of the pull factors (conditions that attract migrants) for First Nations people who move to urban centres?
4. If First Nations people continue to migrate away from reserves, what will be the impact on the health care and education systems in urban areas?

EDUCATION

Elementary and Secondary Schools

Forty years ago, the majority of First Nations children attended residential schools created by the government (see Chapter 5). Today's children attend provincially funded schools, band-run schools, or federal schools. First Nations cultural or language programs are sometimes offered in provincial schools that have high rates of First Nations student enrollment. The local school board receives funding from tuition agreements with the First Nations community.

Federal Schools

At the elementary level, the majority of First Nations children attend federal schools, which are primarily band schools and boarding schools. Band schools are located on-reserve and are administered by the band, based on federal government curriculum guidelines. Courses are often taught in First Nations languages, and children also learn about their cultural heritage.

Of the 503 on-reserve schools in 2003–2004, 496 were band schools. Several First Nations have set up regional organizations that support on-reserve schools through activities similar to those in provincial school boards. In moving toward self-government, some First Nations have gained further control over their education systems.

Boarding schools are generally for First Nations children who live in small, isolated communities with no other schools in the vicinity. Children attending a boarding school live with families in the community where the school is located. They are either integrated into an existing school off-reserve or attend an off-reserve school created specifically for them.

BAND SCHOOLS

Band schools aim to teach skills that will help First Nations children succeed in mainstream Canadian society. They also provide a supportive environment that is culturally relevant. First Nations believe that only an educational system that is entirely implemented and run by First Nations will eliminate the injustices of the residential schools. To achieve this goal, First Nations schools have implemented a number of strategies:

- greater reliance on First Nations learning and teaching styles
- increased exposure to and use of First Nations languages
- greater awareness and sensitivity on the part of teachers and staff to First Nations customs and experiences
- the removal of any biased or distorted texts or educational materials.

Source: J. Fleras and J.L. Elliott, Unequal Relations: An Introduction to Race, Ethnic and Aboriginal Dynamics in Canada *(Toronto: Prentice Hall, 1996).*

Figure 6.5 The Science Laboratory at Pelican Falls First Nation School, Sioux Lookout, Ontario Since the creation of band schools in the 1980s, First Nations student enrollment has increased. The enrollment in elementary and secondary schools increased from 96,594 in 1991–1992 to approximately 119,000 in 2003–2004.

Completion of High School

In 2001, about two out of five Aboriginal people aged 25 to 64 had not completed a high school education—almost twice the proportion of non-Aboriginal people in the same age group. However, this figure represented a significant improvement from 1996. The proportion of Aboriginal people without a high school diploma dropped from 45 percent in 1996 to 39 percent in 2001.

In 1991, 18 percent of First Nations people aged 15 years or older had less than grade 9 education, compared with 37 percent in 1981. Although there is still a significant gap in educational attainment between First Nations students and the general population, the proportion of on-reserve First Nations students who completed high school increased from 31.4 percent in 1991 to 41.4 percent in 2001—an increase of 10 percent. In comparison, the overall high school completion rate increased by 6.9 percent over the same period (from 61.8 to 68.7 percent).

Some of the reasons for increased participation in secondary-level education include

- the introduction of language and cultural classes in schools with large First Nations student populations
- greater awareness and promotion of education by the bands themselves
- the development of First Nations-managed secondary schools.

Postsecondary Education

First Nations and Inuit participation in postsecondary education greatly increased between 1987 and 2001. The number of First Nations and Inuit students enrolled in postsecondary education funded by Indian and Northern Affairs Canada (INAC) almost doubled from approximately 14,000 to 26,000. (Some Aboriginal students who graduate from postsecondary studies are funded by other sources.) About 4,500 postsecondary students graduated each year. Between 1996 and 2001, the First Nations population (on- and off-reserve) with a postsecondary certificate, diploma, or degree increased from 20 to 23 percent. For the general population, it increased from 35 to 38 percent.

The Education Gap

Despite these improvements, First Nations enrollment and participation in education continue to lag behind the average Canadian rate. In 2001, 15.7 percent of the non-Aboriginal population aged 15 and older had a university degree, compared with 4.4 of the Aboriginal population. INAC says that "education programs and services have not kept pace with the needs and

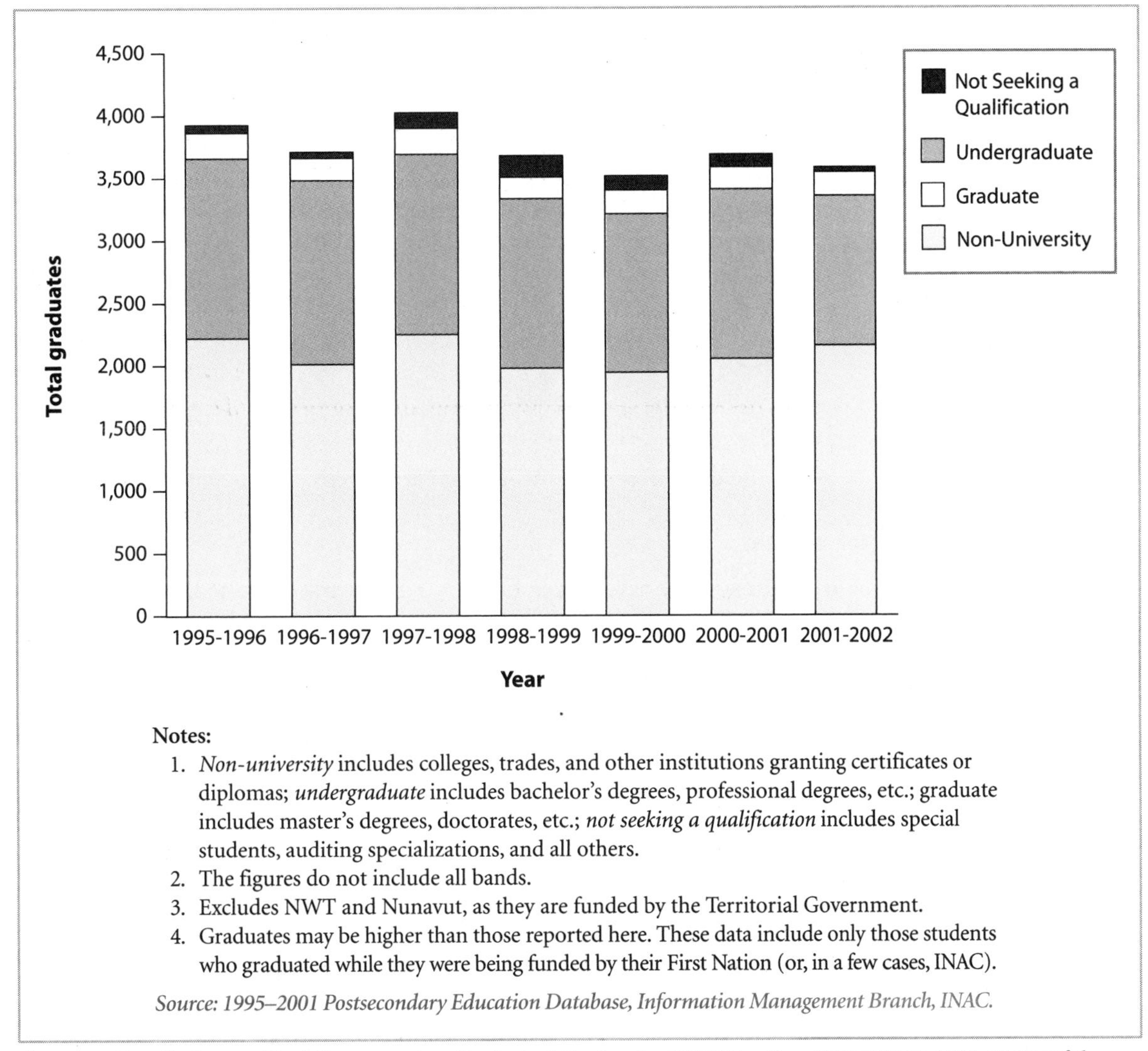

Notes:

1. *Non-university* includes colleges, trades, and other institutions granting certificates or diplomas; *undergraduate* includes bachelor's degrees, professional degrees, etc.; graduate includes master's degrees, doctorates, etc.; *not seeking a qualification* includes special students, auditing specializations, and all others.
2. The figures do not include all bands.
3. Excludes NWT and Nunavut, as they are funded by the Territorial Government.
4. Graduates may be higher than those reported here. These data include only those students who graduated while they were being funded by their First Nation (or, in a few cases, INAC).

Source: 1995–2001 Postsecondary Education Database, Information Management Branch, INAC.

Figure 6.6 First Nations and Inuit Postsecondary Graduates Who Received INAC Funding, 1995–1996 to 2001–2002 Of the 3,584 postsecondary graduates in 2001–2002, 60 percent received a non-university certificate or diploma, and 39 percent received an undergraduate or postgraduate degree from a university.

expectations of First Nations and Canadian society as a whole." It identifies the major challenges to closing the education gap:

- a variety of socioeconomic factors that affect educational attainment
- rapidly increasing populations
- the legacy of residential schools
- the diversity of First Nations communities and needs
- the need for improved support for First Nations' control of their education systems

- the geographic remoteness of First Nations communities
- the fact that 38 percent of on-reserve students attend provincial schools
- the movement of students between on- and off-reserve schools
- the ever-increasing educational expectations of today's knowledge-based economy.

According to INAC, these challenges result in

- many young children coming to school ill-prepared to learn
- significant drop-out rates during high school
- low high school graduation rates
- difficulties making transitions to postsecondary education or the labour market.

Taking Action

Aboriginal leaders and the federal government are working together to develop initiatives for closing the education gap. Two of these initiatives are the First Nation Education Policy Framework and the First Nation Education Management Framework. First Nations and INAC are working jointly on both frameworks. The policy framework will outline a strategic plan for First Nations education and set out roles and responsibilities. The management framework will establish a means of managing educational program delivery. Both will further the final goal of establishing First Nations' jurisdiction over their students' education.

Another education initiative is part of the Canada–Aboriginal Peoples Roundtable process (see page 172). Two sessions on lifelong learning were held in November 2004. Recommendations from these sessions will be presented at a future meeting between members of the Cabinet Committee on Aboriginal Affairs and Aboriginal leaders.

1. What do you think can be done to improve First Nations' enrollment and participation in education? Relate your answer to both on-reserve and off-reserve populations.
2. One of the difficulties in maintaining Aboriginal education is the lack of Aboriginal teachers. Suggest some possible reasons for this shortage.
3. How might small Aboriginal communities offer quality education without closing their schools and transporting students to other areas?

4. Do you think that First Nations students should be educated in the same schools and under the same curriculum as all other Canadian students? Give reasons for your answer.
5. In today's world, students must be knowledgeable about science and technology in order to pursue higher education or prepare themselves for the workforce. How can on-reserve schools, especially those in small communities or isolated areas, incorporate science and technology into their curricula?

HEALTH

Physical Health

Compared with the general Canadian population, the average Aboriginal person experiences a lower standard of health. In this section, you will examine a number of factors that reflect this reality.

Mortality and Morbidity Rates

The **crude mortality rate** for First Nations in 1999 was 354.2 deaths per 100,000 population. The four leading causes of death were injury and poisoning, circulatory diseases, cancer, and respiratory diseases. When compared with the 1991–1993 period, the mortality rate in each of these four categories had decreased significantly.

morbidity rate
the rate of incidence of a disease

crude mortality rate
the number of deaths per 100,000 population in a given year

In her book, *Canada's First Nations: A History of Founding Peoples from Earliest Times*, Canadian historian Olive Dickason quotes from the Jesuit *New Relation of Gaspesia*, then adds her own commentary:

" 'Amerindians are all by nature physicians, apothecaries and doctors, by virtue of the knowledge and experience they have of certain herbs, which they use successfully to cure ills that seem to us incurable.' The process by which the Amerindians acquired their herbal lore is not clearly understood, but there is no doubt about the results. More than 500 drugs used in the medical pharmacopoeia today were originally used by Amerindians."

Report on the Royal Commission on Aboriginal Peoples, *"Chapter 3: Health and Healing," in Volume 3:* Gathering Strength, *April 23, 2004; http://www.ainc-inac.gc.ca/ch/rcap/sg/sim3_e.html.*

The crude mortality rate for First Nations males was 1.3 times higher than the rate for First Nations females in 1999. This difference was largely attributable to higher rates among males for injury and poisoning and circulatory diseases (see Figure 6.7). Age-specific death rates in 1999 were higher for First Nations males than for females in almost all age groups. The largest difference between the sexes occurred in the 5–9 and 20–24 age groups.

Common Illnesses

Aboriginal people have a higher rate of certain types of chronic illness than the general Canadian population. For example:

- Rates of diabetes among Aboriginal people in Canada are three to five times higher than those of the general population. Aboriginal children are now being diagnosed with type 2 diabetes, a condition

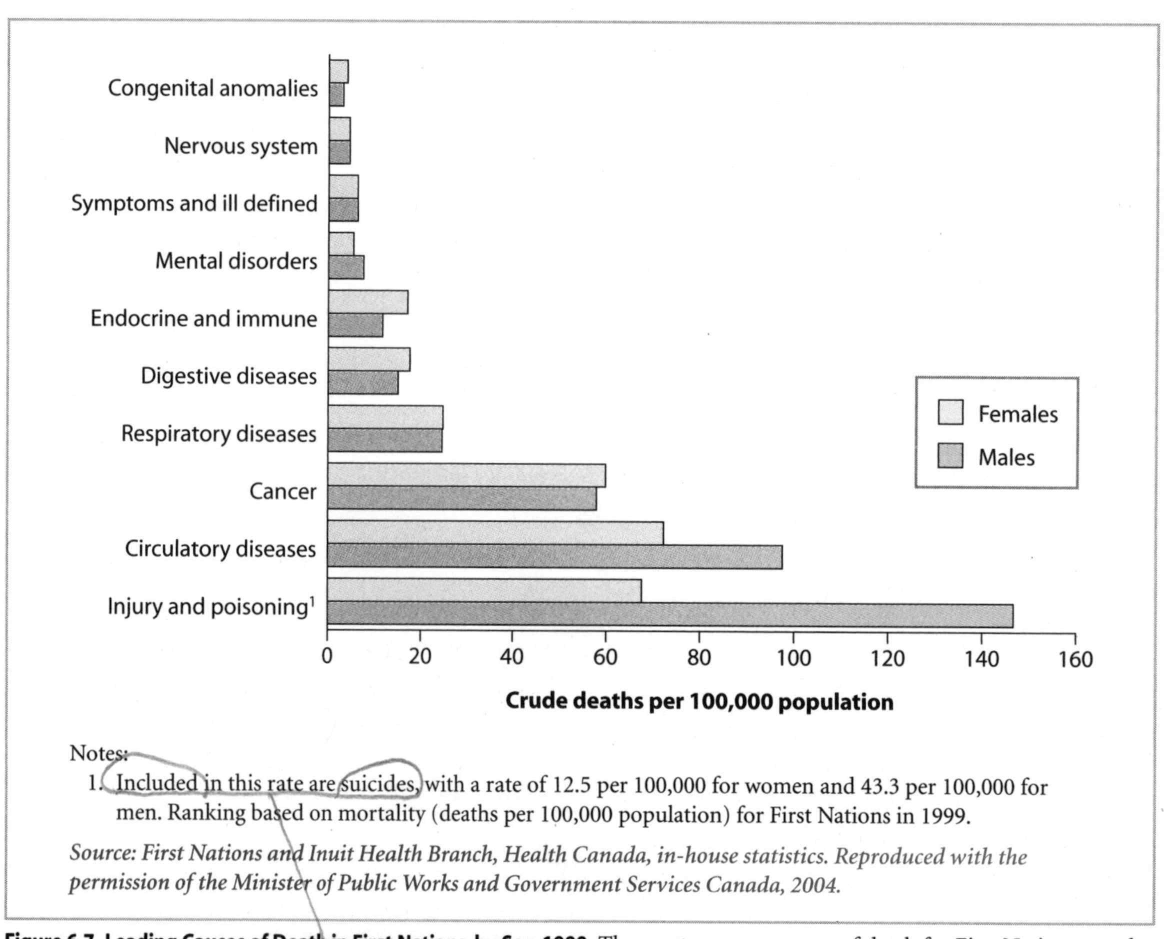

Notes:

1. Included in this rate are suicides, with a rate of 12.5 per 100,000 for women and 43.3 per 100,000 for men. Ranking based on mortality (deaths per 100,000 population) for First Nations in 1999.

Source: First Nations and Inuit Health Branch, Health Canada, in-house statistics. Reproduced with the permission of the Minister of Public Works and Government Services Canada, 2004.

Figure 6.7 Leading Causes of Death in First Nations, by Sex, 1999 The most common cause of death for First Nations people aged 1–44 was injury and poisoning. Suicide and self-injury were the leading causes for youth and adults up to age 44. For First Nations people aged 45 and older, circulatory diseases were the most common cause of death. These trends parallel the Canadian population as a whole.

that, in the past, was mostly associated with older people. While Inuit rates of diabetes are not as high as those of other Aboriginal populations, the rate of type 2 diabetes is increasing among Inuit.

- Among First Nations peoples, the incidence of diabetes is three times the national average. They experience diabetes complications more often and at an earlier age.
- Overall, the annual number of new HIV/AIDS cases has stabilized. However, the number of HIV/AIDS cases among Aboriginal people has grown steadily over the last 10 years. The proportion of Canada's total

ABORIGINAL DIABETES INITIATIVE

The Aboriginal Diabetes Initiative (ADI) was developed in consultation with Aboriginal organizations to address the rising epidemic of diabetes among Aboriginal people. The program's guidelines call for community-based, culturally relevant programs that are respectful of traditional approaches and accountable to Aboriginal communities and the government.

To attain its goals, the ADI has been divided into two components:

- First Nations On-Reserve and Inuit in Inuit Communities Program—improves access to care and treatment services, lifestyle support, and prevention and promotion programs for First Nations living on-reserve and Inuit living in Inuit communities and
- Métis, Off-Reserve Aboriginal, and Urban Inuit Prevention and Promotion Program—provides primary prevention and health promotion programs for Métis and urban Aboriginal and Inuit peoples.

The ADI is designed to provide a more comprehensive, collaborative, and integrated approach to decreasing diabetes and its complications among Aboriginal people. The program is overseen by a national steering committee with representation from national Aboriginal organizations (Assembly of First Nations, Inuit Tapiriit Kanatami, Métis National Council, Congress of Aboriginal Peoples, Native Women's Association of Canada), as well as the National Aboriginal Diabetes Association.

Source: Adapted from Health Topics—Diabetes, Public Health Agency of Canada, November 20, 2003; http://www.phac-aspc.gc.ca/ccdpc-cpcmc/topics/diabetes_e.html and Aboriginal Diabetes Initiative, Community Programs, Health Canada, June 3, 2003; http://www.hc-sc.gc.ca/fnihb/cp/adi/introduction.htm.

HIV/AIDS cases among Aboriginal people climbed from 1.0 percent in 1990 to 7.2 percent in 2001, according to Health Canada.

- Between 1990 and 2001, the tuberculosis rate among First Nations people remained eight to 10 times higher than that of the Canadian population.

Aboriginal Women

The health of Aboriginal women has significantly improved over the past few decades, but there are still imbalances compared with the general population:

- Aboriginal women have higher rates of circulatory problems, respiratory problems, diabetes, hypertension, and cancer of the cervix than the rest of the general female population.
- Most Aboriginal people with diabetes are women (approximately two women for every man).
- Aboriginal women represent a higher percentage of cases of HIV/AIDS than non-Aboriginal women (15.9 compared with 7.0 percent). Fifty percent of female Aboriginal HIV/AIDS cases are related to injection drug use compared with 17 percent of all female cases.
- The mortality rate for Aboriginal women as a result of violence is three times the rate for all other Canadian women. For Aboriginal women aged 25–44, the rate is five times that for all other Canadian women.
- Hospital admissions for alcohol-related accidents are three times higher among Aboriginal females than they are for the general Canadian population.
- More than half of Aboriginal peoples consider alcohol abuse a social problem in their communities. Fetal alcohol syndrome (FAS) and fetal alcohol effects (FAE) have become health and social concerns in some First Nations and Inuit communities.
- Suicide rates are higher for the Aboriginal population than the general Canadian population. Over the five-year period from 1989 to 1993, Aboriginal women were more than three times as likely to commit suicide than were non-Aboriginal women.

Health Canada and Aboriginal communities have set up a number of services and programs to take action on these issues:

- The Canadian Prenatal Nutrition Program (CPNP) supports activities to improve the health of pregnant women and their infants. It is working to prevent FAS and FAE through prevention and public education, and in cooperation with First Nations and Inuit communities, provincial and territorial governments, and other non-governmental organizations.

- HIV/AIDS resources and funding are provided to First Nations and Inuit communities to develop culturally appropriate materials for First Nations and Inuit women.
- The federal government is in the process of establishing an Aboriginal Health Institute in consultation with Aboriginal groups, including the Native Women's Association of Canada.
- The Aboriginal Head Start program fosters child development and school readiness of Aboriginal children living in urban centres and large northern communities.
- The National Native Alcohol and Drug Abuse Program funds prevention programs and treatment services in a holistic manner.
- The First Nations and Inuit component of Brighter Futures provides funds for mental health and child development initiatives with activities in such areas as parenting skills, healthy babies, and childhood injury prevention.
- Building Healthy Communities supports existing health programs and allocates resources to First Nations and Inuit communities who are in urgent need.
- The Indian and Inuit Health Careers Program provides scholarships and bursaries to Aboriginal students pursuing postsecondary careers in health fields, many of whom are women.

Mental Health

Many social concerns that are reported by Aboriginal people are closely tied to mental health issues. Stress, **anomie**, low self-esteem, and poverty contribute to problems such as suicide and substance abuse, including alcohol abuse.

anomie
social instability resulting from the breakdown of standards and values

Suicide

According to Health Canada, suicide rates in First Nations and Inuit communities are three to five times greater than rates in the general Canadian population. All First Nations age groups up to 65 years are at increased risk for suicide when compared with the general population. In 1999, the First Nations suicide rate was 27.9 deaths per 100,000 population. This rate had not declined between the years 1973 and 1999. Notably, the 1999 rate was 2.1 times the suicide rate of the general Canadian population—13.2 deaths per 100,000 population. That same year, suicide was among the leading causes of death in First Nations people aged 10–44.

Henry Zoe is a Member of the Legislative Assembly in the Northwest Territories. He stresses the importance of a holistic approach to health.

"For [people] to be healthy, they must be adequately fed, be educated, have access to medical facilities, have access to spiritual comfort, live in a warm and comfortable house with clean water and safe sewage disposal, be secure in their cultural identity, have an opportunity to excel in a meaningful endeavour, and so on. These are not separate needs; they are all aspects of a whole."

Report on the Royal Commission on Aboriginal Peoples, *"Chapter 3: Health and Healing," in Volume 3:* Gathering Strength, *April 23, 2004; http://www.ainc-inac.gc.ca/ch/rcap/sg/sim3_e.html.*

Youth Suicide

The rate of youth suicide among First Nations is extremely high—up to six times higher than the Canadian average. Among First Nations men between the ages of 15 and 24, the rate is 126 per 100,000, compared with 24 per 100,000 for young Canadian men overall. For young First Nations women, the rate is 35 per 100,000, compared with 5 per 100,000 for young Canadian women overall.

VOICES

Aboriginal Youth Suicide Prevention Walk is a group of young people and their supporters who walk from Nanaimo, British Columbia to Ottawa, Ontario each year. They started this initiative in 2003 and will complete their last walk in 2006.

Figure 6.8 Youth Suicide Prevention Walk Young people who participated in the 2005 walk celebrate in Ottawa.

"Our objective is to raise awareness on the tragic problem of youth suicide on our reserves and in our communities across Canada. In 2004, [we] carried [our] message to at least 50 reserves across Canada. We spoke at junior high schools, high schools, juvenile detention centres and Friendship Centres, and we spoke to over 50 chiefs across the nation. We were on radio and television broadcasts, including APTN and in newspapers across Canada. We even went into caucus in both Alberta and Saskatchewan."

From Aboriginal Youth Suicide Prevention Walk; http://www.theyouthsuicidepreventionwalk.com/2005/information2005.html.

CLOSE-UP

FACTORS IN ABORIGINAL SUICIDE

The Royal Commission on Aboriginal Peoples identified four groups of major risk factors generally associated with suicide: psycho-biological, situational, socioeconomic, and cultural stress. Cultural stress was considered particularly significant for Aboriginal people.

Psycho-biological

While mental disorders and illnesses associated with suicide (such as depression, anxiety disorders, and schizophrenia) were documented less often among Aboriginal people, community health providers have suggested that unresolved grief may be a widespread psycho-biological problem.

Situational

The disruptions of family life experienced as a result of enforced attendance at boarding schools, adoption, and fly-out hospitalizations (often for long-term illnesses such as tuberculosis) were seen as contributing to suicide. To these was added increasing use of alcohol and drugs to relieve unhappiness.

Socioeconomic

High rates of poverty, low levels of education, limited employment opportunities, inadequate housing, and deficiencies in sanitation and water quality affect a disproportionately high number of Aboriginal people. Under these conditions, individuals are more likely to develop feelings of helplessness and hopelessness that can lead to suicide.

Cultural Stress

This term is used to refer to the loss of confidence in the ways of understanding life and living that have been taught within a particular culture. It comes about when the complex of relationships, knowledge, language, social institutions, beliefs, values, and ethical rules that bind a people and give them a collective sense of identity changes. For Aboriginal people, such things as loss of land and control over living conditions, suppression of belief systems and spirituality, weakening of social and political institutions, and racial discrimination have seriously damaged their confidence and thus predisposed them to suicide and other self-destructive behaviours.

Source: Adapted from Turtle Island Native Network, "Suicide Among Aboriginal People: Royal Commission Report"; http://www.turtleisland.org/healing/healing-suicide1.htm, under "The Contributing Factors."

Substance Abuse

Alcohol

There is debate over alcohol misuse among Aboriginal people. Some see it as a major problem in many communities, while others consider it an unfair stereotype.

Aboriginal people had no access to alcohol until 300 years ago. Their vulnerability to alcoholism may be related to the unavailability of the drug in the past. In addition, such factors as income, rate of employment, northern isolation, size of households, and lack of industrial activity may contribute to unhealthy levels of alcohol consumption. Alcohol abuse may contribute to other problems such as violence, suicide, criminal behaviour, and FAS.

The future seems hopeful, however. The National Native Alcohol and Drug Abuse Program (NNADAP) has reported that, while in-patient admissions to treatment centres fluctuated between 4,500 and 4,700 annually through the mid-1990s, and reached a peak of 4,987 in 1996–1997, the admissions rate dropped by 30 percent in 1999–2000. The **recidivism** rate also dropped by 40 percent between 1996–1997 and 1999–2000, and the percentage of clients seeking treatment for alcohol abuse dropped to 43 percent, an 11-year low.

recidivism
a return to a previous pattern of behaviour

Other Substances

Inhalant use (sniffing the fumes from gasoline, nail polish remover, or other substances) is increasingly reported throughout isolated Aboriginal communities and is a cause of major health problems. According to one report in the *Canadian Medical Association Journal*, the median age of children using inhalants was 12, and sniffing was reported among First Nations children as young as four years old. First Nations youths who admitted to using inhalants also reported that they came from communities where financial hardship, neglect, family conflict, or child abuse existed.

Starting in the mid-1990s, the percentage of the NNADAP's clients who reported using hallucinogens and other non-narcotic drugs was on an upward trend, rising to 10 percent and 14 percent, respectively, in 1999–2000. Meanwhile, the percentage of those abusing narcotics decreased after reaching 27 percent in 1995–1996. However, data from 1999–2000 suggest that narcotic abuse has risen again.

Administration of Health Services

After the *Indian Act* was passed in 1876, the federal government assumed jurisdiction for the health of First Nations peoples. By the early 1900s, First Nations and Inuit communities were devastated by smallpox, tuberculosis, and other infectious diseases, but there was no single government organization to deal with this health crisis. Throughout the 20th century, the federal government established various departments and policies to ensure the

NATIONAL NATIVE ALCOHOL AND DRUG ABUSE PROGRAM

The National Native Alcohol and Drug Abuse Program is mainly run by First Nations communities and organizations. It includes a network of 54 treatment centres with in-patient services. As well, there are more than 500 alcohol and other drug abuse community-based prevention programs, with approximately 650 people working in community-based prevention activities. The majority of the NNADAP's resources are managed by First Nations through donations, transfer agreements, or both.

The goal of the NNADAP is to support First Nations and Inuit communities in establishing and operating programs to prevent alcohol, drug, and inhalant abuse among populations living on-reserve. Most of its activities are in the areas of prevention, treatment, training, and research and development.

availability of health services to Aboriginal peoples. In 2000, the Medical Services Branch of Health Canada was renamed the First Nations and Inuit Health Branch (FNIHB).

First Nations and Inuit Health Branch

As part of Health Canada, the FNIHB supports the delivery of public health and health promotion services on reserves and in Inuit communities. It provides drug, dental, and supplementary health services to First Nations peoples and Inuit, regardless of where they live. The branch also provides primary health care on reserves in remote and isolated areas where there are no provincial services.

There are FNIHB regional offices in every province except the Atlantic provinces, which are represented by the Atlantic Region office in Halifax, Nova Scotia. The Northern Secretariat of the FNIHB includes Yukon Territory, the Northwest Territories, and Nunavut. The FNIHB works with First Nations and Inuit organizations to transfer autonomy and control of health programs and resources to Aboriginal peoples.

In partnership with First Nations and Inuit, the Community Programs Directorate of FNIHB offers a wide range of programs in key community health sectors. Two of its programs were discussed earlier in this chapter—the Aboriginal Diabetes Initiative and the National Native Alcohol and Drug Abuse Program. The activities of the directorate are intended to maintain and improve the health of First Nations and Inuit, and to facilitate First Nations and Inuit control of health programs and resources.

Access to Health Services

Despite an increase in the number of health-related services provided to Aboriginal communities, Aboriginal people continue to have less access to health care services compared with other Canadians. Generally, this situation is a result of such factors as geographic isolation, inadequate federal funding, and lack of personnel trained to meet the needs of Aboriginal populations.

In addition, there is a shortage of Aboriginal people within the Canadian health care workforce. An increase in the number of Aboriginal health care professionals with an understanding of related cultural issues would benefit the health of Aboriginal people.

Living Conditions

Overcrowding
An indicator for quality of living is one person per room. If there are more people than rooms in a house, the occupants are considered to be living in overcrowded conditions.

Shelter is a significant issue in First Nations communities. While the percentage of adequate on-reserve housing increased from 45.7 percent in 1994–1995 to 56.9 percent in 1999–2000, it decreased to 53 percent in 2002–2003 (see Figure 6.10). Overcrowding is also a problem. According to INAC, 19 percent of the dwellings on reserves had more than one person per room in 2000, compared with 2 percent of dwellings in Canada as a whole.

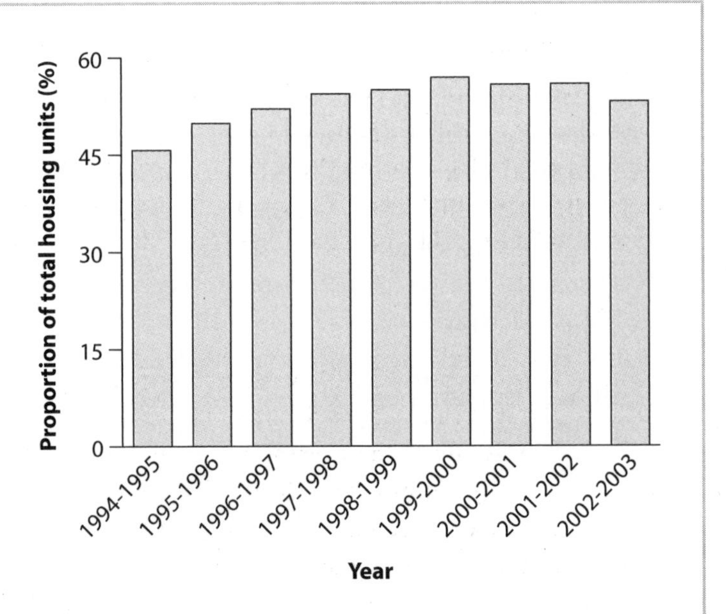

Figure 6.10 Percentage of Adequate On-Reserve Housing, Canada, 1994–1995 to 2002–2003 Despite the general increase in housing over the past decade, Aboriginal people, both on-reserve and off-reserve, experience more overcrowding compared with other Canadians. ("Adequate" is defined as the number of housing units that do not require any minor or major renovations or replacement.)

Source: Indian and Northern Affairs Canada, Information Management Branch, 1994–2003 Capital Asset Management System.

Blueprint for Aboriginal Health

In a special meeting in Ottawa in September 2004, first ministers and national Aboriginal leaders agreed to work together to develop a blueprint for improving the health of Aboriginal peoples. The federal government also committed to provide specific funding for

- an Aboriginal Transition Fund that will devise new ways of integrating and adapting existing health services to meet the needs of Aboriginal people
- an Aboriginal Health Human Resources Initiative that will increase the number of Aboriginal people in the health care professions
- health promotion and disease prevention programs that will focus on suicide prevention, diabetes, maternal and child health, and early childhood development.

Further discussions were expected to take place between governments and Aboriginal leaders at the First Ministers Meeting on Aboriginal Issues, scheduled for fall 2005.

Figure 6.9 Housing on a Siksika reserve near Gleichen, Alberta Overcrowded living conditions are known to contribute to escalating tensions and, ultimately, disintegration of relationships and a higher risk of violence. They may also increase the risk of spreading infectious diseases such as tuberculosis.

Water supply and sewage disposal in First Nations communities have improved dramatically. For example, from 1977 to 1989, only 53 percent of reserve houses had adequate water supplies and only 47 percent had adequate sewage disposal. By 1996–1997, 96 percent of band homes had an adequate water supply and 92 percent had an adequate sewage system. As shown in Figure 6.11, there have been further improvements since then.

The Environment

Many Aboriginal peoples still follow traditional ways of living and eat traditional foods. As a result, environmental pollution may affect them more directly than it affects the general population. According to the National Indian and Inuit Community Health Representatives Organization, environmental damage affects the health and well-being of First Nations peoples and Inuit in three main ways:

- Industry and resource development projects release environmental contaminants into the air, water, and soil, posing hazards to human health.

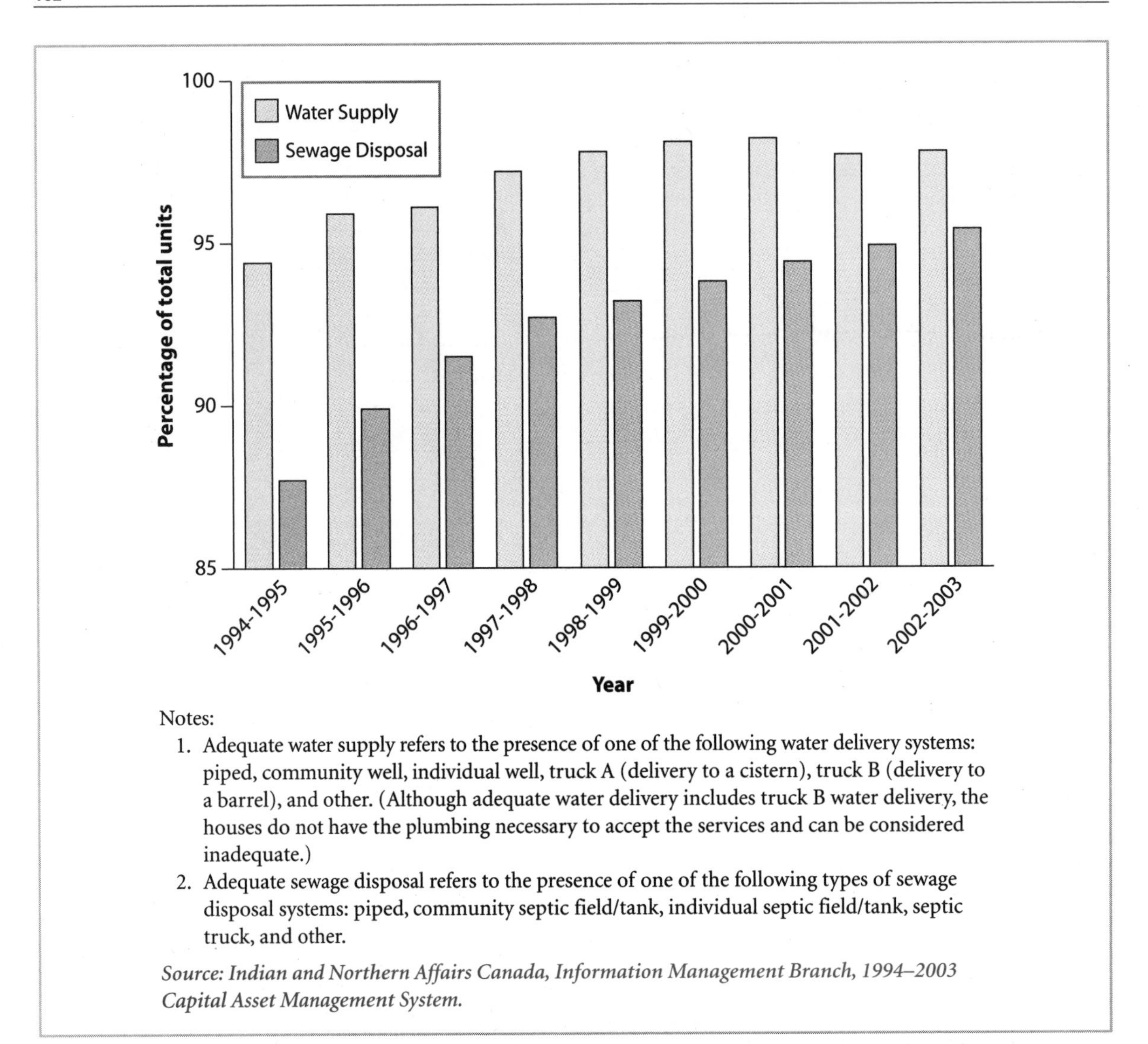

Notes:

1. Adequate water supply refers to the presence of one of the following water delivery systems: piped, community well, individual well, truck A (delivery to a cistern), truck B (delivery to a barrel), and other. (Although adequate water delivery includes truck B water delivery, the houses do not have the plumbing necessary to accept the services and can be considered inadequate.)
2. Adequate sewage disposal refers to the presence of one of the following types of sewage disposal systems: piped, community septic field/tank, individual septic field/tank, septic truck, and other.

Source: Indian and Northern Affairs Canada, Information Management Branch, 1994–2003 Capital Asset Management System.

Figure 6.11 Percentage of On-Reserve Dwellings with Adequate Water Delivery Systems and Sewage Disposal Systems, Canada, 1994–1995 to 2002–2003 Although "outhouses" can still be found on many northern reserves, the federal government has assumed responsibility for installing both water and sewage systems on reserves across Canada.

- The availability and purity of traditional foods and medicines are decreased as a result of industrial contamination and disruption of wildlife habitat.
- Since traditional ways of life depend on the purity of the land, the water, and all living things, their erosion affects the emotional and spiritual health of Aboriginal peoples and causes further cultural disruption.

TALKING CIRCLE

1. What role do you think the government should play in providing training for Aboriginal health care workers? How might health care workers be encouraged to practise on reserves, especially those in isolated areas?
2. Aboriginal people rate their overall health as lower than that of other Canadians. List some reasons why this might be true.
3. In this section, you found out that there is a much higher rate of diabetes and tuberculosis among Aboriginal people than among Canadians in general. What are some of the historical reasons why these diseases occur among Aboriginal people?
4. The health of Aboriginal women is significantly worse than that of the general Canadian population. Based on what you have read so far in this textbook, provide some possible historical reasons for this imbalance.
5. Can suicide, alcoholism, and substance abuse among First Nations peoples be attributed to cultural stress? Give reasons for your answer.

EMPLOYMENT

Unemployment Rate

The unemployment rate for Aboriginal people aged 15 and older fell from 24 percent in 1996 to 19.1 percent in 2001. This 4.9 percent drop was much larger than the 2.7 percent drop for the non-Aboriginal population—its unemployment rate was 7.1 percent. However, the 2001 unemployment rate for Aboriginal people was still close to three times higher than the non-Aboriginal rate.

Employment Rate

While the employment rate for Aboriginal people is relatively low, it has increased at a faster pace than the non-Aboriginal rate. Employment rates for Aboriginal people aged 15 and older increased 5.3 percent between 1996 and 2001, reaching 49.7 percent in 2001. This growth was more than twice the 2.6 percent increase for non-Aboriginal people of the same age—their employment rate was 61.8 percent in 2001. The differences in employment rates between Aboriginal and non-Aboriginal people were not as big among women and people aged 55 and older.

There was a significant difference in employment rates among the three Aboriginal groups. In 2001, the rate for First Nations was 44.6 percent, for Inuit 48.6 percent, and for Métis 59.4 percent. Compared with First Nations and Inuit, a higher proportion of Métis had graduated from high school or completed postsecondary studies.

Level of Education

The employment rate usually increases with level of formal education, according to Statistics Canada. In 2001, the employment rate for Aboriginal people aged 25 to 64 with some high school education or less was 42.9 percent, compared with 82.3 percent for those with a university degree.

Statistics Canada also points out that education appears to reduce the gap in employment rate between Aboriginal and non-Aboriginal people (see Figure 6.12). While the employment rate for Aboriginal people with less than a high school diploma was 17 percent lower than the rate for non-Aboriginal people with the same level of education, there was almost no difference in the employment rates of Aboriginal and non-Aboriginal university graduates.

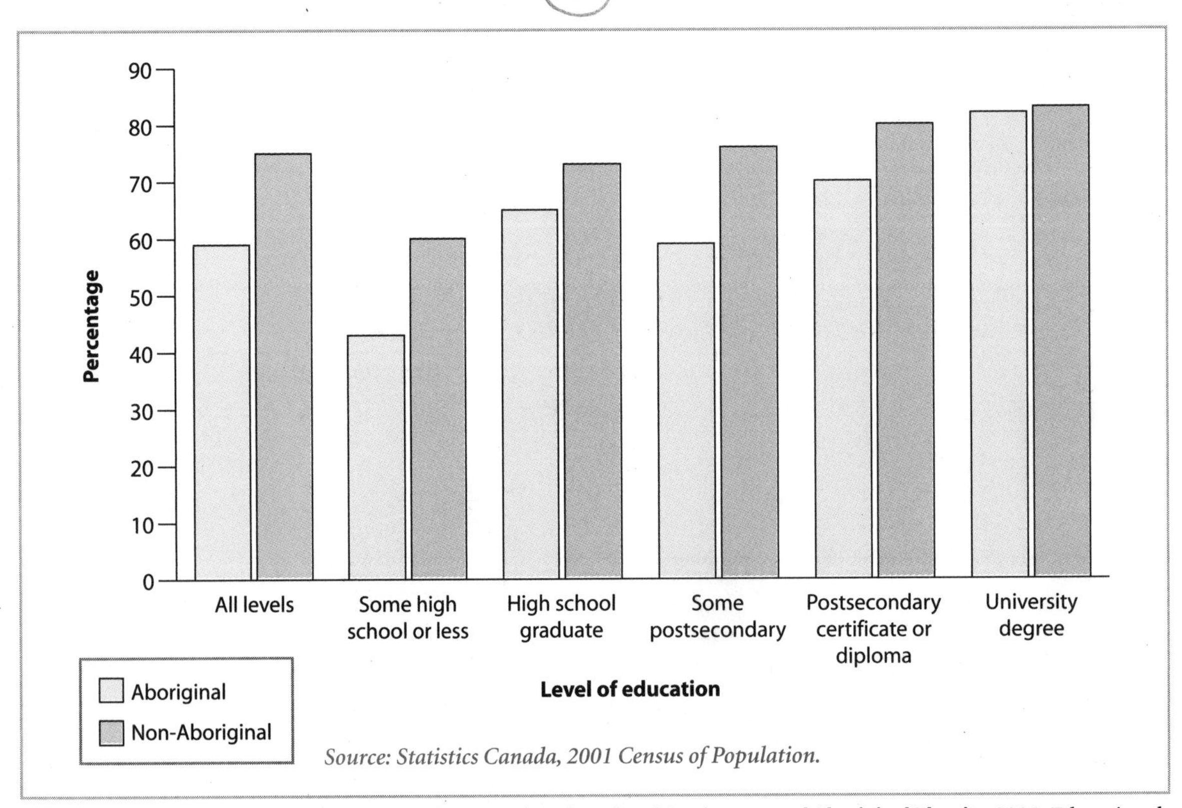

Figure 6.12 Employment Rates of People Aged 25 to 64 by Educational Attainment and Aboriginal Identity, 2001 Educational attainment decreases the employment gap between Aboriginal and non-Aboriginal people.

EMPLOYMENT RATES AND EDUCATIONAL ATTAINMENT

Educational attainment has a considerable positive impact on employment rates of First Nations women and men, according to INAC and the 2001 census:

- Thirty-two percent of First Nations women without a high school certificate were employed, compared with 41 percent of non-Aboriginal women.
- This figure increased to 71 percent for First Nations women with a college certificate, diploma, or degree, compared with 72 percent of non-Aboriginal women.
- Employment rates for First Nations women with a university degree increased to 84 percent, compared with 78 percent for non-Aboriginal women.
- Forty-two percent of First Nations men without a high school certificate were employed, compared with 62 percent of non-Aboriginal men.
- This figure increased to 81 percent for First Nations men with a college certificate, diploma, or degree, compared with 83 percent for non-Aboriginal men.
- Employment rates for First Nations men with a university degree increased to 86 percent, compared with 82 percent for non-Aboriginal men.

Place of Residence

From 1996 to 2001, the employment rate gap between the Aboriginal and non-Aboriginal populations aged 15 and older decreased, particularly in urban areas. In 2001, Aboriginal peoples in urban areas were more likely to be employed than those living elsewhere (see Figure 6.13).

In 2001, the employment rate for the on-reserve Aboriginal population was 37.7 percent, almost the same rate as in 1996. However, 54.2 percent of Aboriginal people living in non-reserve areas had jobs in 2001, compared with 47 percent in 1996. Between 1996 and 2001, the population of working-age Aboriginal people rose by 26 percent both on-reserve and off-reserve, but employment increased by 44 percent for those living off-reserve, compared with 30 percent for those living on-reserve.

Aboriginal Representation in Employment Sectors

Figure 6.14 looks at employment sectors in which Aboriginal people are the most over- or under-represented. It shows that Aboriginal people are under-

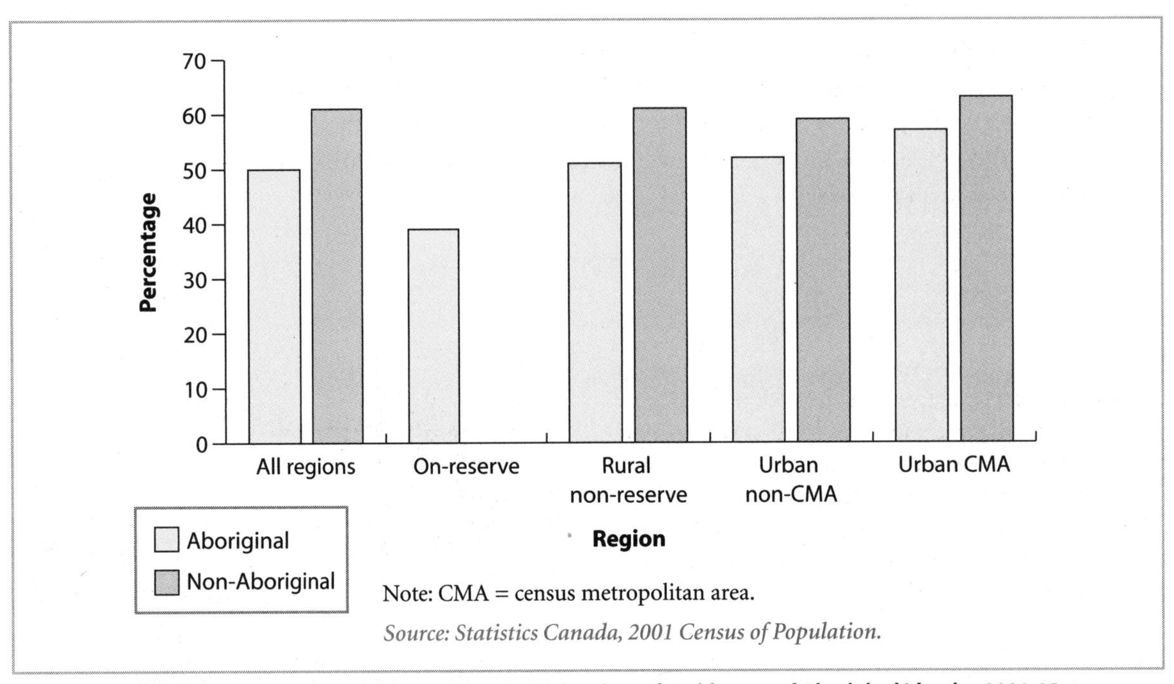

Source: Statistics Canada, 2001 Census of Population.

Figure 6.13 Employment Rates of People Aged 15 and Older by Place of Residence and Aboriginal Identity, 2001 Non-reserve Aboriginal people are more likely to be employed.

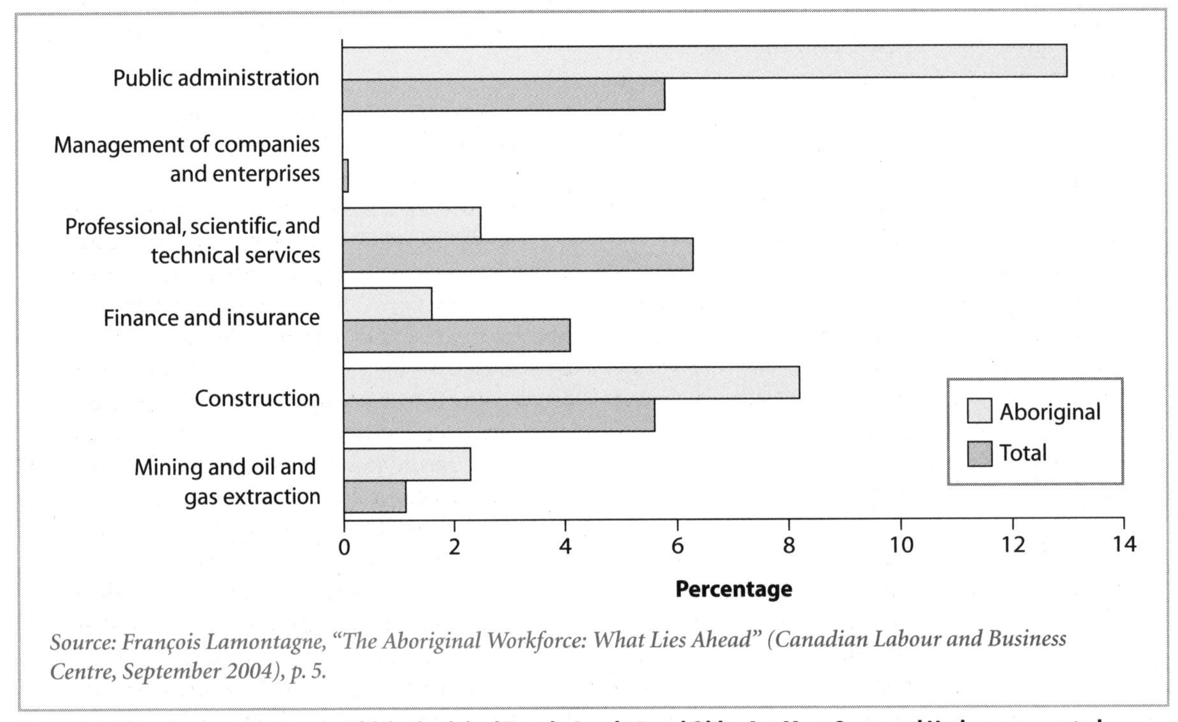

Source: François Lamontagne, "The Aboriginal Workforce: What Lies Ahead" (Canadian Labour and Business Centre, September 2004), p. 5.

Figure 6.14 Employment Sectors in Which Aboriginal People Aged 15 and Older Are Most Over- and Under-represented Compared with people in the total labour force, Aboriginal people are over-represented in public administration (which includes local government such as band administration), mining, oil and gas extraction, and construction.

represented in management of organizations, finance and insurance, and professional, scientific, and technical services. Many of these jobs require university or college degrees; as explained earlier in this chapter, the percentage of Aboriginal people with a university degree is significantly below that of the general population.

Aboriginal Entrepreneurs

Throughout Canada, the businesses founded by Aboriginal entrepreneurs are creating jobs and contributing to the local and national economies. Food, fashion, video production, transportation, and high-technology services are just a few of the areas where dynamic young entrepreneurs are making their mark.

Virtual Circle

Virtual Circle is the inspiration of 25-year-old owner Darrick Baxter, a member of the Martin Falls First Nation near Thunder Bay, who now lives and works in Winnipeg. "I first got the idea back in high school," says Baxter, "when computer-related assignments were the order of the day. Since the notion of 'community' is so central to First Nations, it was natural for me to think of creating a virtual community on the Internet to present authentically Aboriginal perspectives."

He founded Virtual Circle—The Aboriginal Community when he was just 21. "The Web site is a work in progress," says Baxter, who is also completing his BA in political science at the University of Winnipeg. The site changes and grows continuously, he adds, presenting "social, political, and economic theories from an Aboriginal point of view." Visitors can select from a wide variety of topics in the Aboriginal Index, visit the Guest Book, and try the History Quiz. Baxter's latest venture is adding real estate services to Virtual Circle's offerings.

"Virtual Circle—The Aboriginal Community, first and foremost, is a service to mobilize First Nations communities and support the cause of Aboriginal peoples across Canada and the United States. There's absolutely no charge for anyone participating," Baxter emphasizes. "We have a business—Virtual Circle Multimedia—that supports our community work." Virtual Circle Multimedia is a business success in its own right, and a natural spin-off of Virtual Circle.

Figure 6.15 Melanie Goodchild launched the Internet-based Aboriginal Youth Business Council when she was 24.

"The Virtual Circle Web site is the showcase for our Web design work, and the multimedia business is an outcome of getting the Virtual Circle site going in the first place," Baxter explains. Several First Nations professionals look after different aspects of the business while he concentrates on developing and designing Web sites for a wide range of businesses and organizations. These include Industry Canada, the Government of Manitoba, Aboriginal Business Canada, and a fashion designer.

"We pride ourselves on our development and design, and technical savvy," he emphasizes. "Our quality shows. But equally important is our ability to help clients think through every aspect of their Internet future. That's why we stress training to help clients become their own Web site managers. This lowers their costs and also helps them steer their own destinies." Clients also know that when they deal with Virtual Circle [Multimedia], they are contributing to the larger community that is Virtual Circle.

"I think that the Aboriginal community has to look toward politics and other avenues, but most importantly we must think of what Matthew Coon Come said about us missing the Industrial Revolution. Let's not miss the Information Technology Revolution. We have to develop ourselves—our professional selves—in this area, so that Aboriginal businesses are the backbone of our success. Just give us time, and Virtual Circle will prove that virtual reality can come true!"

Karin Lynch, "Virtual Circle—Internet Community Alive and Growing," Indian and Northern Affairs Canada, April 23, 2004; http://www.ainc-inac.gc.ca/nr/ecd/ssd/col29_e.html.

1. Predict what might happen if unemployment among First Nations people remains high.
2. What strategies would you propose that would economically benefit First Nations people in the future, especially since First Nations populations are increasing?
3. Some First Nations have opened casinos in their communities. What do you think are the advantages and disadvantages of casinos for First Nations peoples and their communities?
4. One of the reasons for the high rate of unemployment among First Nations people is that there are few jobs on reserves.
   a) Do you think that First Nations people should leave their reserves in order to work, or should jobs be created on the reserves? Give reasons for your answer.
   b) How would you suggest that jobs be created on reserves?
   c) What might be the effects on the Aboriginal concept of sovereignty of having to work off-reserve?

INCOME

Just under 413,000 people who identified themselves as Aboriginal reported employment income in 2000. This figure represented 63 percent of the total Aboriginal population aged 15 and over. Among the general population, 69 percent of those aged 15 and older reported employment income. One in 15 Aboriginal people reported being without income, compared with one in 23 non-Aboriginal people.

Low-Income Statistics

In 2001, 37.3 percent of First Nations aged 15 and older reported having a low income, compared with only 12.4 percent of the non-Aboriginal population.

Average Employment Income

- According to the 2001 census, the average employment income for Aboriginal people was $32,176, compared with $43,486 for the total non-Aboriginal population.
- The majority of Aboriginal people worked part year or part time. In 2001, just over 25 percent of Aboriginal people who reported employment income worked for the full year on a full-time basis, compared with 37 percent of the total population.
- Regardless of whether Aboriginal people worked full time or part time in 2001, their employment income was considerably lower than the national average. A full-year, full-time Aboriginal worker earned $33,416 on average—23 percent lower than the national average. Aboriginal people working part year or part time earned $13,795—28 percent lower than the national average.
- The average earnings of Aboriginal people were lower in every age and education category. There were also much larger concentrations of Aboriginal people in the education levels that are associated with lower earnings. Approximately 43 percent of Aboriginal people aged 15 and older had not graduated from high school, compared with about 31 percent in the overall population.
- About one of every four Aboriginal earners lived on a reserve. In 2001, 35 percent of these individuals worked full year, full time. Their average employment income was $28,355—18 percent lower than the $34,696 earned by those living off-reserve.

Aboriginal people with employment income report lower incomes than do people in the general population. Describe ways in which a lower income may affect access to health care, education, and consumer products.

SOCIAL ASSISTANCE

Aboriginal people rely on social assistance more than any other group in Canada. To put this fact into perspective, however, the expenditure of social assistance on Aboriginal people represents about 3 percent of total social assistance payments.

INAC's Social Assistance Program helps First Nations people living on reserves to meet their basic needs for food, clothing, and shelter. It also funds special-needs allowances for goods and services that are essential to physical and emotional well-being, for example, basic furniture, physician-recommended foods, and counselling to assist people in becoming independent.

INAC's participation in social assistance is largely to provide funding to First Nations. In turn, First Nations deliver programs and services to community members—78 percent of funding is spent on child and family services and 22 percent is spent on adult care. In 2002–2003, 532 First Nations managed their own programs. (This figure does not include First Nations with self-government arrangements.)

A Cycle of Dependence

Social assistance has created serious problems for Aboriginal people as a group. Factors such as lack of employment opportunities have created a cycle of dependence that is difficult to break. In *Aboriginal Peoples in Canada*, James Frideres says that many Canadians believe that Aboriginal people are responsible for their need for social assistance. The danger in this assumption is that it draws attention away from more critical issues. Laying blame on those needing social assistance ignores such realities as lack of education, discrimination, poverty, lack of employment opportunities, and low self-esteem. According to Frideres, these issues prevent Aboriginal people, as well as other Canadians on social assistance, from fully participating in Canadian society.

Funding of Services and Programs

To understand the services and programs that address Aboriginal issues, it is helpful to know their source of funding. In general, the majority of this funding comes from the federal government. Indian and Northern Affairs Canada, Health Canada, Canada Mortgage and Housing Corporation, and Human Resources Development Canada are collectively responsible for 97 percent of the total federal funding going to Aboriginal people.

INAC's expenditures represent 71 percent of all federal funding, going almost exclusively to Status Indians living on-reserve. As a result of the **devolution** process, 82 percent of INAC's funding for programs is administered by First Nations themselves. It is important to understand that 80 percent of INAC's program expenditures are for basic services provided to other Canadians through provincial, municipal, and territorial governments. The funding from the other departments is directed at Aboriginal populations both on- and off-reserve.

devolution
the surrender of powers to local authorities by a central government

The Future

Despite the efforts that have been made to improve the quality of life of Aboriginal people, much work still needs to be done. In order to experience the same standard of living enjoyed by many Canadians, Aboriginal people

CLOSE-UP

THE HISTORY OF SOCIAL ASSISTANCE FOR ABORIGINAL PEOPLE

Scholars are often driven into research after witnessing the effects of disturbing social realities firsthand. Professor Hugh Shewell at the Atkinson School of Social Work [York University, Toronto] is no exception. Shewell's interest in Aboriginal welfare began in 1983 when he took a job with the federal Indian and Northern Affairs Department overseeing welfare services in British Columbia.

"Whenever I visited reserves," says Shewell, "I was always given this short jarring history lesson concerning injustices suffered by [Aboriginal peoples]." Other members of Shewell's delegation would check their watches or glaze over, bored. Shewell, however, listened carefully. "Our Aboriginal hosts wanted to remind us that they weren't just the vague subjects of some government policy on a piece of paper," he says.

Over time, the history lessons sank in, and two decades later, Shewell's research efforts have yielded the first major history of Aboriginal welfare in Canada, *Enough to Keep Them Alive: Indian Welfare in Canada, 1873–1965.* But far from simply a history of Aboriginal welfare policies, Shewell's book ... charts a troubled relationship, assimilation, and resistance.

The book begins by tracing how the Hudson's Bay Company gave Aboriginal fur traders relief during difficult winters in which fur was not easily obtainable. "Over time," says Shewell, "Aboriginal peoples became dependent on this early form of social assistance. Eventually, the Bay transferred this responsibility to the federal government, and relief policies evolved into welfare policies." These welfare policies were largely based on 19th-century English poor laws—archaic laws that viewed social assistance as a last resort when an individual had failed in the marketplace because of ineptitude or laziness.

"But Aboriginal philosophies were not based on the individual's ability to make it in some capitalist marketplace," explains Shewell. "[Aboriginal peoples] were much more communal, much more community minded. And so our attempts to apply English welfare policies to their way of life represented nothing less than an attempt to assimilate them—an attempt that many have ironically resisted by accepting welfare and refusing to participate in our capitalist economy."

Source: Jason Guriel, "Prof Traces Unsettling History of Aboriginal Welfare," YFile, August 10, 2004 (Toronto: York University); http://www.yorku.ca/yfile/archive/index.asp?Article=3164.

are working toward healing themselves and their communities. Aboriginal communities are continuing to strive for greater autonomy over services provided to them. Many Aboriginal people see education as a key component in the process toward self-determination.

Improving the overall health and prosperity of Aboriginal people depends largely on improving their economic and social conditions. This can be accomplished through Aboriginal self-determination strategies—the abilities to identify their own needs and to develop and implement their own strategies. By doing so, Aboriginal communities can assume greater responsibility for the overall well-being of their people.

WORKING TOWARD SELF-DETERMINATION

A two-day gathering that brought together over 100 Aboriginal and non-Aboriginal business leaders, as well as experts and practitioners who deal with Aboriginal business, wrapped up today [December 14, 2004] in Ottawa. The session tackled a set of issues and proposed ideas for action toward economically stronger, healthier and self-reliant Aboriginal people and communities.

"This is an unprecedented opportunity for Aboriginal people and for Canada to take a fresh look at how to build on existing Aboriginal entrepreneurial capacity and economic performance," said the Honourable David L. Emerson, Minister of Industry. With a 30 percent increase in the number of Aboriginal [people who are] self-employed since 1996, a 25 percent rise in the number of working-age Aboriginal people and a business creation rate nine times the Canadian average for self-employment, the consensus at the session was that there is momentum that must be sustained and built upon.

"There are many challenges to moving forward, and we cannot ignore the [size] of the task ahead, but significant results have been achieved by the various players working together—governments, organizations, the private sector, and individuals," said Minister Emerson. "Aboriginal people must be part of developing the solutions to key economic challenges."

As a result of the Canada–Aboriginal Peoples Roundtable held on April 19, 2004, the Government of Canada and roundtable partners committed to following up with six sectoral sessions on lifelong learning, health, housing, negotiations, accountability and results, and economic opportunities. Sectoral follow-up sessions to extend the work of the roundtable have been implemented over the fall, and will conclude in January. The sessions are jointly planned by the federal, provincial, and territorial governments, along with the five national Aboriginal organizations [Assembly of First Nations, the Inuit Tapiriit Kanatami, the Métis National Council, the Congress of Aboriginal Peoples, and the Native Women's Association of Canada]. They are designed to generate recommendations to government and Aboriginal leadership so that further development and consideration of options may occur at a spring 2005 policy retreat and subsequent First Ministers Meeting on Aboriginal Issues.

Source: Industry Canada, "Minister of Industry Leads Session on Aboriginal Economic Opportunities," news release, December 14, 2004; http://www.ic.gc.ca/cmb/welcomeic.nsf/ICPages/NewsReleases.

Affirmative Action

A number of the social problems and health issues in Canada's Aboriginal communities are rooted in the past mistreatment of Aboriginal peoples. In order to redress this mistreatment, many people believe that the government must take responsibility for its actions in the past. They maintain that Aboriginal people should be given as many opportunities as necessary in order to integrate into the larger community. This includes funding for Aboriginal education, Aboriginal-oriented criminal justice programs, and compensation.

It is feared that Aboriginal cultures will be lost if the Canadian government does not help to preserve them. Affirmative action is seen by some as an acceptable way of "levelling the playing field." Historical wrongs against Aboriginal peoples have created a cycle of poverty, under-education, and unemployment. Quotas for university seats and public service positions, among other things, can help rectify past mistakes and create a stronger Aboriginal identity.

1. In this section, you learned that Aboriginal people rely on social assistance more than any other group in Canada. Draw a diagram of the cycle of dependence that illustrates why this situation exists. For example, limited access to health care means that people are unable to work; people unable to work have little income; little income means that people can't pay for higher education; a lack of education results in lower-than-average income; lower-than-average income results in stress and poor health, etc.
2. What can be done to alleviate Aboriginal people's reliance on social assistance? Refer to the Close-Up feature on page 172 in your answer.

Aboriginal Peoples and Affirmative Action Programs

Courts in Canada and the United States have upheld affirmative action programs; in fact, affirmative action is written into the *Canadian Charter of Rights and Freedoms.* However, there are two sides to this issue. You explored one side on page 173 of this chapter. The other side maintains that affirmative action, either in an employment or educational setting, does not necessarily lead to advancement for the affected group. Further, it can create resentment among the general population. Aboriginal people should not be told that their historical hardship justifies lower standards and automatic acceptance.

From the University of Alberta, "Admission of Aboriginal Students":

> 14.1.1 General Statement
> The University of Alberta is committed to the recruitment, retention and graduation of Aboriginal students. The University also recognizes that Aboriginal applicants have traditionally been underrepresented in higher education, and has adopted the Aboriginal Student Policy (see Section 108.13 of the GFC Policy Manual) with a view to having the University's Aboriginal student population attain a level that is at least proportionate to the Aboriginal population of the province.
>
> In order to facilitate appropriate representation of Aboriginal students on campus, additional qualified applicants may be considered over and above the Aboriginal students who are admitted in the regular competition for places in a Faculty. Aboriginal applicants who wish to be considered for such additional places must attain the minimum admission requirements of their chosen program as prescribed by the University and its Faculties and Schools. To assist the University in achieving this overall goal, Faculties are encouraged to set aside places specifically for Aboriginal applicants, the number being consistent with the available pool, student interests, and available teaching and learning support services.

For more information on University of Alberta admissions, see www.registrar.ualberta.ca/calendar.

Use the general statement above to write two fictional letters to the editor of your local newspaper and one real letter to the editor (see the instructions below). Keep in mind that the Canadian government has a treaty obligation to pay for secondary education for Aboriginal students.

1. Pretend that you are an Aboriginal student who is attempting to gain admission to the University of Alberta's law school. Write a fictional letter to the editor in support of the University of Alberta's affirmative action program. Be sure you support your position.
2. Pretend that you are a non-Aboriginal student who is applying to the same law school. Write a fictional letter to the editor against affirmative action, expressing your concern about someone's being admitted to the school with a lower scholastic average than your own. Be sure to outline clear arguments that someone against affirmative action might use.
3. Finally, write a real letter to the editor, expressing your own views on affirmative action.

CHAPTER 7

Aboriginal Peoples and the Canadian Justice System

LEARNING OBJECTIVES

In this chapter, you will

- discover the traditional forms of social control used by First Nations and Inuit societies
- understand how European contact created conflict with traditional Aboriginal concepts of justice
- recognize ways in which the Canadian government imposed its laws on Aboriginal societies
- understand why Aboriginal peoples want to maintain their traditional rights
- explore the issue of domestic violence in Aboriginal communities
- recognize that Aboriginal peoples are disproportionately represented in the Canadian prison system
- investigate alternative forms of justice designed to meet the needs of Aboriginal peoples

INTRODUCTION

In this chapter, you have the opportunity to learn about the traditional methods of social control that were practised in Aboriginal societies before the arrival of Europeans in North America. You'll come to understand the difference between Aboriginal peoples' traditional concepts of law and justice and those of the mainstream Canadian justice system. You'll see how the government of Canada has imposed its standards of justice on Aboriginal peoples and the challenges this has created for them. You'll also look at some of the key legal issues in Aboriginal society, in particular, Aboriginal rights and domestic violence. Finally, you'll have the opportunity to explore alternative approaches to justice that reflect traditional Aboriginal values.

TRADITIONAL SOCIAL CONTROL

Prior to European contact, First Nations and Inuit peoples were self-governing societies. Each culture had its own system of government and law that reflected its values, practices, and traditions. Traditional systems of social control regulated personal and community interaction within three key areas: property laws, interpersonal conflicts, and international relations.

Contrary to the European stereotype of First Nations and Inuit cultures as lawless societies, each culture had its own social controls for enforcing laws and administering justice:

"There were no written laws, of course, merely rules and injunctions handed down by word of mouth. ... Persuasion and physical force were the only methods of arbitrating disputes. ...

"Fear of the blood-feud was a powerful restraint on murder, and social disapproval, more keenly felt in small communities than in large, checked the commission of many lesser crimes. ..."

Diamond Jenness, Indians of Canada, *7th ed. (Toronto: University of Toronto Press, 1989), p. 125.*

mediation a method of resolving conflicts in which a neutral third party facilitates a mutually acceptable solution between disputing parties

restitution giving back or compensating for something that has been lost or taken away

Historically, First Nations and Inuit cultures resolved disputes in their societies through **mediation**. Offenders were confronted directly to help them understand the consequences of their actions and to settle conflicts to the satisfaction of all concerned. The focus was on healing communities rather than punishing offenders.

In most Aboriginal societies, offenders were expected to make **restitution** for their crimes. If they failed to do so, the families of the offenders and the victims intervened. If their efforts failed, communities applied their collective disapproval by shunning or admonishing the offenders until they agreed to make amends. If they still failed to do so, the offenders were banished from their communities for a period of time. In extreme or chronic cases, repeat offenders were permanently exiled. In a harsh environment, this was equal to the death penalty because individuals relied on the community for survival.

Resolving Disputes in Selected Cultures

Although the goal of all First Nations and Inuit cultures was to heal their communities, each culture had its own unique methods for resolving disputes. In the Dene Nation, social control was based on a three-tiered system. When two people came into conflict, they first attempted to resolve the problem themselves. If they were unable to do so, they approached an Elder to act as a mediator. If this failed, the community applied its collective public opinion to force the offender to act toward resolving the conflict. In most cases, community disapproval was enough to motivate the offender to make restitution.

During the annual buffalo hunt in the Nehiyaw (Plains Cree) and Anishnaabe (Plains Ojibwe) cultures, several hunters were assigned to maintain order, watch out for enemies, and prevent eager young hunters from rushing ahead and frightening the herd. If a hunter broke the rules of the hunt, his possessions were seized and his tipi was slashed. In extreme cases, the offender was flogged. If the hunter accepted the consequences of his actions without rebellion, his possessions were returned. If he offended again, he was banished or killed.

The Anishnaabe (Ojibwe) lived in a harsh environment with a cold climate. Their survival depended upon obtaining the resources they needed. Cooperation among community members was vital to their survival, so acts of aggression were carefully monitored. Aggressive behaviour was minimized in Anishnaabe society because the people believed the spirits used their supernatural powers to punish offenders. They believed that great misfortune would befall a person, or even an entire community, if people acted inappropriately. Therefore, Anishnaabe society was able to function without a structured system of social controls.

Although each Aboriginal culture had its own method of resolving disputes, the focus was always on atonement and forgiveness rather than punishment and incarceration. This approach contrasts sharply with the concepts of law held by the Europeans who would eventually settle in North America and impose their values and governmental systems on the people who already lived here.

39

EARLY JUDICIAL CONFLICTS BETWEEN ABORIGINAL AND NON-ABORIGINAL LAWS

Imposing Foreign Laws

When Europeans came to North America, they brought their own values and concepts of law with them. At first, they applied these laws only to themselves. Over time, however, Europeans and some First Nations formed alliances. These relationships sometimes led to confusion because the French and British systems of justice, which differed from each other, both conflicted with Aboriginal concepts of law.

In time, the Europeans took over more and more land in what is now Canada. As they did so, they increasingly imposed their laws and concepts of justice upon all those who lived here. The First Peoples protested against the newcomers' interference with their traditions and customs. Ultimately, however, they were powerless to stop it as they struggled to understand a system of justice that was foreign to them.

VOICES

Today, many Aboriginal peoples argue that the enforcement of foreign laws on their cultures reflects the cultural bias that Europeans first brought to North America over 500 years ago:

"The imposition of foreign laws as supreme is totally unjust. The notion that English Common Law and French Civil Law supersede First Nations Law was and is based on racist and colonial attitudes. To imagine inviting a person into your home and having that person dictate to you that your authority and your laws are of no value and that theirs are supreme is totally racist and borders on insanity."

Carl Roberts, former chief of the Roseau River Band, in The Report of the Aboriginal Justice Inquiry of Manitoba *(Winnipeg: Aboriginal Justice Implementation Commission, November 1999), Chapter 7.*

As you discovered in Chapter 5, when the new nation of Canada was created, the federal government was given responsibility for First Nations peoples. It used the powers of the *Indian Act* to assimilate them into mainstream Canadian society. One of the ways they attempted this was to ban many of the First Nations' sacred ceremonies and celebrations.

Banning the Potlatch

One ceremony that the federal government was determined to eliminate was the potlatch. This was an important ritual in West Coast First Nations' cultures. It served many purposes, such as mourning the death of a chief, acknowledging a new chief, and celebrating a marriage. During the potlatch, gifts such as masks, copper plates, artwork, clothing, jewellery, and food were bestowed upon the guests. Traditionally, gift giving was a means of improving one's social status within the community—the more a person gave away, the greater was the person's status. The potlatch also served an important economic function because it redistributed community wealth.

Historically, the Canadian government did not understand the potlatch or its significance. Missionaries disapproved of it because they believed it created an obstacle to their efforts to convert people to Christianity. The government disapproved because it believed such ceremonies stood in the way of assimilating West Coast First Nations. So in 1884, the government banned the potlatch.

The ban forced the ceremony underground as many communities continued to hold potlatches in secret. Those who were caught were charged, convicted, and jailed. Ceremonial masks and gifts were seized and sold to museums and art collections across North America.

The potlatch ban was not lifted until 1951. Since then, the ceremony has been restored in many West Coast communities as part of the cultural revival taking place in Aboriginal societies across Canada.

VOICES

In 1884, a group of missionaries issued the following report to the government:

"During the whole winter, schools are deserted by all those children whose parents attend the dance. ... When the winter is over they have squandered all their summer earnings and are compelled to leave their homes and roam about in their canoes in search of food, and thus neglect cultivating their lands and sending their children to school. ... Church and school cannot flourish where potlatching holds sway."

Figure 7.1 Tlingit Potlatch Ceremony Dancers pose in traditional ceremonial attire at the Tlingit Village of Chilkat, 1895.

1. How does the traditional Aboriginal concept of justice differ from the Euro-Canadian system?
2. Consider this scenario: Serina and her three children live in their own home next door to a neighbour who often has loud parties that last late into the night. One night, Serina is awakened by loud music coming from her neighbour's backyard. Her children are awakened, too, and the youngest begins to cry because of the noise. An angry Serina goes over to the neighbour's house to ask him to turn down the music. An argument breaks out, and the neighbour—a large man—shoves Serina away. She falls to the ground, breaking her arm.
   a) How would this situation be resolved under the traditional Aboriginal concept of law?
   b) How would this situation be resolved under the mainstream Canadian justice system?
3. Why did the Canadian government ban the potlatch? What impact do you think this ban had on West Coast cultures? What impact do you think it had on the younger Aboriginal generations?
4. Today, many First Nations people want the sacred artifacts that were seized during the potlatch ban returned to them. Do you think the federal government has an obligation to buy back these artifacts and return them to First Nations? Give reasons for your answer.

LEGAL RIGHTS

Some of the key legal issues in Aboriginal societies involve the preservation of traditional rights and the desire for self-government.

Hunting and Fishing Rights

Among the legal issues in today's Aboriginal communities is the maintenance of traditional hunting and fishing rights. Historically, hunting and fishing were the primary means by which Aboriginal peoples obtained food. While the introduction of new foods and technologies has reduced the need to hunt and fish, these activities continue to play an important role for many Aboriginal peoples, especially in northern communities. Hunting and fishing are symbolically important, both as a legal right and as part of a people's cultural identity.

The issue of Aboriginal hunting and fishing rights has led to legal battles as well as violent confrontations in many parts of Canada. While federal treaties recognize Aboriginal hunting and fishing rights, other laws passed since the treaties were signed have restricted hunting and fishing. Aboriginal peoples have argued that they are exempt from these laws because of the provisions in the treaties. However, the courts have not always agreed.

Treaty Rights versus the Law

In 1916, the federal government passed an act restricting the hunting season on migratory birds. For years, however, this law was not applied to Aboriginal hunters. Then, in 1968, the treaty promises that guaranteed First Nations hunting rights were called into question. In a precedent-setting case, an Aboriginal hunter in the Northwest Territories was charged under the act after killing a duck out of season. Although his First Nations band was protected under the terms of Treaty 11, the man was convicted of the charge. The court ruled that even though the federal government had signed Treaty 11, the legislation banning the hunting of birds out of season superseded treaty promises. This decision set the stage for ongoing legal battles over hunting and fishing rights.

Today, Aboriginal peoples continue to fight for the right to hunt and fish. In most cases, the courts consider whether the people traditionally relied on hunting and fishing for their livelihood. If they did, their rights to hunt and fish today are usually upheld.

Land Claims and Self-Government

Many Aboriginal peoples believe they have the right to govern themselves because they never willingly gave up their **sovereignty**. In recent years, some Aboriginal groups have succeeded in negotiating a degree of self-government. In 2000, for example, the Nisga'a of British Columbia signed a treaty that granted them self-government over land, resources, and their culture, language, and family life (see Chapter 4).

sovereignty
having independence and freedom from external control; the right to self-government

The Creation of Nunavut

The most far-reaching agreement to date, however, was the creation of the territory of Nunavut in 1999. The new territory gave the Inuit 2 million square kilometres in the central and eastern Arctic, with direct ownership of 350,000 square kilometres, along with a cash settlement of $1.4 billion and a $13 million trust fund. The government of Nunavut was given a wide range of powers over the territory's natural resources and its education and justice systems. It was also given the power to enact laws affecting wildlife and the environment.

BIOGRAPHY

JOHN AMAGOALIK (1947–)

Figure 7.2 John Amagoalik

The people of Nunavut often refer to John Amagoalik as the "Father of Nunavut" for his determination in creating Canada's newest territory. Amagoalik joined a team of Inuit leaders in 1975 to negotiate the Nunavut Land Claim Agreement. He then served as chief commissioner of the Nunavut Implementation Commission, which designed and planned the new territorial government.

Amagoalik has always worked to represent the Inuit in Canadian politics and society. Between 1981 and 1991, he held two terms as president of the Inuit Tapiriit Kanatami. He was also a driving force behind the Inukshuk Project, which became the Inuit Broadcasting Corporation. In 1998, Amagoalik received the National Aboriginal Achievement Award in recognition of his significant contributions to Inuit political rights in Canada.

VOICES

The desire of many Aboriginal groups to gain self-government does not mean that they are seeking independence from Canada. It means they want the right to govern themselves within Canada:

"I recognize that we live within the country called Canada. … So we recognize that Canada is going to be in control over certain matters. We recognize that the province is going to be in control over certain matters. And we recognize that we are in control over certain matters in our own reserves. And where there's overlapping, there's going to be joint sharing of that responsibility with the Canadian or provincial governments."

Louis Stevenson, chief of the Pequis band in Manitoba, in Pauline Comeau and Aldo Santin, The First Canadians *(Toronto: Lorimer, 1995), p. 71.*

A number of violent confrontations have occurred between First Nations and federal and provincial governments over hunting and fishing rights. These include incidents at Ipperwash in Ontario and Burnt Church in New Brunswick.

1. Find out more about these confrontations. What were the root causes? Why did the people resort to violence?
2. Do you think there are times when violence is justified? Give reasons for your answer.

DOMESTIC VIOLENCE

One of the biggest legal and social problems in Aboriginal communities today is domestic violence. While domestic violence cuts across all demographics in Canada, it is particularly widespread among Aboriginal families. No other social problem is more debilitating in these communities. Domestic violence takes many forms: **physical abuse**, **psychological abuse**, **sexual abuse**, **incest**, **financial abuse**, and **spiritual abuse**. It affects all family members, but the most obvious victims are women and children.

physical abuse a physical act intended to harm, injure, or inflict pain on a person

psychological abuse the use of psychological tactics to break down a person's morale and self-esteem in order to control that person

sexual abuse any act of unwanted sexual attention or exploitation toward a person

incest any form of sexual contact between family members

financial abuse the deceitful use of another person's money or assets

spiritual abuse the erosion of a person's cultural or religious beliefs

The Roots of Domestic Violence

The roots of this disturbing problem run deep. They are closely connected to the loss of Aboriginal culture and traditions. Today, poverty, unemployment,

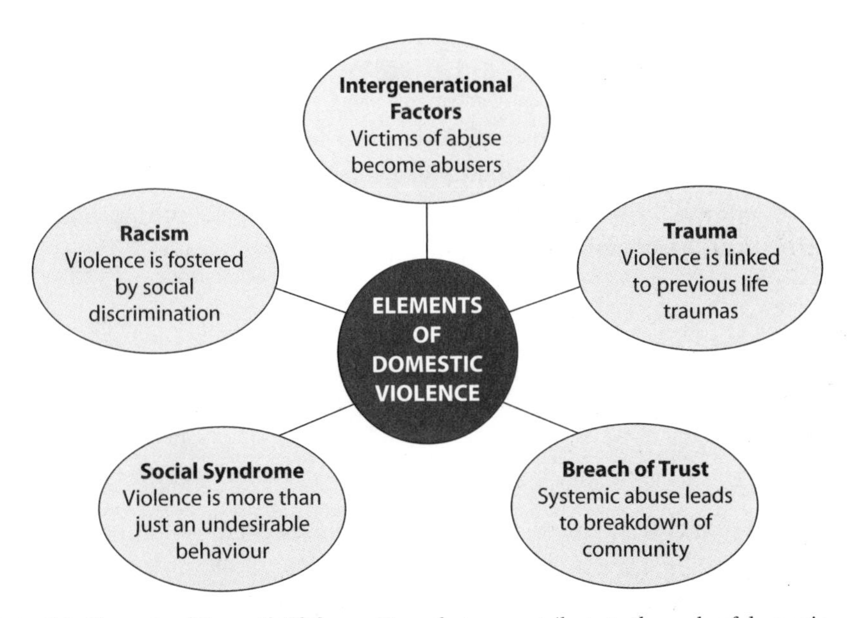

Figure 7.3 Elements of Domestic Violence Many factors contribute to the cycle of domestic violence in Aboriginal communities.

VOICES

Domestic violence is not part of traditional Aboriginal cultures. In 1996, the Royal Commission on Aboriginal Peoples noted the root causes and impact of domestic violence on Aboriginal communities:

"The pattern of family violence experienced by Aboriginal people shares many features with violence in mainstream society. [However,] it also has a distinctive face. ... First, Aboriginal family violence is distinct in that it has invaded whole communities and cannot be considered a problem of a particular couple or an individual household. Second, the failure in family functioning can be traced ... to interventions of the state deliberately introduced to disrupt or displace the Aboriginal family. Third, violence within Aboriginal communities is fostered and sustained by a racist social environment that promulgates demeaning stereotypes of Aboriginal women and men and seeks to diminish their value as human beings and their right to be treated with dignity."

Royal Commission on Aboriginal Peoples *(1996), pp. 54–56.*

lack of education, poor housing, and other social issues all contribute to this devastating pattern of violence. The situation is critical on many reserves and in enclaves of Aboriginal populations in urban centres.

A Culture of Violence

Domestic violence often spreads from generation to generation. In many Aboriginal families, abuse is a chronic problem that has been passed down through three and even four generations. Women who are abused by their husbands often respond by becoming abusive themselves, usually toward their own children. In turn, children who face violence and abuse often grow up to become violent and abusive teenagers and adults. As a result, today domestic violence is ingrained in many Aboriginal communities, creating a **culture of violence**.

culture of violence a community or society in which violence is a distinguishing characteristic

Spiritual Abuse

Some Elders use their position of power and influence to cover up acts of abuse. They misrepresent spiritual teachings to persuade their victims that inappropriate acts are acceptable. Because people are taught to honour and respect their Elders, it is difficult for them to confront an Elder who is behaving inappropriately. And so the abuse continues unchecked.

In some instances, imposters who claim to have the right to perform certain spiritual ceremonies pose as healers and shamans. Some of these imposters defraud people of their money by charging high fees to perform healing ceremonies. Others use their false positions to violate women and children.

Addictions and Violence

Substance abuse is closely linked to domestic violence. In fact, alcohol is involved in most cases of domestic violence. Often, the level of violence is in direct proportion to the level of alcohol use, or use of other dangerous substances. Gambling addictions also contribute to domestic violence as a family's limited financial resources are squandered by the gambler. Family arguments over money often erupt into violent confrontations.

Eliminating Domestic Violence

Leaders in the Aboriginal community believe that the only effective way to deal with the problem of domestic violence is to reclaim traditional ways.

FACTS ABOUT DOMESTIC VIOLENCE

It is difficult to be precise about the number of cases of domestic violence, because abuse often goes unreported. However, the following statistics provide "snapshots" of violence among Aboriginal families:

- Between 1991 and 1999, spouses were responsible for killing 62 Aboriginal women and 32 Aboriginal men—a rate eight times higher than for non-Aboriginal women and 18 times higher than for non-Aboriginal men (Canadian Centre for Justice Statistics, 2001).
- Aboriginal women between the ages of 25 and 44 are five times more likely to die from violence than non-Aboriginal women in the same age group.
- In 1999, 25 percent of Aboriginal women and 13 percent of Aboriginal men reported acts of violence from a current or former spouse in the previous five years (Statistics Canada, 1999).
- In 2001, 49 percent of Aboriginal women who were physically abused reported physical injuries; 23 percent required medical attention, and 39 percent feared for their life (Canadian Centre for Justice Statistics, 2001).
- In 2001, 37 percent of Aboriginal women and 30 percent of Aboriginal men reported experiencing psychological abuse in the past five years (Canadian Centre for Justice Statistics, 2001).

They believe that their communities will heal by reclaiming languages, storytelling, ceremonies, and other expressions of traditional culture. In order for this healing to occur, women must regain their place in Aboriginal societies as givers of life. Elders and senior members of the community must be honoured and respected. The value of families must be recognized and strengthened. Only by healing Aboriginal communities and societies will the pattern of domestic violence be broken.

The goal of the National Aboriginal Circle Against Family Violence is to eliminate domestic violence.

WOMAN OF THE DAWN

by Wenona Gardner

I am the heart of my family.
I am the centre of my community.
I carry the nation on my back.
I carry the life of tomorrow in my soul.

I rise above the violence.
Bones heal. Bruises fade. My fear I face.
The rage I channel to protect myself.
To protect my children.
I walk away from the destruction
With my Great Creator by my side.

I am the one who can change the tide.
I am the one who will say STOP!
No more forever.

For I am the Woman of the Dawn.
I rise with the morning sun,
Blazing with light, love, and hope.
I hold the future within me.

The National Aboriginal Circle Against Family Violence; http://www.nacafv.ca.

1. Create a web diagram illustrating the factors that contribute to domestic violence.
2. What do you think should be done to eliminate domestic violence?

ABORIGINAL PEOPLES AND THE JUSTICE SYSTEM TODAY

Aboriginal people in Canada are more likely than non-Aboriginals to have some contact with law enforcement. They are more likely to be victims of crime, to be witnesses to crime, and to be arrested for committing crimes than non-Aboriginal people.

Why are Aboriginal people more likely to come into conflict with the law? Historically, the inequities in Canadian society have left Aboriginal children, youth, and families without the support services they need. They have been deprived of their land, their cultural traditions, and their way of life. These inequities and injustices have created great challenges for Aboriginal people. The lack of educational opportunities leads to high levels of unemployment. As a result, many Aboriginal people are forced to live in poverty, and their poor living conditions often lead to substance abuse and domestic violence. These, in turn, contribute to a higher incidence of crime.

This explanation only partly illustrates the problem. Aboriginal people have endured prejudice and discrimination by political institutions, the judicial system, and society at large. In many communities, over-policing contributes to high rates of incarceration. An Aboriginal person is more likely to be charged with an offence than a non-Aboriginal person in a similar situation.

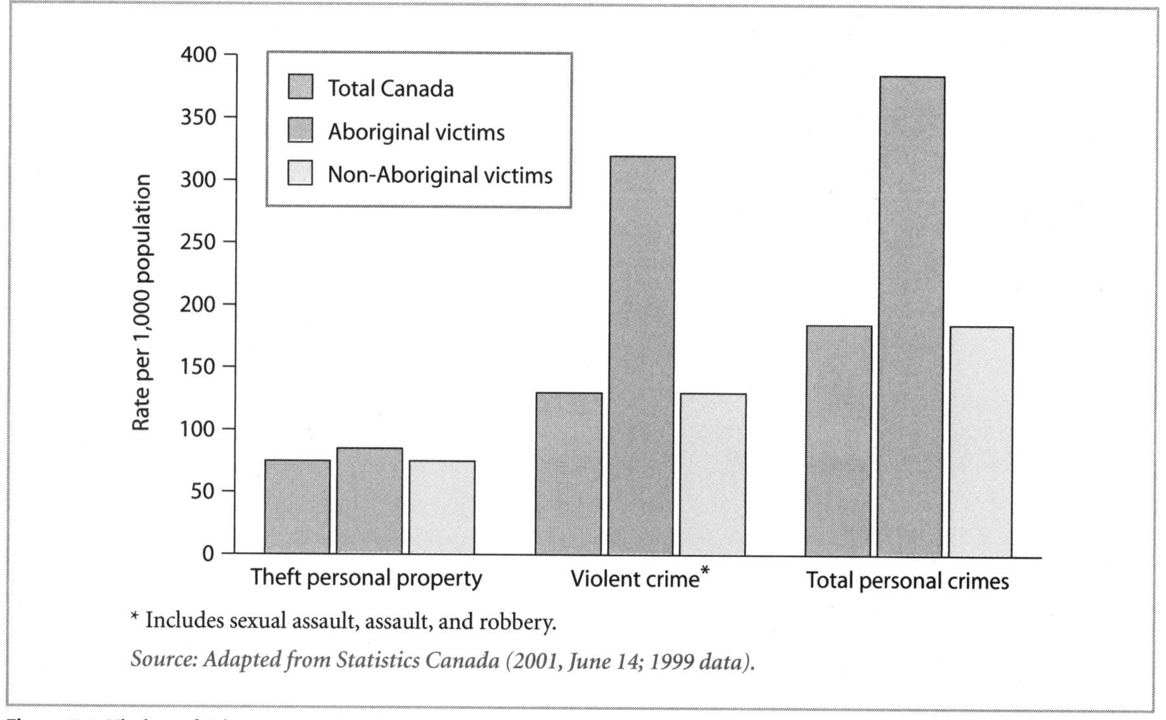

* Includes sexual assault, assault, and robbery.

Source: Adapted from Statistics Canada (2001, June 14; 1999 data).

Figure 7.4 Victims of Crime, 2001 This graph shows the rates of theft and violent crimes for Aboriginal and non-Aboriginal people in Canada.

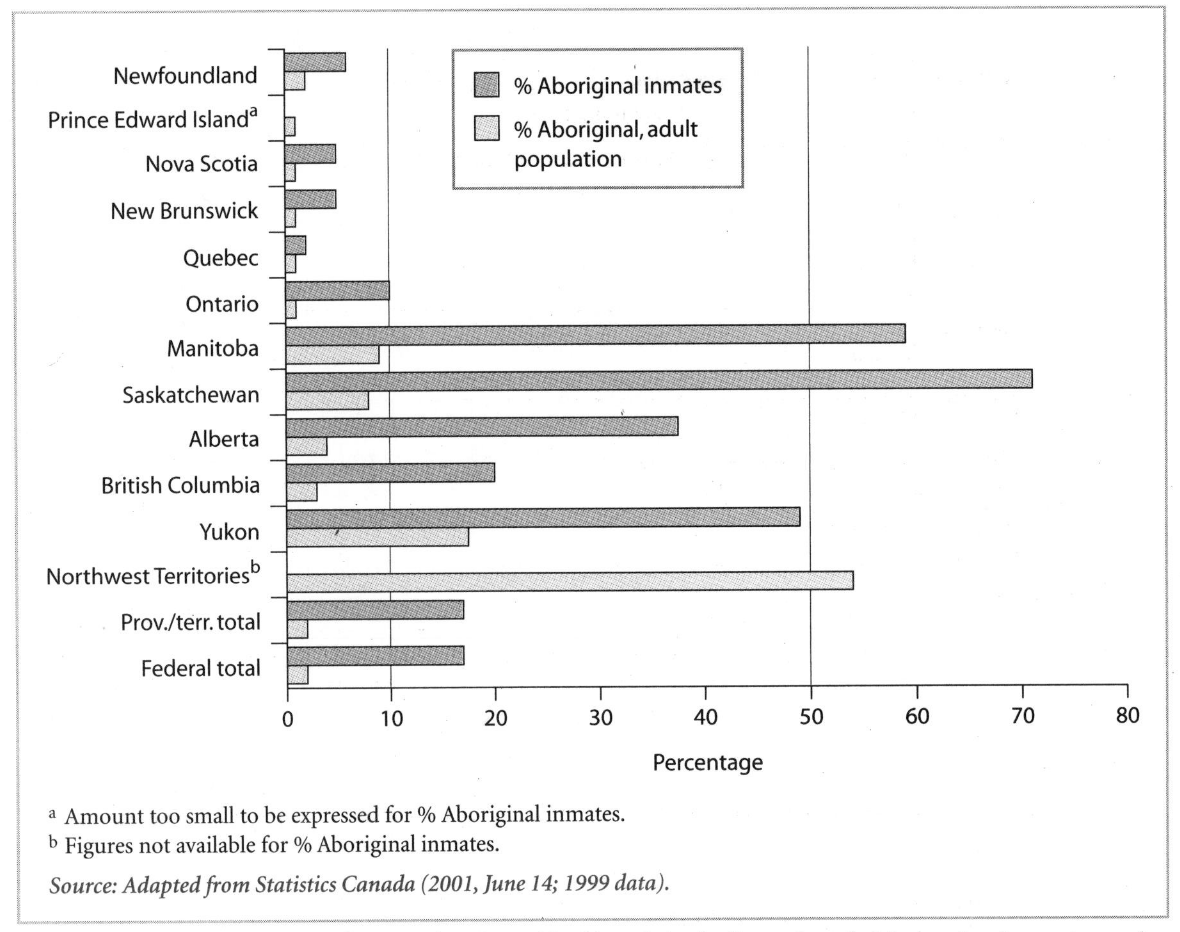

Figure 7.5 Aboriginal Adults in Custody, 2001 There is considerable variation in the number of adults in prison by province and territory. In some prisons in the western provinces and the territories, up to 95 percent of the inmates are Aboriginal people.

racial profiling focusing on a particular race or culture

Studies have found that while on patrol, police often apply **racial profiling** to determine whom to arrest and detain. In cities with significant Aboriginal populations, police often patrol bars and streets in Aboriginal neighbourhoods with greater frequency than they patrol non-Aboriginal neighbourhoods. This practice increases the likelihood that Aboriginal people will be arrested.

Aboriginal people are also arrested more frequently than non-Aboriginal people for minor offences. While police rarely arrest non-Aboriginals for being intoxicated in public, Aboriginal people frequently face such charges. They are concerned that they are over-policed for such minor offences, while their communities are under-policed when it comes to more serious crimes, such as assault and domestic violence. Many people believe that the police do not do enough to intervene in cases of domestic violence.

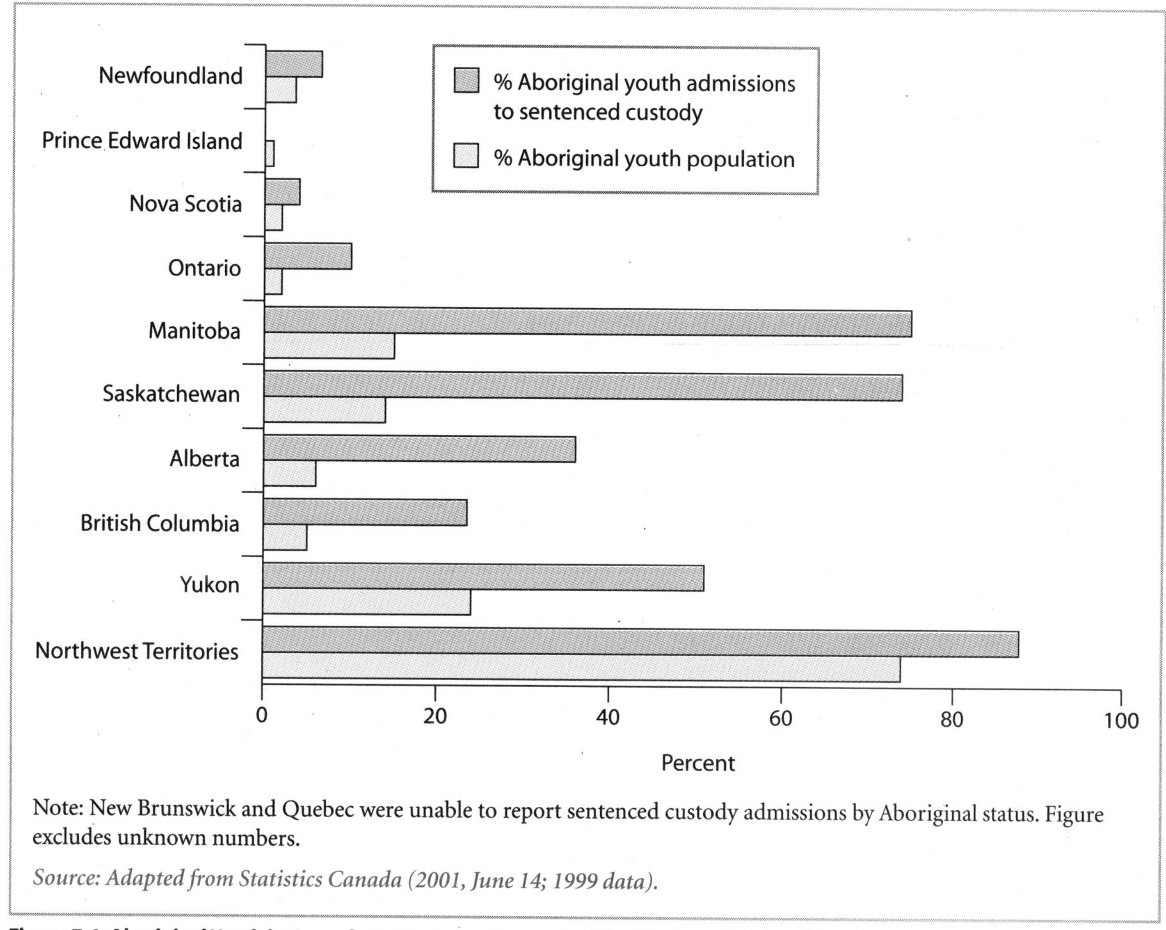

Note: New Brunswick and Quebec were unable to report sentenced custody admissions by Aboriginal status. Figure excludes unknown numbers.

Source: Adapted from Statistics Canada (2001, June 14; 1999 data).

Figure 7.6 Aboriginal Youth in Custody, 2001 According to the First Nations Child and Family Caring Society, First Nations youth in Canada are more likely to be incarcerated than to graduate from high school.

Crime among Aboriginal Youth

As more Aboriginal people move to urban centres, young people are increasingly exposed to crime, including criminal gangs in which violence and abuse flourish. As a result, a disproportionate number of Aboriginal youth are arrested for a variety of criminal acts, including assaults and murders. In prison, they learn to identify with the values of prison gangs and other criminals. Upon their release, they take these values with them to their communities, where they perpetuate the cycle of violence and crime.

Aboriginal Peoples within the Justice System

Although Aboriginal peoples are overrepresented in the criminal justice system, they are dramatically underrepresented in the system as staff. Less

CLOSE-UP

FACTS ABOUT ABORIGINAL PEOPLES AND THE JUSTICE SYSTEM

- Aboriginal people are overrepresented in Canada's prison system. Although they represent 4.4 percent of the adult population, they account for nearly 18 percent of Canadians who are incarcerated.
- Aboriginal people who are arrested and incarcerated are usually unemployed and have low levels of education.
- Aboriginal youth are overrepresented in the criminal justice system and account for 25 percent of all juvenile offenders sentenced to custody.
- On the prairies, 40 percent of federal inmates are Aboriginal. In some Manitoba prisons, the percentage is as high as 60 percent.
- More Aboriginal women than men are in provincial jails. In Saskatchewan, Aboriginal women are eight times more likely to be arrested than non-Aboriginal women.
- Aboriginal offenders are less likely to receive parole and temporary passes and are less likely to be accepted into halfway houses.
- Aboriginal people are three times more likely than non-Aboriginals to be victims of violent crime and are at even higher risk for being victims of assault, sexual assault, robbery, and domestic violence.

than 1 percent of all police officers in Canada are Aboriginal. Provincially, only 2.7 percent of people working in correctional services are of Aboriginal heritage. This figure is only slightly higher at the federal level, with 4 percent of employees with Correctional Service Canada being Aboriginal. The number of Aboriginal justices of the peace and judges is also extremely low.

Although professionals in the justice system have the power to use discretion in cases involving Aboriginal people, lack of cultural sensitivity continues to contribute to high rates of incarceration. Aboriginal offenders face **systemic discrimination** and are more likely to be found guilty of crimes regardless of the strength of the evidence. In many cases, simply being an Aboriginal person contributes to guilty verdicts and subsequent sentences.

systemic discrimination laws and policies that are inherently prejudicial to a group or culture

For most Aboriginal peoples in Canada, the mainstream legal system does not reflect their traditional perceptions of justice. The courts, police services, corrections centres, and other services are foreign concepts. Aboriginal peoples believe that there have been limited attempts to recognize or understand their concepts of law and justice. They feel that the justice system has rejected them. In turn, they have rejected the justice system.

BIOGRAPHY

FAUNA KINGDON (1985–)

Many young people in Aboriginal communities are working to make a difference. One such person is Fauna Kingdon. A Métis born in Manitoba, Kingdon and her family moved to Iqaluit when she was five years old. She began volunteering to help others at the age of 14. By the time she was 16, she was a volunteer for the Nunavut Kamatsiaqtut Help Line, where she provided help and counselling for troubled youth and served as a juror for the Youth Court Advisory Panel. Kingdon has received many awards in recognition of her achievements and contributions, including the National Aboriginal Achievement Award in 2005.

Figure 7.7 Fauna Kingdon

Concepts of Law in Aboriginal Societies	Concepts of Law in the Mainstream Canadian Justice System
• Community values should be taught by Elders and other respected members of the community • Offenders should be counselled by community leaders and councils • Elders, community members, and clan leaders should mediate and negotiate disputes and reconcile offenders with their victims • Offenders or their families should compensate victims and their families • Offenders are reluctant to testify on their own behalf and/or they plead guilty to avoid confrontation	• Society has the right to protect itself from those who threaten to harm its members or its property • Punishment should be directly proportional to the offence, with judgment imposed by legal authorities • Retribution and incarceration punish offenders and deter potential offenders; rehabilitation helps them re-enter society • Offenders should admit to their wrongdoing and express remorse • Offenders must defend themselves in the adversarial setting of a courtroom

Figure 7.8 Two Concepts of Law This table highlights the differences in the concepts of law in Aboriginal societies and in Canada's mainstream criminal justice system.

Many Aboriginal leaders argue that the only way to ensure Aboriginal justice is to establish an Aboriginal legal system based on traditional values and concepts:

"We ... believe that our own laws are important and need to be respected and applied in our daily lives. Unfortunately, neither Parliament, the legislature, nor the judiciary fully understand our rights and laws."

Ovide Mercredi, former national chief of the Assembly of First Nations, in The Report of the Aboriginal Justice Inquiry of Manitoba *(Winnipeg: Aboriginal Justice Implementation Commission, November 1999), Chapter 7.*

TALKING CIRCLE

1. Look at Figure 7.4. What patterns can you identify? What might explain the reason that rates for theft among Aboriginal and non-Aboriginal people are similar, while the rates for violent crimes are not?
2. Are you aware of any instances of racial profiling in your community? Do you think that there are ever any circumstances under which racial profiling is justified? Give reasons for your answer.
3. How might systemic discrimination be eliminated from the Canadian justice system?

ALTERNATIVE METHODS OF JUSTICE

Since the report of the Royal Commission on Aboriginal Peoples in 1996, many initiatives have aimed to adapt Canada's mainstream justice system to meet the needs and reflect the cultural traditions of Aboriginal peoples.

Community Policing

Community policing applies a holistic approach to law enforcement in both Aboriginal and non-Aboriginal communities. The duties, responsibilities, and activities of the police are part of the public and social institutions of the community. The police act in partnership with the community to share the responsibility for maintaining law and order.

The focus of community policing is on the prevention of crime. Aboriginal police officers take a proactive

Aboriginal Police Officers
In the 1970s, Aboriginal police forces were created to supplement mainstream law enforcement. Today, Aboriginal police officers have replaced most non-Aboriginal officers on First Nations reserves. The number of Aboriginal people in the general police population remains small, however. Only 2.5 percent of RCMP officers are Aboriginal.

approach to resolving underlying problems in the community rather than reacting to events after the fact. This decentralization of community policing allows resources to be managed locally so that police can respond to local issues. It is also flexible to reflect changes in the community and adaptable so that it can be applied to diverse customs and practices in various communities across Canada.

Court Workers

More Aboriginal court workers are available to help Aboriginal defendants. These justice employees ensure that Aboriginal defendants have legal counsel. They explain the court process, offer advice about postponements and appeals, write pre-sentencing reports, and translate proceedings into Aboriginal languages. Court workers also provide support services to Aboriginal inmates in jail.

Legal Clinics

Community clinics provide legal advice and representation at no cost to any Canadian who cannot afford a lawyer. Today, some Aboriginal communities

BIOGRAPHY

ROBERTA JAMIESON (1953–)

Figure 7.9 Roberta Jamieson Roberta Jamieson has earned a reputation as a skilled negotiator and mediator in resolving conflicts.

Roberta Jamieson was born on the Six Nations reserve at Grand River near Brantford, Ontario. Throughout her life, she has worked to become a leader in First Nations and Canadian society. She has been a pioneer in both politics and law, achieving a variety of "firsts": the first female First Nations lawyer in Canada, the first non-MP to be appointed to a House of Commons committee, the first female **ombudsman** in Ontario, and the first female chief of the Six Nations.

Jamieson is highly regarded in Canada for her work promoting non-adversarial methods of conflict resolution. Internationally, she is respected for advancing democracy through institutional change in countries around the world. Roberta Jamieson is known as a committed and passionate leader who is a role model for all Canadians.

ombudsman
a government official appointed to investigate citizens' grievances against the government

have legal clinics serving Aboriginal clients. Legal representation is critical to ensure that Aboriginal people understand the Canadian justice system and that their spiritual beliefs are not exploited in an attempt to gain a confession.

Justices of the Peace

The Aboriginal Justices of the Peace Program was developed to train, recruit, and appoint Aboriginal justices of the peace. Today, many of these justices serve in areas with large Aboriginal populations, both on reserves and in urban centres. While justices of the peace must abide by federal and provincial laws, they can use their discretionary powers to incorporate an Aboriginal perspective to ensure that the quality of justice better reflects Aboriginal values.

Restorative Justice

Restorative justice programs take a community-centred approach to rehabilitation. They are consistent with traditional Aboriginal values and concepts of law because they focus on healing rather than punishment.

sentencing circle a form of community justice for offenders practised in some Aboriginal communities

The most common form of restorative justice is the **sentencing circle.** A sentencing circle is made up of court officials, members of the community, the offender, and the victim. All participants gather in a circle to listen to the facts of the case. Then they discuss how to determine an appropriate sentence

Figure 7.10 A Sentencing Circle in Winnipeg Volunteers from Aboriginal Ganootamaage Justice Services of Winnipeg take part in a sentencing circle. Such restorative justice programs are increasingly used in many Aboriginal communities as well as some courtrooms. The concept has also been adopted in many public schools in partnership with local law enforcement.

CLOSE-UP

A SENTENCING CIRCLE IN ACTION

In 1999, two 18-year-old Inuit boys set fire to a school in Kangiqsualujjuaq, a small town of 450 people in northern Quebec. The school was destroyed in the blaze, and the boys pleaded guilty to the crime. The judge imposed a sentencing circle to determine the fate of the young offenders. The judge, court officials, a missionary, a teacher, and 13 members of the community sat on the sentencing circle, along with the two boys. In an emotional meeting that lasted more than four hours, the sentencing circle reached a decision: the boys should be placed on probation for two years, during which time they would serve 15 hours a week doing community service while attending school regularly. The judge accepted the sentence, but added that the boys had to apologize to the community on the local radio station.

for the offender that satisfies all concerned. The objective is to administer a sentence that reconciles the offender with the victim and acts as a deterrent to committing future crimes. Sentencing circles last for as long as it takes to reach consensus (in which everyone agrees with the final outcome), although the judge remains the final authority.

The sentence that is handed down typically depends on the severity of the crime. It may include community service, mandatory counselling, admission to a treatment facility, monetary fines, or other forms of restitution. If the defendant complies with the conditions of the sentencing circle, the charges are dropped in the courts. If the defendant fails to comply, the court process is resumed.

Decisions reached in sentencing circles are sensitive to local cultural needs and issues. They provide Aboriginal people with a vehicle for a greater degree of self-determination, and they help the community develop the ability to handle problems and assume responsibility for the actions of its members.

Young Offenders and the Justice System

Canada's Department of Justice has developed the Youth Justice Renewal Initiative to help Aboriginal communities deal with young offenders using a restorative justice approach. The communities receive funds to help them develop their capacity to participate in the sentencing options outlined in the *Youth Criminal Justice Act*, implemented in 2002. The new Act is modelled in part on the Aboriginal healing circle. It provides non-judicial sanctions for first-time offenders who are charged with non-violent crimes. These sanctions include restitution, community service, and anger management programs. They must be agreed to by all parties, including the victim, and in all cases the offender must write a letter of apology to the victim. Young offenders who complete their sentences during the prescribed period do not receive a criminal record.

Creating a Fairer System of Justice

Today, many initiatives to create a fairer system of justice—one that takes into account the needs of Aboriginal people—are beginning to make an impact. Progress is being made toward addressing Aboriginal rights and reducing the high rate of crime and incarceration among Aboriginal communities. It is the responsibility of both governments and Aboriginal leaders to continue to foster a relationship of mutual respect in order for Aboriginal peoples in Canada to gain equal status with all Canadians.

1. In what ways do you think community policing can help reduce crime rates in a community?
2. Do you think the sentence that the two Inuit boys received for setting fire to the school was fair? What impact might this sentence have on their future behaviour? Give reasons for your answer.
3. Do you think that sentencing circles are appropriate for all types of crimes? Why or why not?
4. Under the Youth Justice Renewal Initiative, offenders are required to write a letter of apology to their victims. What effect do you think this might have on the offender? On the victim?

CHAPTER 7 CULMINATING ACTIVITY

Conflict over Hunting and Fishing Rights

In 1999 and 2000, confrontation between Mi'kmaq fishers and non-Aboriginal fishers erupted at Burnt Church, New Brunswick. Provincial governments in Atlantic Canada had placed restrictions on the fishing and hunting activities of First Nations peoples. Their actions defied treaties established in 1725, 1752, and 1760 that recognized First Nations' right to hunt and fish in traditional lands. However, in 1999, the Supreme Court of Canada overturned the provinces when it ruled that the Mi'kmaq had the right to fish to earn a "moderate livelihood."

The Mi'kmaq responded by making plans to regulate the fishery by working together with non-Aboriginal fishers. However, at Burnt Church, conflict erupted after the Mi'kmaq laid a small number of lobster traps in fall 1999. Non-Aboriginal fishers responded by destroying the traps and attacking the Mi'kmaq and their property.

In 2000, the federal government intervened and told the Mi'kmaq at Burnt Church that they could lay a total of 40 lobster traps. The non-Aboriginal fishery, however, was allowed to lay 300 traps. The Mi'kmaq responded by claiming that they had the right to regulate their own fishery, and they made plans to lay 6,000 traps.

The federal Department of Fisheries and Oceans then launched an armed campaign against the Mi'kmaq. Its agents sank Mi'kmaq boats and destroyed their lobster traps. The government's rationale for its actions was that it was defending its right to regulate the fishery. From the Mi'kmaq's point of view, however, setting a limit of just 40 lobster traps violated the Supreme Court's requirement that First Nations be allowed to earn a moderate living, because the quota applied to their entire reserve. They also believed that the regulation violated their historic hunting and fishing rights.

As a class, debate the two sides of this legal issue. Divide into two groups, one representing the Mi'kmaq fishers and the other representing the federal government. Do some additional research into the positions of both sides, including the treaties of the 1700s. Then, conduct a class debate over this ongoing issue. After the debate, discuss how traditional Aboriginal justice might have handled this dispute.

The Resurgence of Aboriginal Cultures

LEARNING OBJECTIVES

In this chapter, you will

- learn about the decline of Aboriginal languages and efforts to rebuild them
- discover why Aboriginal peoples want to reclaim ancient artifacts and ancestral remains
- see how artists of Aboriginal heritage have led a cultural resurgence
- understand how traditional cultures blend ancient traditions with modern technologies to build successful communities
- discover how Aboriginal tourism contributes to cultural revival

INTRODUCTION

In the second half of the 20th century, oppressed peoples around the world challenged the remnants of colonialism and demanded equality. Some proclaimed their independence and forged new nations. Others, like the First Nations, Inuit, and Métis in Canada, demanded the right to sovereignty and self-determination within the framework of their country.

In this chapter, you will discover how Aboriginal peoples today are embracing their traditions and reviving their languages. You will see that they are celebrating their age-old ceremonies and expressing their unique cultures through the arts and the media. As they do so, they give all Canadians the opportunity to explore their rich traditions and to gain a greater understanding of their experiences, beliefs, and values.

REBUILDING LANGUAGES

Loss of the ability to speak heritage languages is one of the key factors that has contributed to the breakdown in transmission of cultural knowledge, values, and beliefs from generation to generation. Today, the number of people speaking Aboriginal languages across Canada is in decline, particularly off reserves. Retaining and transmitting languages is difficult. There are few opportunities to practise these languages, and even fewer opportunities to learn them. The 2001 census in Canada indicated that the percentage of non-reserve First Nations people with the ability to speak their native language fell from 20 percent in 1996 to 16 percent in 2001. Similarly, the number of Métis who were able to speak an Aboriginal language dropped from 8 percent in 1996 to 5 percent in 2001. Only in the far North is the use of an Aboriginal language still strong. In 1996, 82 percent of Inuit knew Inuktitut well enough to conduct a conversation. This figure remained unchanged in 2001, although the census indicated that Inuktitut was being spoken at home less often than in the past.

VOICES

Canada has a history of cultural and linguistic diversity that is an integral part of our heritage:

"Today, there are still about 50 to 70 native languages still functioning in the country and which are in danger of disappearing. … [W]hether these languages are spoken by large groups or only five people, each of these languages [is] part of … our heritage and [is] an important part of the complexity that is our country. When [languages] disappear, a door closes on our understanding of part of what we are because [they] give us access to the complexity of the non-monolithic nature of this country."

John Ralston Saul, in an address to the Canadian Association of Second Language Teachers, May 2, 2002; http://www.caslt.org/Info/may2b.htm.

The 2001 census highlighted the state of Aboriginal languages in Canada. Figure 8.1 shows the percentages of people who speak an Aboriginal language and use it regularly at home. At first glance, the numbers look promising: some languages are holding their own, and usage in a few languages is increasing.

Aboriginal Language	Know the Language % change 1996–2001	Speak It as Primary Language % change 1996–2001
Cree	−3.1	−6.2
Inuktitut	8.7	7.5
Ojibwe	−6.0	−10.1
Dene	10.2	6.8
Montagnais–Naskapi	10.2	8.0
Mi'kmaq	8.2	2.3
Blackfoot	−20.2	−27.1
Algonquian	−8.4	−12.6
Dogrib	−6.8	−7.7
Carrier	−29.3	−34.8

Source: Adapted from Statistics Canada, January 31, 2003.

Figure 8.1 Percentage Change in Selected Language Use between 1996 and 2001 These figures show the percentage of Aboriginal people who know an Aboriginal language and those who speak an Aboriginal language as their primary language.

However, these figures are offset by the rapid rate of decline in many more languages as more and more people speak English or French as their primary language. Today, knowledge of English or French is essential in business, education, and social communications. It is not surprising, therefore, that Aboriginal languages have given way to these larger linguistic groups. When any language disappears, however, it is lost forever.

Relearning and Renewing

In spite of this downward trend, many Aboriginal peoples are determined not to let their languages die. According to the 2001 Aboriginal Peoples Survey, the majority of Aboriginal people believe that retaining and relearning Aboriginal languages is important.

Today, language classes are offered on reserves and at Friendship Centres, women's centres, and preschool and daycare centres. Immersion schools provide the opportunity for Aboriginal youth to learn their native languages. Many secondary schools offer Aboriginal language instruction to people living off reserves. Aboriginal dictionaries, language and grammar texts,

Figure 8.2 Heritage Language Class A teacher of Aboriginal languages gives a lesson in Anishnaabe (Ojibwe) to a grade 12 student. To help Aboriginal peoples retain and relearn their languages and cultures, many communities have developed Aboriginal Head Start programs designed to develop cultural awareness in preschool children.

electronic books, and children's books all help to foster language renewal. However, young people cannot learn their languages in schools and from books alone. They must have the opportunity to speak their languages with others in their homes and communities on a daily basis. Only then can Aboriginal languages recover.

Aboriginal Languages Initiative

In December 2002, the federal government announced plans to commit $172.5 million over 11 years to the Aboriginal Languages Initiative. This program is designed to increase the number of people who speak an Aboriginal language, to encourage the passing down of these languages from generation to generation, and to expand the use of Aboriginal languages in communities.

1. Some people believe that the loss of a language leads to the loss of a culture. Others believe that although culture and language are closely linked, culture extends beyond language. Do you think a culture can survive the loss of its language? Give reasons for your answer.

2. Canada is a land of immigrants, where people from many countries and cultures speak many different languages. What do you think individuals can do to maintain their native languages while still learning to speak one or both of Canada's official languages?

RECLAIMING ANCIENT ARTIFACTS

Another way in which Aboriginal peoples are rebuilding their cultures is by reclaiming their ancient artifacts. After European contact, Aboriginal art treasures, artifacts, and human remains were systematically removed from the societies that created them and taken for display in museums and private collections around the world. Today, Aboriginal peoples are reclaiming these priceless artifacts as they strengthen and rebuild their societies and cultures. They are negotiating with museums and other organizations to have their cultural artifacts returned to them. Some museums have given back these artifacts; others have decided to keep them, but have agreed to their use in special Aboriginal ceremonies. While progress has been made, however, there are still many thousands of Aboriginal treasures in the hands of foreign cultures.

HAIDA REPATRIATION (*YAGHUDANGANG*—TO PAY RESPECT)

After centuries of loss, the Haida of northwestern British Columbia on the Queen Charlotte Islands (called the Haida Gwaii by First Nations) are restoring their culture. Part of this cultural renewal involves repatriating thousands of Haida artifacts and hundreds of human remains that were taken from Haida villages, mostly by collectors at the turn of the 20th century.

Since 1976, when the Royal British Columbia Museum returned 10 totem poles, entrusting them to the Haida Gwaii Museum, the Haida have successfully repatriated many artifacts and ancestral remains. All known human remains in North American museums have been returned to Haida Gwaii for reburial, and 485 individuals have now been laid to rest. An End of Mourning ceremony was held in 2005 to commemorate this achievement. Repatriating human remains is particularly important to the Haida. They believe that when ancestral remains are stored in museums and other unnatural burial sites, the people's souls are left wandering and unhappy. Only when they are laid to rest with respect and honour in their homeland will these souls find peace.

(Concluded on next page.)

CLOSE-UP (concl.)

Many museums, including the Royal British Columbia Museum, the UBC Museum of Anthropology, and the Canadian Museum of Civilization, have cooperated with the Haida's requests for repatriation. Some museums, however, are unable or unwilling to return remains and artifacts. British law, for example, prevents repatriation from its museums, including the extensive collections of the British Museum. But because of the partnerships and goodwill established through the successful efforts to bring home ancestral remains, the Haida are optimistic that, with continued negotiation, museums will agree to return a portion of their collections to Haida Gwaii.

Figure 8.3 Repatriation of Ancestral Remains Members of the audience join Haida dancers during a 2003 ceremony at Chicago's Field Museum. The ceremony celebrated the return by the museum of some 150 human remains to descendants for re-interment in Haida Gwaii, their ancestral homeland.

1. a) In what ways are the artifacts of your culture unique? Give examples.
   b) As an individual, what value do you place on your cultural artifacts? What steps would you take to regain important artifacts that were in the possession of another culture?
2. Do you think that museums and other collectors should return Aboriginal artifacts to the cultures that created them? Why or why not?
3. Why is it important to the Haida to have their ancestral remains returned for reburial?
4. What role do you think the Canadian government should take to persuade foreign countries to allow the repatriation of Aboriginal artifacts?

A RESURGENCE IN THE ARTS

The arts have always played an important part in Aboriginal cultures. Traditionally, they reflect a people's history, their society, and their spiritual world. Art was often both decorative and practical, as many of the tools that people used and the clothing they wore reflected their artistic expressions.

By the dawn of the 20th century, however, many of these rich artistic traditions had been weakened or lost. The misguided attempts to assimilate Aboriginal peoples into mainstream Canadian society meant that many ceremonial objects created by artists were no longer produced. As these artistic treasures disappeared, so did the skills needed to create them. Still, amid this cultural turmoil, a few artists struggled to keep the ancient ways alive. By the middle of the century, the cultural flame of artists of Aboriginal heritage began to be rekindled. They began teaching themselves the artistic traditions and symbols of the past. By the 1980s, this artistic cultural revival had gained strength as Aboriginal leaders and activists demanded that their voices be heard and that their rights be respected. Since then, the art of Aboriginal peoples in Canada has gained recognition and acclaim around the world.

Blending the Old with the New

Many young artists of Aboriginal heritage train as apprentices with older, more experienced artists. They learn traditional techniques that have been handed down from the past and blend these with modern techniques to produce unique art that is both traditional and contemporary.

VOICES

The art created by artists of Aboriginal heritage reflects their societies, both past and present:

"Contemporary [Aboriginal] art is an art of survival, of resistance, of celebration, deeply rooted in the great and sacred tradition of the millennium. The art of the indigenous peoples is neither folkloric nor backward-looking: on the contrary, it is the carrier of meaning and the creator of modernity, and is resolutely turned towards the future."

Robert Houle, Anishnaabe (Saulteaux) artist, "Aboriginal Voices in Canadian Contemporary Art"; http://cybermuse.gallery.ca/cybermuse/teachers/plans/intro_e.jsp?lessonid=44.

BIOGRAPHY

JANE ASH POITRAS (1951–)

Jane Ash Poitras was born into the Mikisew Cree Nation in the remote northern community of Fort Chipewyan, Alberta. When she was just five years old, her mother died of tuberculosis and she was fostered by an elderly German Canadian widow. For the next 20 years, she was denied her cultural heritage.

Figure 8.4 Jane Ash Poitras A popular lecturer at the University of Alberta, Poitras is much in demand as a guest lecturer and speaker at universities and art forums across the continent. She has been an exhibitor and speaker at the invitation of Foreign Affairs Canada at Canadian embassies in Paris, Amsterdam, Washington, and Mexico City.

Poitras graduated from the University of Alberta in Edmonton with a degree in microbiology. Then, in 1981, she reconnected with her First Nations ancestors and decided to study art, first at the University of Alberta, where she completed a bachelor's degree in fine arts, then at Columbia University in New York City, where she completed her master's degree.

Since then, Poitras has become an accomplished and internationally acclaimed artist. Her work, featured in many prestigious collections around the world, explores the continuing impact of colonialism on Aboriginal peoples in North America. It reflects the deep spiritual connection between Aboriginal peoples and the land, and the strength that they gain from this relationship. Poitras's highly expressive mixed-media works place her at the forefront of the Canadian art world. *(Concluded on next page.)*

BIOGRAPHY (concl.)

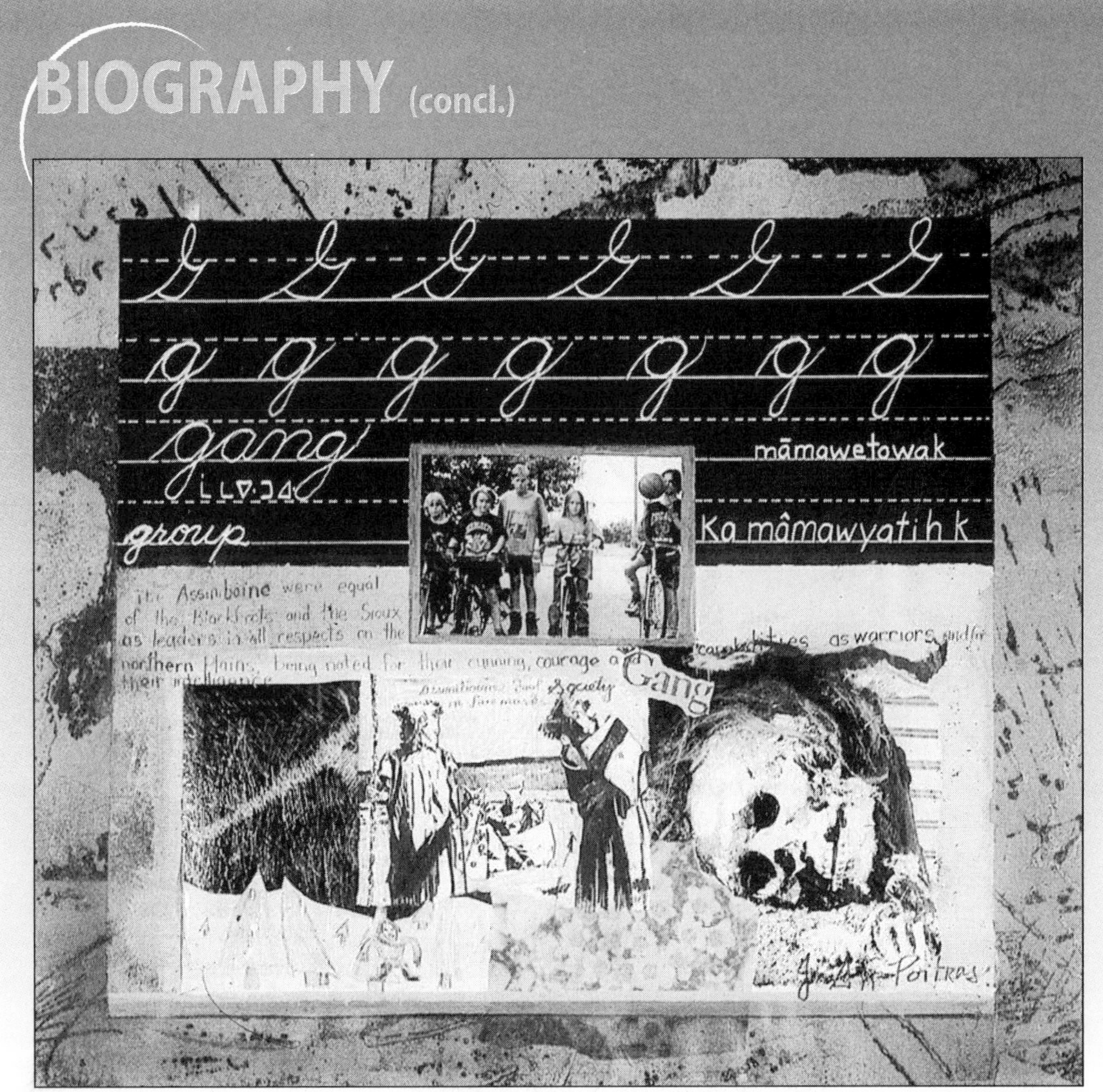

Figure 8.5 Assiniboine-Fool-Society by Jane Ash Poitras What do the images in this work convey to you? Explain.

Métis Cultural Revival

For hundreds of years, the Métis struggled against discrimination, indifference, and ignorance to achieve recognition as a distinct Aboriginal nation. They finally achieved their rightful status when they were officially recognized as one of three Aboriginal cultures in Canada in the *Constitution Act, 1982.*

Over the past two decades, a vital Métis culture has emerged as the people join in the Aboriginal cultural renaissance taking place in Canada. Michif,

Figure 8.6 Lucie Idlout With her hard-hitting lyrics and primal energy, Inuit rock songwriter Lucie Idlout and her band, The Angry Best, have broken free of the musical stereotypes typically associated with Aboriginal people, transcending barriers of culture and geographic location.

Aboriginal Rock Music

The development of Aboriginal rock music has its roots in both culture and politics. Many of the lyrics in Aboriginal songs reflect the oppression, persecution, and displacement of Aboriginal peoples and the clash between traditional and modern values. Their music reflects the increasing confidence of Aboriginal musicians as they entertain and also educate and empower their audience.

the Métis language that blends French, English, and Anishnaabe (Ojibwe), is taught in Métis schools. Métis music and dance, with its roots in the fiddle music of the Red River colony, flourish in their communities and celebrations. Contemporary recordings perform, preserve, and teach the unique Métis musical heritage.

The Métis cultural revival extends to all types of artistic expression. Métis writers produce books, plays, and television and film scripts that tell the stories of their heritage. Métis painters, illustrators, and sculptors keep their culture alive by creating works that reflect both traditional and contemporary culture and values.

Flower Beadwork People

Métis women are well known for their skill in the traditional arts of beading, embroidery, quilling, and finger weaving. The Plains peoples called them the "Flower Beadwork People" because of their skill and agility in creating beadwork.

Blending Past and Present in Inuit Society

The Inuit people of the Arctic have succeeded in blending their traditional values with modern technologies to build a prosperous society. Today, Inuit of all ages rely on such modern technologies as snowmobiles and all-terrain vehicles for land transportation. Community airstrips have state-of-the-art navigational equipment to facilitate air transport. Even in small communities, satellite dishes and communications towers dot the horizon. Most family homes are equipped with the technologies needed to communicate anywhere in the world. Yet, the Elders and the traditional stories they tell are still the spiritual foundation of these communities. Inuit values and traditions are integrated with the realities of the modern world to ensure a productive and prosperous past, present, and future.

BIOGRAPHY

MARIA CAMPBELL (1940–)

Maria Campbell was born in Spring Valley, Saskatchewan, to parents of Cree, Scottish, and French heritage. In her best-selling autobiography, *Halfbreed*, Campbell told the story of her struggle as a Métis woman in Canada and the racism and discrimination that she and all Métis people faced.

At the age of 12, Campbell was forced to quit school to raise her siblings following the death of their mother. To keep her family together, she married a Euro-Canadian man at the age of 15. He turned out to be an abusive husband. He reported her family status to welfare authorities, who promptly placed her siblings in foster care.

After losing custody of her family, Campbell moved to Vancouver, where her husband abandoned her. Desperate and unfamiliar with city life, she descended into a nightmare of alcohol and drug abuse. After being hospitalized following two suicide attempts and a nervous breakdown, Campbell entered Alcoholics Anonymous and began her long journey back from hopelessness and despair. *Halfbreed* recorded the pain, frustration, and anger of those first 33 years of her life.

Since then, Maria Campbell has transformed her life to become an accomplished and acclaimed author, playwright, filmmaker, and university professor.

Figure 8.7 Maria Campbell
Today, Campbell works with the Indigenous Peoples Health Resource Centre at the University of Saskatchewan, and lobbies as a political activist for Aboriginal rights in Canada.

Aboriginal Tourism

Another way in which Aboriginal peoples are reviving their cultures is through tourism. Aboriginal peoples no longer accept being a tourist "attraction." Today, they are leading the way in offering tourist activities that extend beyond hunting, fishing, and trapping to include cultural explorations, heritage parks, village sites, adventure sports, and ecotourism in some of the most beautiful natural settings in the world.

Tourism supports the long-term well-being of Aboriginal communities. It promotes the revival and preservation of Aboriginal cultures and languages and gives Aboriginal peoples the opportunity to design their own businesses. It encourages young people to learn and practise their language and cultural traditions while fostering a sense of pride in their heritage. Aboriginal tourism benefits all Canadians, as it provides an opportunity to learn about

HEAD-SMASHED-IN BUFFALO JUMP

Tourists visiting Alberta have the unique opportunity to learn about and experience the ancient traditions of the buffalo hunt at Head-Smashed-In Buffalo Jump outside Fort Macleod. A designated UNESCO World Heritage Site, Head-Smashed-In was used continuously as a site to hunt and trap buffalo by the Siksika, Kainai, and Piikunii First Nations for over 5,500 years. Today, the site is a leading teaching facility where people can experience the traditional lifestyle, technology, and ecology of the Plains peoples.

Head-Smashed-In Buffalo Jump offers an interpretive centre that blends into the natural environment of the Alberta foothills, where the Rocky Mountains meet the plains. During the summer, visitors have the opportunity to experience life on the prairies, living in traditional tipis from one to three days. They learn at first hand what it was like to live off the land from First Nations guides. At the end of the day, they sit around the campfire as they listen to traditional storytellers.

Figure 8.8 Head-Smashed-In Buffalo Jump The Head-Smashed-In Buffalo Jump Interpretive Centre is ingeniously built into the sandstone cliff at the site near Fort Macleod, Alberta.

Canada from an Aboriginal perspective and contributes to the economic success of the Canadian tourism industry.

Conclusion

In their quest for sovereignty and self-determination, First Nations, Inuit, and Métis peoples are focusing on healing their communities as the first step in rebuilding their nations. They have served notice that they will no longer be tied to the colonial constraints of the past and will no longer accept decisions and laws created without their consent or participation.

> No longer will Aboriginal people stand meekly by as others run things to suit themselves, without taking into serious account the people who were on the scene first. As the case of Canada so well illustrates, its confederation may be young, but it has components that are ancient.
>
> *Olive Dickason,* Canada's First Nations, *3rd ed. (Toronto: Oxford University Press, 2002), p. 430.*

Today, as a new millennium lies before them, First Nations, Inuit, and Métis peoples of Canada are rebuilding their cultures to make them strong again, and are reclaiming their status in the land they have called home since time began.

TALKING CIRCLE

1. Why do you think art has played such an important role in the cultural resurgence of Aboriginal societies?
2. In what ways do you think Aboriginal tourism can help restore a people's sense of identity?
3. Many Aboriginal peoples are concerned about the **appropriation** of Aboriginal culture. Do you think they should be concerned when non-Aboriginal people practise their ceremonies or tell their stories? How would you personally feel if someone who was not a member of your culture appropriated your traditions?

appropriation taking or using as one's own

CHAPTER 8
CULMINATING
ACTIVITY

The Resurgence of Aboriginal Cultures

Throughout this text, you have had the opportunity to learn how Aboriginal societies first flourished all across the land we now call Canada. You have seen how their fortunes changed after outsiders came and took over their land and imposed their own rules. In this final chapter, you have had the opportunity to see how Aboriginal peoples have struggled to overcome these injustices and restore their cultures. Today, Aboriginal peoples want to remain in Canada, but they want to be recognized and respected for their unique cultural identity and their contributions to the nation.

enculturation the process by which the values and norms of a society are passed on

Over the years, the forces of **enculturation** have been at work in Canada. As a class, brainstorm some examples of the ways in which elements of Aboriginal culture have become part of Canadian society. Compile your ideas in a poster, using visuals and colours to enhance your presentation. Consider the contributions of Aboriginal peoples in such areas as food, sports and entertainment, language, and technologies.

The following section highlights some of the contributions of the indigenous peoples of Mexico to North American popular culture.

MEXICAN ACCULTURATION IN THE UNITED STATES

Mexicans have often been called the "forgotten people" of American history because of their lack of inclusion in history books. When they are included, Mexicans are often portrayed in a negative or stereotyped way. This fosters a lack of knowledge and understanding of the contributions that Mexicans have made to North American society and culture. Here are just a few things that originated in Mexico and have been adopted into North American culture.

Food

Enchilada: a tortilla with chili sauce and a filling, usually meat

Taco: a fried corn tortilla folded over and filled with ground meat, tomatoes, shredded cheese, lettuce, and guacamole

Tamale: seasoned ground meat wrapped in cornmeal dough and steamed or baked in corn husks

Margarita: a drink made from tequila and lime juice served in a salt-rimmed glass

Sports and Entertainment

Oscar de la Hoya: A professional boxer who won a gold medal at the Barcelona Olympics and is considered by many to be one of the best prizefighters of all time

Carlos Santana: Leader of the rock band Santana since 1966 who is renowned for his guitar playing

Salma Hayek: Actor born in Mexico who has lived in both Mexico and the United States while pursuing her career

Anthony Quinn: Actor who was confined to small film roles portraying stereotypical characters until he received the Academy Award for the film *Viva Zapata!* in 1952

Language

bronco: wild horse

ranch: from the word *rancho*

chaps: from the word *chaparajos*

hasta la vista: so long

adios: goodbye

the whole enchilada: something in its entirety

the big enchilada: a person or thing of great importance

Glossary

Aboriginal
in Canada, includes Indian, Inuit, and Métis peoples

Aboriginal rights
special rights held by Aboriginal peoples of Canada based on their ancestors' longstanding use and occupancy of the land; for example, the rights of certain Aboriginal peoples to hunt, fish, and trap on ancestral lands

acculturation
the modification of the culture of a group or an individual as a result of prolonged contact with a different culture

allegory
a story in which the meaning or message is represented symbolically

annuity
a sum of money paid yearly

anomie
social instability resulting from the breakdown of standards and values

anthropologist
a scientist who studies human beings, their societies, and their customs

appropriation
taking or using as one's own

archaeologist
a scientist who studies human history and prehistory through the excavation of sites and the analysis of physical remains

artifacts
products of human skill or activity

assimilation
a process in which a cultural group is absorbed by another and takes on its distinctive cultural traditions

autonomy
the right of self-government; personal freedom

birth rate
the number of live births per 1,000 population in a given year

cede
to surrender possession of, especially by treaty

clan
a group of people who share a common ancestor

consensus
general agreement of the group

Crown
the government under a constitutional monarchy

crude mortality rate
the number of deaths per 100,000 population in a given year

cultural genocide
the mass extermination of a people's culture and way of life

culture
the abstract values, beliefs, and perceptions of the world that are shared by a society and reflected in the behaviour of its people

culture of violence
a community or society in which violence is a distinguishing characteristic

demographics
statistics on population numbers, distribution, and trends

devolution
the surrender of powers to local authorities by a central government

ecosystem
a biological community of interacting organisms in a physical environment

egalitarian
promoting human equality, especially with respect to social, political, and economic rights and privileges

enculturation
the process by which the values and norms of a society are passed on

erosion
the wearing away of the Earth's surface by wind, water, or glacial action

evolutionary
gradually developed from a simple to a more complex form

expropriation
the takeover (especially by the government) of property from its owner

extinguish
to nullify a right, claim, etc.

fast
to abstain from food and, in some cultures, water to purify one's self and to connect with the spiritual world

fiduciary
holding something in trust for another

financial abuse
the deceitful use of another person's money or assets

First Nations
an Indian band or community, excluding Inuit and Métis

First Peoples
First Nations and Inuit peoples

genesis
the origin of something

holistic
balanced in all aspects of life—physical, emotional, mental, and spiritual

immorality
under the *Indian Act*, living in a common-law relationship, having a child born out of wedlock, or conducting an extramarital affair

incest
any form of sexual contact between family members

indigenous
people born in a region

inherent
existing, as in a permanent quality; e.g., a natural right

intemperance
the making, selling, purchasing, or drinking of alcohol

interdependence
the state of being influenced by or dependent on one another

Inuit
an Aboriginal people living in the Arctic regions of Canada

jurisdiction
the power or right to exercise authority

kayak
a traditional Inuit sea vessel used for hunting

legacy
something that is handed down from a predecessor

legislation
a law or series of laws passed by the federal or provincial governments

life expectancy
the average lifespan of an individual

lineage
a group of people who share a common ancestor

litigation
legal proceedings

mediation
a method of resolving conflicts in which a neutral third party facilitates a mutually acceptable solution between disputing parties

missionary
a person sent to another country to spread a religious faith and to engage in charitable work

monopoly
exclusive control of the trade in a product or service in a certain market

morbidity rate
the rate of incidence of a disease

mutations
distinct forms produced by genetic change

mythology
traditions or stories involving supernatural characters that embody popular ideas about nature and society

net migration
the effect of in-migration and out-migration on an area's population in a given period, expressed as an increase or decrease

nomadic
moving from place to place in search of food and fresh pasture

ombudsman
a government official appointed to investigate citizens' grievances against the government

oral tradition
information that is passed from one person to another by word of mouth

paternalism
a policy or practice of treating or governing people in a fatherly manner, especially by providing for their needs without giving them rights or responsibilities

physical abuse
a physical act intended to harm, injure, or inflict pain on a person

Prohibition
a period during the 1920s in North America when it was illegal to manufacture, sell, or consume alcohol

provisional government
a government that is serving temporarily until a permanent government comes into power

provisioning station
a place where necessary goods, especially food, can be obtained

psychological abuse
the use of psychological tactics to break down a person's morale and self-esteem in order to control that person

racial profiling
focusing on a particular race or culture

recidivism
a return to a previous pattern of behaviour

restitution
giving back or compensating for something that has been lost or taken away

scrip
a certificate issued to Métis people entitling the holder to land or money for the purchase of land, issued as compensation for lands lost by the Métis after the Northwest Rebellion

sentencing circle
a form of community justice for offenders practised in some Aboriginal communities

Seven Grandfathers
traditional teachings of the Anishnaabe that describe the qualities of wisdom, love, respect, bravery, honesty, humility, and truth that should guide a person's life

sexual abuse
any act of unwanted sexual attention or exploitation toward a person

shaman
a person who has access to the spiritual world

Six Nations Confederacy
an alliance of the Kanien'Kehaka (Mohawk), Oneida, Onondaga, Cayuga, Seneca, and Tuscarora nations

sovereignty
having independence and freedom from external control; the right to self-government

spirituality
in Aboriginal cultures, a belief that all things in the world are alive, have a role in the land, and are therefore worthy of respect

spiritual abuse
the erosion of a person's cultural or religious beliefs caused by another

subculture
a group that has the general characteristics of a culture, but also has distinctive features in its values, norms, and lifestyle

systemic discrimination
laws and policies that are inherently prejudicial to a group or culture

theory
a system of ideas based on general principles that explains a fact or event

Three Sisters
corn, beans, and squash, which were planted together in the same mound so that the corn stalks supported the climbing beans and the leaves of the squash discouraged weeds

treaty
an agreement between two states that has been formally concluded and ratified

umiak
a large, flat-bottomed boat used by the Inuit to hunt and carry freight

usufructuary right
the right to use and benefit from the land

vision quest
a sacred ceremony in which a person goes to a secluded place to communicate with the spirit world

ward
a person under the protection or care of another

worldview
a group's view of the world and its relationship to it

Index

Abenaki, 5
Aboriginal Diabetes Initiative, 153
Aboriginal Head Start program, 155
Aboriginal Health Human Resources Initiative, 161
Aboriginal Justices of the Peace Program, 196
Aboriginal peoples, *see also* First Nations; Inuit; Métis
    2001 census data
    identity, 140
        language usage, 202–203
        migration to cities, 144–145
        population distribution, 143–144
        population growth rate, 141
    birth rate, 142
    Canadian justice system, and, 189–194
        alternatives to, 194–198
    defined, 3
    domestic violence
        addictions, and, 187
        culture of, 186
        elimination of, 187
        facts about, 187–188
        roots of, 185
    education
        band schools, 147
        education gap, 148–150
        elementary and secondary, 146–148
        employment rates, and, 165
        federal schools, 146
        initiatives, 150
        postsecondary, 148
    employment
        employment rate, 163–164
        employment sectors, Aboriginal representation, 165–166
        entrepreneurship, 167
        level of education, 164–165
        place of residence, and, 165
        unemployment rate, 163
    health
        administration of services, 158–160
        environment, 161–162
        living conditions, 160–161
        mental health, 155–158
        physical health, 151–155
    income, 168–169
    legal rights
        hunting and fishing rights, 182–183, 199
        land claims, *see* land claims
        self-government, *see* self-government
    life expectancy, 142
    seniors, 142–143
    social assistance
        affirmative action, 173
        cycle of dependence, 170

Aboriginal peoples *(cont.)*
social assistance *(cont.)*
funding, services and programs, 170
history of, 171
self-determination, future of, 172
traditional social control, 178–179
Aboriginal police officers, 194
Aboriginal rights, 102, 126
Aboriginal rock music, 210
Aboriginal tourism, 211–213
Aboriginal Transition Fund, 161
Aboriginal Youth Business Council, 167
acculturation, 56, 214–215
affirmative action, 173
Ah-ah-nee-nin, 5, 63, 69
alcoholism, 158
Algonquian, 34
allegory, 9
Allied Tribes of British Columbia, 126
Alnombak, 5
Amagoalik, John, 184
American genesis theory, 12–13, 14
Amoskapi Piikunii, 5, 66
animism, 28
Anishnaabe, 5, 6, 8, 28, 94, 96, 97, 99, 179
annuities, 95
anomie, 155
anthropologist, 9
Apatohsi Piikunii, 5, 66
appropriation, 213
archaeologist, 9
archaeology, 24
Archaic culture, 26
Archibald, Adams, 97
Arctic peoples, 46–47
artifacts, 12, 205–206
Assembly of First Nations, 108, 128, 133, 172
assimilation, 56, 114–115
Athapaskan, 34
Attiwandaron, 5, 36
autonomy, 87

band schools, 147
barter system, 77
Baxter, Derrick, 167
Benton-Benai, Edward, 78
Beothuk, 52–53
Beringia theory, 10–12
Big Bear (Mistahimaskwa), 68, 98
Bill C-6
background, 106–107
introduction, 107
opposition to, 107–108
birth rate, 142
Blackfoot Confederacy, 63, 98
bois-brûlé, 72
Brighter Futures, 155
British North America Act, 94, 95, 114
buffalo culture, 40
buffalo hunt, 72
Building Healthy Communities program, 155

Cabot, John, 52
Campbell, Maria, 211
Canada–Aboriginal Peoples Roundtable, 150
Canadian Métis Council, 130
Canadian Prenatal Nutrition Program, 154
Cartier, Jacques, 53
Cayuga, 34, 36
ceded, 97
Chinook, 5, 60
clan system, 78
Columbus, Christopher, 52, 54
community policing, 194–195
Compagnie du Nord, La, 57
Congress of Aboriginal Peoples, 130, 172
consensus, 30
Constitution Act, 1867, 94, 114
Constitution Act, 1982, 106, 131, 132, 141
Coon Come, Matthew, 168
coureurs de bois, 56
court workers, 195
creation stories, 6, 7
Crowe, K.J., 83
Crowfoot (Isapo-muxika), 64
Crown, 87
crude mortality rate, 151
cultural genocide, 120
cultural groups
Arctic peoples, 46–47
Interior Plateau peoples, 41–42
Pacific Coast peoples, 43–44
Plains peoples, 38–41
Subarctic peoples, 44–46
Woodland peoples, 36–37

cultural periods
  archaeology, and, 24
  Archaic period, 26
  Palaeo-Indian period, 24–25
  Wisconsin Glaciation period, 24
  Woodland period, 26–27
culture
  defined, 3
  European settlement, and
    barter system, 77
    clan system, 78–79
    Europeans, dependence on, 79
    fur trade collapse, 80
    government, dependence on, 81
    leadership selection, 79
    missionaries, 81–83
    wealth, notion of, 77–78
  rebuilding initiatives
    artifact reclamation, 205–206
    arts, resurgence in, 207–209
    language, 202–204
culture of violence, 186

Dakota, 5
demographics, 140
Dene, 5, 70–71, 98, 99, 130, 179
Dene-thah, 5, 70, 99
devolution, 170
Dickason, Olive, 151
Dominion Lands Act, 75
Douglas, James, 94
Douglas, Thomas, 72
Dumont, Gabriel, 76
Dunne-za, 5, 69–70

ecosystem, 15
egalitarian society, 29
enculturation, 214
erosion, 15
Eskimo–Aleut, 34
European contact
  Aboriginal culture, effect on, 77–83
  acculturation, 56
  assimilation, 56
  Beothuk, and, 52–53
  coureurs de bois, 56
  first Europeans, 52
  Jacques Cartier, 53
  Métis, and, 52
  North America, opportunities in, 54
  settlements, growth of, 54–55
evolution, 12
expropriation, 105
extinguish, 93

fast, 6
Federation of Saskatchewan Indians, 100
fiduciary relationship, 104
Fiedel, Stuart, 62
financial abuse, 185
First Nation Education Management Framework, 250
First Nation Education Policy Framework, 150
First Nations, *see also* Aboriginal peoples
  children, role of, 30
  code of ethics, 29
  connection to land, 27–32
  cultural groups, 35–47
  defined, 3
  gender roles, 30
  language families, 33–34
  status, reinstatement of, 140
  trade, 31
First Nations and Inuit Health Branch, 159
First Peoples, *see also* Aboriginal peoples; First Nations; Inuit
  theories of origins, 10–12
Flower Beadwork People, 210
Frideres, James, 104, 170
fur trade, 58–62, 80, 89

Gardner, Wenona, 188
gender roles, 30
genesis, 12
Goodchild, Melanie, 167
Goodman, Jeffrey, 12–13
Gradual Enfranchisement Act, 114, 115
Great Law of Peace of the People of the Longhouse, 90
Great Peace Treaty of 1701, 88
Gwich'in, 99

Haida, 5, 6, 7, 34, 205
Haida Gwaii Museum, 205
Hare, 99
Haudenosaunee, 5, 8, 31, 36, 79, 88
Head-Smashed-In Buffalo Jump, 212
Henday, Anthony, 59, 62
hieroglyphics, 8

holistic, 29
Homo sapiens, 24
Hopewell culture, 27
horses, 40
Hudson's Bay Company, 57, 58, 71, 73, 89, 171
hunting and fishing rights, 182–183, 199

Idlout, Lucie, 210
immorality, 115
incest, 185
Indian Act
- alcohol prohibition, 116
- band system under, 117
- impact of, 116
- "Indian" defined under, 116
- land claims, and, 105
- passage, 95, 115

Indian agents, 115–116
Indian and Inuit Health Careers Program, 155
Indian Association of Alberta, 100
Indian Claims Commission, 106
Indian Department, 93
indigenous peoples, 12
inequality, 116
inherent right, 129
intemperance, 115
interdependence, 15
Interior Plateau peoples, 41–42
Inuit, *see also* Aboriginal peoples
- children, role of, 30
- code of ethics, 29
- cultural groups, 35–47
- connection to land, 27–32
- defined, 3
- gender roles, 30
- language families, 33–34
- modern technology, use of, 210
- Nunavut, creation of, 183
- trade, 31

Inuit Broadcasting Corporation, 184
Inuit Tapiriit Kanatami, 131, 172, 184
Inukshuk Project, 184
Inuna-ina, 5
Iroquoian, 34
Isaac-Downey, Darlene, 121
Isapo-muxika (Crowfoot), 64, 67

Jamieson, Roberta, 195
James Bay and Northern Quebec Agreement, 104
Jenness, Diamond, 52
Joe, Rita, 122–123
jurisdiction, 94
justices of the peace, 196

Kainai, 5, 63, 65, 105, 212
Kanien'Kehaka, 5, 34, 36
kayak, 47
Kingdon, Fauna, 193
Ktunaxa, 5, 34, 63, 65

Lakota, 5, 75
land claims
- Bill C-6, 106–108
- comprehensive land claims, 104
- Nisga'a Final Agreement, 109
- northern and southern, 104
- prior to 1973, 103–104
- resolution of, 105–106
- specific land claims, 105
- usufructuary right, 103

language
- 2001 census data re use, 202–203
- retention efforts, 203–204

language families, 33–34, 203
Laurel culture, 27
Laurentian culture, 26
Laurier, Wilfrid, 75
League of Indians of Canada, 100
legacy, 6
legal clinics, 195–196
legislation, 100
life expectancy, 142
lineage, 78
litigation, 107

Macdonald, John A., 74, 75, 95, 114
Mackenzie, Alexander, 70
Manitoba Act, 74
McDougall, William, 74
Meadowood culture, 27
mediation, 178
"medicine chest" clause, 98
Medicine Wheel, 15–18
Mercredi, Ovide, 132
Métis, *see also* Aboriginal peoples
- Bill of Rights, 74
- buffalo hunt, 72
- constitutional recognition, 131

cultural revival, 209–210
Numbered Treaties, and, 98
origins, 52
population growth rate, 141
Red River Rebellion, 74
Red River Settlement, 72, 73
Union nationale Métisse Saint-Joseph du Manitoba, 127
Western settlement, 71
Métis National Council, 130, 172
Michif, 210–211
Mi'kmaq, 5, 53, 91, 199
missionaries, 81–83
Mistahimaskwa (Big Bear), 68, 98
monopoly, 80
morbidity rate, 151
mutations, 12
mythology
defined, 9
origins, and, 13

Nakoda, 5, 58, 63, 68–69, 98
National Aboriginal Achievement Award, 184, 193
National Aboriginal Circle Against Family Violence, 188
National Indian and Inuit Community Health Representatives Organization, 161
National Indian Brotherhood, 128
National Indian Council, 128
National Inuit Women's Association, 131
National Native Alcohol and Drug Abuse Program, 155, 158, 159
Native Council of Canada, 130
Native Women's Association of Canada, 155, 172
Nehiyaw, 5, 6, 8, 58, 60, 63, 65, 66, 79, 96, 98, 99, 179
net migration, 145
Nisga'a, 5, 183
land claim, 103–104, 109, 183
nomadic culture, 26
non-status Indian, 116
Norris, Malcolm, 127
North West Company, 58, 71
Northwest Rebellion, 75, 124
Numbered Treaties
1 through 5, 96–97
6, 98
7, 98
8 through 11, 98–99
inclusions, 95
Nunavut, 183

Odawa, 5
Office of Native Claims, 104
Oka crisis, 142
ombudsman, 195
Oneida, 34, 36
Onondaga, 34, 36
oral tradition
defined, 4
storytelling, 4, 6–9
overcrowding, 160

Pacific Coast peoples, 43–44
Palaeo-Indian culture, 24–25
Palliser, John, 73
Palliser Triangle, 73
paternalism, 81
Peace and Friendship Treaties, 91
pemmican, 41
petroglyphs, 8
physical abuse, 185
pictographs, 8
Piikunii, 5, 63, 66, 212
Pitikwahanapiwiyin (Poundmaker), 67, 98
Plains people
Ah-ah-nee-nin, 69
as a cultural group, 38–41
Nakoda, 68–69
Nehiyaw, 66
Soyi-tapix Nation, 63–66
Tsuu T'ina, 66–68
Point Peninsula culture, 27
Poitras, Jane Ash, 208
Potawatomi, 5
potlatch, 180–181
Poundmaker (Pitikwahanapiwiyin), 67, 98
Princess Point culture, 27
prohibition, 116
Province of Canada Treaties, 94
provisional government, 74
provisioning station, 72
psychological abuse, 185

Queen Anne's War, 57

racial profiling, 190
recidivism, 158
Red Crow, 65
Red River Rebellion, 74, 76
Red River Settlement, 72, 73, 76

residential schools
    abuse at, 121–123
    creation of, 118
    impact of, 120–121
    structure of, 119–120
restitution, 178
restorative justice, 196
Rich, E.E., 59
Riel, Louis, 74, 75, 76
Royal Commission on Aboriginal Peoples, 133, 157, 186, 194
Royal Proclamation of 1763, 58, 91–93, 95, 114, 116
Rupert's Land purchase, 73, 74

Saint Brendan, 52
Salishan, 34
Salteaux, 78, 79
Saugeen culture, 27
Scott, Duncan Campbell, 126
Scott, Thomas, 74
scrip, 123
Sealey, D.B., 60
Sechelt Government Indian District, 134
self-government, 132–134, 201–213
Selkirk Settlement, *see* Red River Settlement
Seneca, 5, 34, 36
sentencing circle, 196–197
Seven Grandfathers, 28
Seven Years' War, 57
sexual abuse, 185
shaman, 9
Shewell, Hugh, 171
Shield culture, 26
Siksika, 5, 6, 7, 59, 60, 63–64, 98, 105, 212
Siouan, 34
Sitting Bull, 75
Six Nations Confederacy, 34, 36, 93
So-sonreh, 5, 63, 65
sovereignty, 51, 93, 183, 201–213
Soyi-tapix Nation, 63–66
Specific Claims Resolution Act, 107–108
spiritual abuse, 185, 186
spirituality, 6, 27
status Indian, 116
storytelling
    common characteristics, 6
    creation stories, 6
    interpretation, stories, 7, 9
    oral tradition, and, 4
    reliability, oral stories, 7
    value of, 9
Subarctic peoples, 44–46
    Dene, 70–71
    Dene-thah, 70
    Dunne-za, 69–70
subculture, 3
substance abuse, 158
suicide, 155–157
Sun Dance, 63, 66, 100
systemic discrimination, 192

tapirisat, 131
Tecumseh, 94
theory, 10
Three Sisters, 36
Tionantati, 5, 36
Tlingit, 34
travois, 38
trade
    fur trade, 58–62, 80
    pre-European contact, 31–32
trading posts, 59, 80
treaties
    between First Nations, 90
    defined, 88
    European motives for, 90
    First Nations' motives for, 90
    fur trade, and, 89
    Great Peace Treaty of 1701, 88
    land and resources, and, 89
    Numbered Treaties
        1 through 5, 96–97
        6, 98
        7, 98
        8 through 11, 98–99
        inclusions, 95
    pre-Confederation
        Peace and Friendship Treaties, 91
        Province of Canada Treaties, 94
        Royal Proclamation of 1763, 91–93, 95
        Upper Canada Treaties, 93
        Vancouver Island Treaties, 94
    treaty rights versus the law, 183
treaty adhesions, 96
treaty Indian, 116
Tsimshian, 34
Tsuu T'ina, 5, 63, 66–68
Tuscarora, 34, 36

umiak, 47
Union nationale Métisse Saint-Joseph du Manitoba, 127
Universal Declaration of Human Rights, 101
Upper Canada Treaties, 93
usufructuary right, 103

Vancouver Island Treaties, 94
Virtual Circle, 167
vision quest, 66
voyageurs, 56

Wakashan, 34
wampum, 8
ward, 81
Wendat, 5, 34, 36
Wheel of Life, 20–22
White Paper on Aboriginal Issues, 129, 130
Wisconsin Glaciation period, 24
Woodland peoples, 36–37
Woodland period, 26–27
worldview, 6
Wuastukwiuk, 5

Yukon First Nations Final Agreements, 104
Youth Criminal Justice Act, 198
Youth Justice Renewal Initiative, 197, 198
Youth Suicide Prevention Walk, 156

Zoe, Henry, 156

Credits

Images

British Columbia Archives: Figure 2.13 (G-00754); *Calgary Herald:* Figure 6.9 (Terry Cioni); *Canadian Heritage Gallery* (www.canadianheritage.ca): Figures 2.8 (ID#10044, Archives of Ontario-373), 2.15 (ID#10049, National Archives of Canada PA-11214); *Canadian Pacific Railway Archives:* Figure 3.8 (#8615); *Canadian Press:* Figures 4.4 (Ryan Remiorz), 4.5 (Nick Procaylo), 6.15 (Tom Hanson), 7.9 (John Ulan), 7.10 (Winnipeg Free Press/Joe Bryksa), 8.2 (Winnipeg Free Press/Marc Gallant), 8.3 (M. Spencer Green); *Corbis:* Figures 7.1 (Museum of History & Industry), 8.8 (Dave G. Houser); *Courtesy of Maria Campbell:* Figure 8.7; *Courtesy of Jane Ash Poitras:* Figures 8.4 (Clint Buehler); 8.5; *Glenbow Archives:* Figures 1.2 (NA-2956-4), 2.2 (NA-3241-10), 2.3 (NA-3878-93), 2.10 (NA-1093-1), 2.11 (NA-395-10), 2.17 (NA-239-22), 2.19 (NA-1964-5), 3.6 (NA-118-52), 3.10 (NA-1138-3), 4.3 (NA-47-41), 5.2 (NA-1406-240), 5.3 (PA-2218-183), 5.4 (NA-5-16); *Library and Archives of Canada:* Figures 3.4 (PA-66536), 3.7 (C-5181), 3.9 (C-1873), 3.11 (1982-188-1), 3.12 (C-7376); *National Aboriginal Achievement Foundation* (www.naaf.ca): Figure 7.2; *Nunatsiaq News* (www.nunatsiaq.com): Figure 7.7; *Pelican Falls First Nation School,* Sioux Lookout, Ontario: Figure 6.5; *Provincial Archives of Alberta:* Figure 3.5 (P.129); *Saskatchewan Archives Board:* Figures 3.3 (R-B 1627), 5.1a (R-A8223-1), 5.1b (R-A8223-2); *Starfish Entertainment:* Figure 8.6 (Clint Adams); *The Youth Suicide Prevention Walk* (www.theyouthsuicidepreventionwalk.com/2005): Figure 6.8.

Text

Page x: Courtesy of the Estate of Chief Dan George; Page 4: From "Journey Through Daylight-land: Through Ojibwa Eyes." *Laurentian University Review,* 8, 31–43, February 1976; Page 7: From *Origins, Canadian History to Confederation,* 5th ed., by Francis/Smith/Jones. © 2004. Reprinted with permission of Nelson, a division of Thomson Learning: www.thomsonrights.com. Fax 800-730-2215; Pages 12, 52–53, 176: Canadian Museum of Civilization, taken from *The Indians of Canada,* by Diamond Jenness, Ottawa, National Museum of Canada, 1932; Pages 13, 14 (Figure 1.4): Adapted from *Knots in a String: An Introduction to Native Studies in Canada,* by Peggy Brizinski. Copyright 1993 University Extension Press. Reprinted by permission of University Extension Press, University of Saskatchewan; Page 31: Adapted from Harris, R.C. (ed.). (1987). *Historical Atlas of Canada: Vol. 1, From the Beginning to 1800.* Toronto: University of Toronto Press; Page 32 (Figure 2.4): P.V. Beck, A.L. Walters and N. Francisco, *The Sacred Ways of Knowledge: Source of Life* (Tsaile, AZ: Navajo Community College Press, 1992. Reprinted by permission of Dine College Press; Page 62 (Figure 3.1): From Stuart Fiedel, *Prehistory of the Americas* (Cambridge, UK: Cambridge University Press, 1987). Reprinted with permission from Cambridge University Press; Page 88: Adapted from William B. Henderson, *The Canadian Encyclopedia,* Copyright © 2005; Page 109: Source: Chronology of Events Leading to the Final Agreement with the Nisga'a Tribal Council, 2004. Reproduced with the permission of the Minister of Public Works and Government Services Canada, 2005; Page 121: Reprinted by permission of Gord Atkinson; Pages 122–123: Source: *We Are the Dreamers: Recent and Early Poetry* (Wreck Cove, NS: Breton Books, 1999). Reprinted by permission of Breton Books; Pages 141 (Figure 6.1), 143 (Figure 6.2): From the Statistics Canada publication, *Aboriginal Peoples of Canada: A Demographic Profile, 2001 Census* (Analysis Series), Catalogue 96F0030XIE, January 21, 2003, available at http://www12.statcan.ca/english/census01/products/analytic/companion/abor/pdf/96F0030XIE2001007.pdf, page 20. Data are adapted in part from the Statistics Canada publication, *Population Projections for Canada, Provinces and Territories, 2002–2026,* Catalogue 91-520, March 13, 2001; Pages 144 (Figure 6.3), 145 (Figure 6.4): From the Statistics Canada publication, *Aboriginal Peoples of Canada: A Demographic Profile, 2001 Census* (Analysis Series), Catalogue 96F0030XIE, January 21, 2003, available at http://www12.statcan.ca/english/census01/products/analytic/companion/abor/contents.cfm; Pages 164 (Figure 6.12), 166 (Figure 6.13): From Statistics Canada, 2001 Census of Population, available at: http://www.statcan.ca/english/freepub/71-222-XIE/2004000/chart-080-big.htm and http://www.statcan.ca/english/freepub/71-222-XIE/2004000/chart-081-big.htm; Page 166 (Figure 6.14): Reprinted by permission of Canadian Labour and Business Centre; Page 174: Reprinted by permission of University of Alberta; Page 187: From Statistics Canada, Canadian Centre for Justice Statistics, 2001; Page 188: Reprinted by permission of Wenona Gardner; Pages 189 (Figure 7.4), 190 (Figure 7.5), 191 (Figure 7.6): From the Statistics Canada publication, *Aboriginal People in Canada,* 1999, Canadian Centre for Justice Statistics Profile Series, Catalogue 85F0033MIE, June 14, 2001, available at http://www.statcan.ca/english/85F0033MIE2001001.pdf; Page 203 (Figure 8.1): From the Statistics Canada publication, *Aboriginal Peoples of Canada: A Demographic Profile, 2001 Census* (Analysis Series), Catalogue 96F0030XIE, January 21, 2003, available at http://www12.statcan.ca/english/census01/products/analytic/companion/abor/contents.cfm.